ORGANIZING ORGANIC

ORGANIZING ORGANIC

Conflict and Compromise
in an Emerging Market

MICHAEL A. HAEDICKE

Stanford University Press
Stanford, California

Stanford University Press
Stanford, California

Printed on acid-free, archival-quality paper

Printed and bound in Great Britain by
Marston Book Services Ltd, Oxfordshire

Library of Congress Cataloging-in-Publication Data
Names: Haedicke, Michael A., author.
Title: Organizing organic : conflict and compromise in an emerging market /
    Michael A. Haedicke.
Description: Stanford, California : Stanford University Press, 2016. |
    Includes bibliographical references and index.
Identifiers: LCCN 2016000333 (print) | LCCN 2016000801 (ebook) |
    ISBN 9780804795906 (cloth : alk. paper) | ISBN 9780804798730 (ebook)
Subjects: LCSH: Natural foods industry--United States--History. | Food
    industry and trade--United States--History. | Industrial
    organization--United States--History.
Classification: LCC HD9005 .H24 2016 (print) | LCC HD9005 (ebook) | DDC
    338.4/76413020973--dc23
LC record available at http://lccn.loc.gov/2016000333

Typeset by Bruce Lundquist in 10.5/15 Adobe Garamond Pro

Contents

List of Tables

Acknowledgments

I DEPENDED ON the support, advice, and good spirits of many people while writing this book. First, thanks are due to the many members of the organic foods sector who shared their time and knowledge with me. Although most of these individuals remain anonymous in the text, I hope that my respect for their work is clear. I would especially like to thank Elizabeth Henderson, whose decision to share her personal archive of documents related to the development of federal organic regulations greatly increased my understanding of this important time in the sector's history. Also, I am grateful to the staff and directors of the store that I refer to as Pacific Foods Co-op, who welcomed me as an observer at board meetings and other events during this research.

Mentors of mine at the University of California, San Diego guided this project while it was in its early stages, and many of them have remained involved in its later development. Richard Biernacki kindled my interest in the intersection of culture and economic life and provided unwavering support through research and writing. Amy Binder was my guide through the world of organizational theory and helped me see this book's potential when I was in doubt. Maria Charles applied her careful reading and rigorous logic to the improvement of my drafts, and Kit Woolard and David Serlin showed me how to enrich my scholarship with insights from anthropology and cultural theory.

More recently, Tim Hallett has given valuable advice and provided opportunities for collaboration that deepened my understanding of contemporary institutional theory. I have also benefited from the support of my colleagues in the Department for the Study of Culture and Society at Drake University and from comments that attendees at the Drake University Center for the Humanities Colloquium offered on versions of chapters. Melisa Klimaszewski,

Kevin Lam, and Amahia Mallea—fellow book writers, all—also provided encouragement and advice. The work was also supported by grants from the College of Arts and Sciences, the Office of the Provost, and the Center for the Humanities at Drake University.

Margo Beth Fleming, my editor at Stanford University Press, guided me through the Press's submission, revision, and publication process with aplomb. She has a gift for setting a high bar and providing a novice writer with the encouragement and guidance needed to clear it. James Holt contributed able editorial assistance and much-needed help when it came to the technicalities of formatting, documentation, and permissions. Jeffrey Haydu, Paul-Brian McInerney, and one anonymous reviewer read drafts of the manuscript and provided rigorous and important critical feedback. I have also given presentations based on this work at meetings of the American Sociological Association, the Midwest Sociological Society, the Association for the Study of Food and Society, the Law and Society Association, and the Society for the Study of Symbolic Interaction. Audiences at these venues helped me sharpen my arguments in multiple ways.

Writers live in a world of metaphor, and many of those metaphors have to do with the process of writing itself. Anne Lamott compares writing to bathing a cat, while for E. L. Doctorow it is like driving at night, and for Katherine Cowley, like taking care of sick kids. None of these things are fun to do alone, and I am grateful for the support of many friends, near and far. My parents, David and Susan Haedicke, have provided inspiration, encouragement, and good advice, as have my brothers, Stephen Oshyn and Daniel Haedicke, and their families. My wife, Kathleen Gillon, has managed to challenge and support me at the same time, which as any good teacher knows, is how you grow. It would take another book to express my love, gratitude, and admiration for her. For now, I will just say thank you. Let's keep on creating.

List of Abbreviations

CCOF	California Certified Organic Farmers
FTC	Federal Trade Commission
FVO	Farm Verified Organic
IFOAM	International Federation of Organic Agriculture Movements
MOSES	Midwest Organic and Sustainable Education Service
NCGA	National Cooperative Grocers Association (later National Co+op Grocers)
NCSA	National Campaign for Sustainable Agriculture
NOFA	Natural Organic Farmers Association (later Northeast Organic Farming Association)
NOP	National Organic Program
NOSB	National Organic Standards Board
OCA	Organic Consumers Association
OCIA	Organic Crop Improvement Association
OFAC	Organic Farmers Associations Council
OFPA	Organic Foods Production Act
OFPANA	Organic Foods Production Association of North America
OGF	*Organic Gardening and Farming*
OTA	Organic Trade Association
UNFI	United Natural Foods, Inc.
USDA	United States Department of Agriculture
WFM	Whole Foods Market

ORGANIZING ORGANIC

.

Visions of Transformation and Growth

Institutional Logics and Social Processes in the Organic Sector

IN EARLY 2004, an organic farmer named Elizabeth Henderson gazed out into a crowded hall at the Midwest Organic and Sustainable Education Service (MOSES) annual meeting and issued an ultimatum. Henderson had many years of experience in the organic field. In the late 1970s, she had left a position at Boston University and moved with her young son and several friends to a dilapidated dairy farm in rural Massachusetts. The group gradually restored the farm, and Henderson cobbled together a living from selling the farm's produce and teaching mail correspondence classes. She also attended meetings of a small group known as the Natural Organic Farmers Association (NOFA), which at the time was working to develop a shared definition and set of standards for organic foods production. As consumer demand for organic foods grew during the 1990s, Henderson published several books about sustainable farming and frequently contributed to *The Natural Farmer*, NOFA's quarterly newsletter. Now, facing an audience of small-scale farmers and community food activists, as well as pioneers in the organic farming world, she focused on a theme that had often appeared in her writing. "We need to make a decision," she explained. "Are we an industry? Or are we a movement?"

Henderson's questions came at a pivotal moment in the history of the organic foods sector. Barely one year earlier, the U.S. Department of Agriculture had implemented its National Organic Program (NOP), a set of rules for the production and processing of foods marketed as organic in the United States. The federal rules were meant to facilitate trade in organic foods by eliminating variations in state and regional definitions of organic production, by curtailing instances of fraud in which conventionally grown products were marketed as organic, and by enhancing consumers' confidence in organic marketing claims. When Henderson gave her speech, the NOP had begun to accomplish these goals. In 2004, the value of organic foods sales in the United States amounted to $11.9 billion, up from $3.5 billion in 1997, according to statistics collected by the Organic Trade Association (OTA), an industry group. While just over 2 percent of the food products sold in the United States were organic, the market's growth during the preceding decade had attracted investments from mainstream food companies and from venture capital firms. Farmers who had previously grown only conventional crops were turning to organic cultivation, and processed, brand-name organic products were appearing on store shelves in greater numbers. It was a dramatic change for a sector that had historically emphasized its opposition to and difference from the mainstream food and agriculture industry.

The preceding years had also witnessed a number of challenges to these developments in the organic sector. In 1998, hundreds of thousands of angry organic farmers and consumers had written to the Department of Agriculture to protest a proposed version of the NOP. Among other things, they claimed that the rules would open the door for the use of genetically engineered seeds and sterilizing irradiation in organic foods production. Additionally, there were underlying concerns about the viability of regional organic foods systems, farmer-run certification groups, and alternative organizational ideals in a federally regulated organic sector. The outcry led the agency to withdraw the draft and devote several more years to its revision. Even once the revised rules were finally implemented, they faced a court challenge from an organic farmer named Arthur Harvey. A number of agricultural and consumer advocacy groups signed on to support Harvey's lawsuit, which was making its way through the courts at the time of Henderson's speech.

By asking her audience to consider whether they thought of themselves as members of an industry or as participants in a movement, Henderson was joining her voice with the voices of those who questioned the sector's growth and convergence with the mainstream food industry. When the audience indicated by raising their hands that they thought of themselves as members of an organic movement, she explained that the agricultural practices associated with organic farming, such as the use of composted fertilizers and complicated crop rotations, were only one part of a deeper transformation that would substitute the principles of democracy and decentralization for those of industrial efficiency. She offered an ambitious program of social change to the MOSES audience:

> As organic farmers it behooves us to be radicals. Our anchoring taproot connects us with the indigenous farmers who over millennia built up the seed stock for domestic grains and vegetables, domesticated livestock, and discovered that rotations, composting and biodiversity make it possible to provide adequate harvests to feed their families and communities . . . While it may be more efficient in industrial terms to grow food on a few thousand high-tech farms, organic agriculture offers an alternative vision of prosperous, self-reliant villages with trade only in surpluses and regional specialties . . . One of my daydreams is that our movement will somehow find a democratic and participatory way to create a set of holistic goals for our future, so that we can grow into a great healthy tree, spreading our branches over all the people, uniting, nourishing and enriching.[1]

Two years later, another organic pioneer faced an audience at a different organic foods conference. Like Henderson, Joe Smillie had entered the organic field by "dropping out" of mainstream society. A Canadian native, he had moved to rural Québec in 1974 and started a company that provided composted fertilizer to organic farmers. He also traveled to New England to participate in NOFA conferences during the early 1980s. By the 1990s, his career path had diverged from Henderson's. After leaving the fertilizer company, Smillie began to work as an organic inspector, examining the operations of farms and companies that produced organic foods for long-distance trade and making sure that they were in compliance with formal rules of organic production. This led to a job with Quality Assurance International, an inspection and certification company that provided services to some of the largest organic producers in the United States and Mexico.

Smillie offered his thoughts about the organic foods sector to a group at the Natural Products Expo West, an annual meeting of manufacturers, retailers, and others involved in the natural and organic foods industry. The expo was far larger than the MOSES meeting that Henderson had addressed, and it also differed in atmosphere. While the MOSES group had met in gritty La Crosse, Wisconsin, the expo took place in the glittering Anaheim Convention Center, across from Disneyland in Anaheim, California. The business suits and corporate advertising in evidence at the expo contrasted with the jeans and political messages that appeared at the MOSES meeting. While a highlight of the MOSES meeting was a buffet meal created from items donated by local organic farms, the expo featured a three-day trade show, where attendees could sample the latest innovations in retail-ready branded organic foods. And finally, Smillie's message about the nature and potential of the organic sector differed from Henderson's in important ways. He explained:

> My whole purpose is to stop the poisoning of the planet. It's really for me that simple. For me organic is about agriculture. It is an agriculture-based system, an agricultural methodology . . . And even though organic is extremely successful the planet is still being poisoned by the use of chemicals. So that is why I do what I do every day. That's why I love my work and that is why I'm committed to it. So as a consumer, as a person on this planet, anything that helps convert acreage away from chemical use is good . . . I believe that our main purpose in organics is to change the ways of farming on the planet and I believe that organic supports that. So I tend to lean towards ways that allow conventional farmers to enter the organic field. I really believe that we have to move all farmers, conventional farmers, to organic.[2]

Set side by side, these two speeches offer a snapshot of cultural divisions in the contemporary organic sector. Henderson and Smillie both justified organic foods production in moral terms, rather than in purely commercial ones, by asserting that the benefits of organic farming transcend the success or failure of organic products on the market. However, the details of their arguments differed. While Henderson suggested that organic farming promises a "democratic and participatory way" to accomplish "holistic goals," Smillie characterized organic farming as an "agricultural methodology" that mainly seeks to "convert acreage away from chemical use." Smillie sought to bring conventional (i.e., non-organic) farmers into the organic fold, while Henderson, judging by her vision of a food system based on "prosperous, self-reliant villages," wished to revolutionize the structure of agriculture entirely. In the specifics of their moral visions, the speeches contradicted each other. How can the organic sector simultaneously welcome conventional farmers and advocate revolutionary changes in the food system as a whole? If chemical use is the main problem, as Smillie suggested, why is a radical vision like Henderson's necessary at all?

What This Book Is About

This book examines how these different cultural understandings of organic agriculture have developed over the history of the organic sector, as well as how they inform identities and interactions of people who make a living from producing and selling organic foods. It devotes particular attention to how people in the organic sector create cultural meanings in economic and organizational settings and to how they bring those meanings to bear in everyday life and during periods of sector-level change. The book is anchored in qualitative data that I collected during a six-year period, including interviews with a spectrum of sector participants, archival material ranging from records of regulatory meetings to documents from private collections, and notes from observations at trade conferences and business meetings. Taken together, these data provided me with the means to create a rich portrait of the sector's organization and of the patterns of conflict and compromise between different cultural understandings that exist within it.[3]

My study differs from many popular books about organic foods because its goal is not to determine which vision is "right" or, to put it differently, more worthy of popular support. As the sector expanded in the early 2000s, Michael Pollan's best seller *The Omnivore's Dilemma* questioned whether the growing number of large, market-oriented farmers and retailers in the sector had "cost organic its soul" (2006c, 139). Barbara Kingsolver, in a memoir of her family's year of homesteading and eating locally on a Virginia farm, noted soon afterward that "the rising consumer interest in organic food has inspired most of the country's giant food conglomerates to cash in . . . [but] the larger the corporation, the more distant its motives are apt to be from the original spirit of organic farming" (2007, 121–122). Maria Rodale (2010), the granddaughter of the indefatigable organic foods booster J. I. Rodale, fired back with a book that praised the ability of voracious organic shoppers and savvy businesspeople to convert ever-increasing acres of farmland to more environmentally sustainable organic management. These ongoing efforts to define the story of the organic sector—whether tragic or triumphant—testify to its cultural significance and growing economic importance. Yet, they simplify the ways in which different visions of organic production have shaped the sector's history and contributed to its trajectory of economic and institutional development. This book aims to offer an analytic contribution that looks beneath the dramatic and engaging stories that circulate in the public sphere.[4]

The analysis that I develop relies on—but also extends—the important scholarly work about organic agriculture and the organic movement that began to emerge in the late 1990s. In addition to numerous articles, scholars in this area have produced two book-length studies. Julie Guthman's (2004a) landmark *Agrarian Dreams* applied a conceptual framework derived from agricultural political economy to the evolution of organic farming in California. Guthman demonstrated that the state's history of specialized, market-oriented agriculture, as well as the inflated land values that this history produced, has pushed organic farmers to employ some of the same intensive techniques used by conventional growers. She also argued that private and state-level certification programs that emphasize technical compliance have supported this trajectory toward conventionalization. More recently, Brian K. Obach, in *Organic Struggle* (2015), used insights from the sociology of social movements to track the coalition-building and political work of organic farming advocates during the decades that preceded and followed the creation of the NOP. Focusing on the tensions that emerged around the federal regulations, Obach divided advocates into growth-seeking "spreaders" and locally oriented "tillers." Like Guthman and Obach, I am interested in patterns of market and institutional development within the organic sector, but I extend their work by exploring how sector members who are immersed in the day-to-day concerns of doing business and running organizations interpret these changes and how their interpretations shape their interactions with others.

Through this focus, the book links an analysis of the organic sector to discussions that are occurring in the academic subfields of organizational studies and economic sociology. Researchers in these areas have increasingly conceptualized markets and businesses as sites of complex moral reasoning (Fourcade and Healy 2007), negotiation between multiple rationalities (Townley 2002), and contentious social interaction (King and Pearce 2010). Markets and businesses are not simply economic institutions, these arguments run, but they are also cultural ones, and cultural templates, alongside economic forces, shape patterns of interaction and organization in market settings (DiMaggio 1994; Spillman 1999). These insights raise important questions. How do multiple rationalities persist in market settings? How do they shape organization and action? How do the people who "inhabit" (Hallett and Ventresca 2006) markets and organizations navigate cultural pluralism and find pragmatic resolutions to the contradictions that it entails? These questions multiply when we bring consumers' behavior and participation into the picture. Some scholars have suggested that markets for organic foods and other ethically resonant products represent new arenas of political engagement, as consumers blend critical reasoning and the pursuit of social change with the everyday activity of shopping (Micheletti 2003; Stehr 2008). To what extent does the contemporary organic sector support this argument? How do consumers participate in debates about the sector's direction and future, and in what ways do sector members respond to and try to channel consumers' claims?

In the chapters that follow, I marshal the qualitative data that I collected to engage with these questions in two ways. First, the book traces the historical arc of the organic sector's development in the United States from a fringe of countercultural farmers and food purists to a lucrative, deeply institutionalized niche within the broader food industry. I show that different ways of thinking about organic farming were present in the sector's early years, although the sector's decentralized, loosely organized character eased the tensions that existed between these cultural understandings. The sector's growth during the 1990s and 2000s advanced understandings that were compatible with market expansion to a dominant position, while also sparking well-organized efforts to resist the convergence of organic markets with the mainstream food industry. As a result of these two factors, market growth has coincided with increased conflict between different approaches to organic foods production. Many of the sector's earliest members find themselves caught between these competing visions, striving to survive economically while also maintaining a degree of integrity by connecting their actions to their understandings of the mission of organic farming.

Second, the book examines the relationship between these cultural understandings and the activities of participants in the organic sector. Participants do not simply "act out" one set of understandings or the other; rather, their actions incorporate a variety of considerations, but they mobilize these understandings to account for the things that they do and to interpret and try to influence the behavior of others (Scott and Lyman 1968). This argument is especially important when it is put in the context of many people's sense that the organic sector is an arena of increasing ideological polarization. Popular (and some social scientific) accounts portray the sector as occupied by people who vigorously advocate for market growth at the expense of organic farming's countercultural heritage, as well as by others who are equally dedicated to defending the cultural and organizational boundaries between the organic sector and the conventional food industry (Guthman 2004a, 57). A significant amount of conflict about the legitimacy of market growth and mainstream forms of business organization does occur within the organic sector, and I will discuss a number of examples of this conflict in the chapters that follow. However, the complex relationship between culture and action also appears in the ways in which members of the sector have managed to combine different understandings in discourse and action, despite the contradictions between these understandings and despite the conflicts that they have engendered. Examples of this phenomenon appear in the design of organic regulations, in the organization of businesses, and in the accounts that members of the organic sector provide of their work. The reverse of conflict is "pragmatic compromise" (McInerney 2014, 19), and this book unpacks the dynamics of both conflict and compromise as they appear in this intricate organizational field.

I lay the theoretical foundation of the study in the remainder of this introduction, focusing especially on work in organizations scholarship that uses the concept of institutional logics to examine culture in markets and organizational settings. In subsequent chapters, I will mine this theory for the building blocks of my analysis of the organic sector, but I will also leverage my data about the organic sector to suggest modifications to and extensions of theoretical arguments. In addition to illustrating the usefulness of certain concepts for understanding the organic sector and similar settings, this book connects qualitative case analysis to the project of theory building.

Visions of Transformation and Expansion

The speeches by Henderson and Smillie that I described at the outset were not simply expressions of individual, idiosyncratic views. They tapped into shared repertoires of symbols, ideas, and metaphors to articulate different understandings of organic farming and different visions of an organic foods system.[5] The concept of institutional logics offers insight into the nature and persistence of these multiple, contradictory visions (Kraatz and Block 2008; Thornton, Ocasio, and Lounsbury 2012). This concept derives from the late twentieth-century work of Roger Friedland and Robert Alford (1991, 248), who defined institutional logics as socially derived and historically distinctive assemblages of "material practices and symbolic constructions [that provide] organizing principles" for human activity.[6] Friedland and Alford argued that these material and symbolic constructs vary in important ways across what they called the interinstitutional order. For example, modern capitalist markets are organized around the logic of commodification and ownership, democratic political systems around the logic of participation and popular control, and nuclear family units around the logic of cooperation and interdependency of members. Within these institutional arenas, the symbols and practices that constitute an institutional logic hang together in a mutually reinforcing way: when an investor buys a share of a company, when a citizen makes a donation to an activist organization, when a parent pays for a child's music lessons, they affirm and reproduce the "transrational symbolic systems" that give these actions comprehensible and legitimate meanings (Friedland and Alford 1991, 250). At the same time, logics contradict one another across the interinstitutional order, which sets the stage for political conflicts "over the appropriate relationships between institutions, and by which institutional logic different activities should be regulated and to which categories of persons they apply" (Friedland and Alford 1991, 256).

Friedland and Alford examined variations and contradictions between logics across institutional arenas, but many subsequent researchers adopted a more fine-grained approach that focused on mapping out contradictory logics within particular industries and organizational fields. Just as societies contain different logics that define legitimate goals and actions, these scholars argued, so too do many fields of activity possess warring cultural templates for organizing their members (Marquis and Lounsbury 2007; Rao, Monin, and Durand 2003; Townley 2002). These field-level logics are analogous to societal ones in that they consist of linked cultural understandings and material practices that are anchored in the field's history and structure and that organize the actions and identities of participants in recognizable ways (Thornton 2004).

Moreover, these field-level templates display the influence of overarching societal logics, even as they accommodate the unique character and history of the field (Thornton and Ocasio 2008). People in particular industries and sectors draw on generalized symbols and practices related to markets, democracies, families, and other institutional arenas, while also adapting these logics to local goals and challenges. Finally, contradictions between different field-level logics, which are often heightened by changes in the field's size, composition, or relationship with other fields in society, can fuel important episodes of conflict and change (Clemens and Cook 1999; Seo and Creed 2002).

The institutional logics approach offers two important insights when it is brought to bear on the different cultural understandings that exist in the contemporary organic sector. First, the approach provides a framework for making sense of the internal consistency of these different understandings, as well as the contradictions between them. Like the societal-level logics that Friedland and Alford discuss, different visions of organic farming are anchored in "transrational symbolic systems": the principles of local diversity and decentralized organization figure in the vision articulated by Henderson, while those of methodological standardization and market growth form the foundation of Smillie's account. In the context of the different visions, these principles are understood to be fundamental to the moral mission of organic agriculture and provide benchmarks against which to evaluate developments in the organic sector. Contradictions between the different understandings exist at the level of these basic principles. Decentralized organization tends to impede rapid market expansion, while methodological standardization is impossible in a field characterized by local diversity in experiences and practices. In addition, the institutional logics approach draws attention to the historical development of these different understandings. Like other organizational fields that contain multiple and contradictory logics, the organic sector straddles different institutional arenas (Dunn and Jones 2010; Lee 2015). Over the course of the sector's development, understandings of organic farming have been shaped by its relationships with transformative social movements, as well as with the commercial world of expansionary, profit-seeking enterprise.

Second, by conceptualizing culture in both symbolic and practical terms, the institutional logics approach highlights ways that members of the organic sector try to "concretize" different cultural understandings of organic farming in the structure of the organizations that they run and in the institutions that govern behavior in the sector as a whole. Sector members do not only assert different understandings of organic foods production in public speeches. They also attempt (with more or less success) to operate their businesses and to design regulatory arrangements in ways that reflect the value that they place on decentralized organization and local diversity or on market growth and methodological standardization (Clemens 1996). These organizational manifestations of cultural understandings contribute to the persistence of cultural pluralism in the organic sector by providing concrete examples of particular visions of the sector's purpose and future development. As I will explain in greater detail below, examining the practical side of these different cultural understandings enables a deeper comprehension of the patterns of conflict and compromise that exist in the sector.

With these insights from the institutional logics perspective in mind, I find it helpful to attach shorthand labels to the two different cultural understandings that appeared in Henderson's and Smillie's speeches. In the chapters to come, I will refer to the organizational principles expressed in Henderson's speech, which called for a restructuring of the food and agriculture system, as *transformative*. On the other hand, I will refer to the principles expressed in Smillie's speech, which emphasized market growth and quantifiable environmental goals, as *expansionary*. Both sets of principles position organic agriculture as a solution to problems created by mainstream farming practices, but they diagnose these problems in different ways. They also call for different sorts of relationships between members of the sector and between food producers and food consumers, and they identify different sorts of organizations and individuals as having a legitimate role within the organic sector. In Table I.1, I outline the key elements of these two visions of the organic sector in an abstract, schematic way.[7]

Transformative understandings rest on the argument that contemporary agriculture and the modern food industry are systemically flawed and inherently destructive. They produce economic inequalities in the form of market concentration and exploitative labor relationships, health and environmental problems that result from the disruption of the natural ecologies of farmland, and cultural alienation by distancing farmers and food consumers from the land and from each other. Organic agriculture represents a holistic alternative

TABLE I.1 Two Cultural Visions of the Organic Foods Sector

Organizational and Cultural Elements	Transformative Vision	Expansionary Vision
Critique of the conventional agrofood system	Systemic: The conventional system produces social inequality and cultural alienation as well as health and environmental problems	Limited: The conventional system produces health/environmental problems because of flawed technologies and practices
Scope of organic agriculture	Holistic: Organic agriculture includes changes in farm size, labor relations, farming practices, and producer-consumer relationships	Technical: Organic agriculture involves the substitution of benign for dangerous inputs and sustainable for destructive practices
Legitimate organizational forms	Farms and businesses of limited size and complexity that are anchored in local environments and communities	Efficient, competitive farms and businesses that provide organically grown foods to a large and geographically dispersed consumer market
Legitimate mode of growth	Gradual construction of alternative food systems	Rapid conversion of existing farms and businesses to organic production
Sources of authority about organic goals and practices	Experienced organic farmers	Scientists, technical experts, and market leaders
Governance mechanisms	Farmer knowledge, integrity, and ethical commitment	Formal rules and enforcement mechanisms
Cultural model for the organic sector	Civic community	Enlightened marketplace

to this system. Constructing an organic foods system, therefore, requires not only new farming techniques, but also changes in farm size, labor relations, and interactions between producers and consumers. Legitimate organizational forms include small-scale farms and local markets that are "embedded" in social relationships of cooperation, trust, and reciprocity and that steward the welfare of communities and local environments (Lyson 2004). Organic foods systems are understood to germinate slowly as farmers in different regions and localities exchange ideas, share techniques, and enlist the support of dedicated customers. Farmers who work directly with the land are authorities about the sorts of practices that should exist in an organic system, and their knowledge, integrity, and ethical commitment form the foundation of the organic sector's governance. The transformative logic gives rise to a vision in which building the organic sector is not primarily a commercial project. Rather, it is a project that is modeled along the lines of civic community, in which close relationships and shared, deliberative activities advance the collective good (Johnston 2008).

Expansionary understandings point to the intensive use of synthetic pesticides and other agricultural inputs that harm the environment as the central problem of mainstream agriculture. This vision suggests that because organic farming techniques reduce the use of these inputs, the increasing adoption of these techniques correlates with environmental improvement. It places a premium on market growth and treats the adoption of organic methods by large farms and the purchase of organic products by a growing number of consumers as clear victories. Instead of emphasizing relationships of cooperation and trust between farmers and consumers, it allocates a central role in the sector's governance to technical assessments and formal rules and standards. Consumers are understood to support the mission of organic agriculture through their purchases—by "voting with their dollars," as one of my interview respondents put it—but close relationships with organic farmers are neither essential nor, in some cases, even desirable. Whereas the transformative vision depicts the organic sector as a civic community, the expansionary vision tends to portray it as an enlightened marketplace in which consumerism and profit-seeking promote environmental welfare.

In the chapters that follow, I trace the development of these understandings and the changing relationship between them, from the organic sector's origins after World War II, to its initial growth in the 1970s and 1980s, to the development of federal regulations in the 1990s and the sector's subsequent expansion and convergence with the mainstream food industry. In the starkest terms, the story is one of the increasing dominance of expansionary ideas and arrangements and the gradual retreat of transformative ones from the sector's center to its margins. The roots of both cultural understandings can be found in the sector's early years. On the one hand, ideas about the value of small-scale agriculture, the robust moral character of farmers, and the importance of close connections between communities and the land frequently appeared in calls for alternative agriculture and natural foods consumption, which influenced the thinking of pioneering organic advocates (Beeman and Pritchard 2001). The countercultural and environmental movements of the 1960s and 1970s also brought into the world of organic farming a rich questioning of hierarchical organization, a greater skepticism of technology and non-experiential expertise, and new ways of talking about cultural alienation (Belasco 1989). On the other hand, participants in the sector often embraced the goal of selling increasing amounts of organic foods to an expanding circle of consumers and looked to mainstream businesses for ideas about how to accomplish this task. Although market growth was usually discussed as a means to increase the environmental and social benefits of organic farming, rather than as an end in itself, some farmers' groups and national organic farming advocacy organizations worked intently to increase consumers' desire for and confidence in organic foods.

The organic sector's decentralized character during the 1970s and 1980s hampered efforts that aimed at market expansion, even as it eased conflicts between cultural understandings of organic production. The move toward federal regulation of the organic market, which began with the passage of the Organic Foods Production Act (OFPA) in 1990, had the opposite effect. While setting the stage for more rapid market growth, regulation also heightened tensions between members of the sector who felt that organic farming should be organized differently from the mainstream food industry and others who argued that the goals of organic agriculture would be accomplished most effectively through rapid market growth. Since federal regulation meant that everyone would be playing by the same rules, the cultural principles behind those rules became hugely important. The organic farmers and other sector participants who contributed to the legislation and to the federal rulemaking process worked with some success to build compromises into the regulations, although the final version of the rules clearly leaned in the direction of market expansion. A sector-wide protest over the initial draft of the regulations failed to alter this expansionary orientation, although it did lay a foundation for ongoing public conflicts within the sector.

These conflicts characterize relationships between newly arrived businesspeople and organic farming activists in the contemporary organic sector. Mainstream food companies, drawn both by consumer demand for organic products and by the stability promised by federal oversight, entered the organic sector in increasing numbers as the regulations moved toward completion. These companies brought with them business professionals who often had an active interest in organic farming but less knowledge of the sector's history. Their training and the demands of their employers attuned the new arrivals to the imperative of market growth. From their perspective, expansionary understandings of organic farming's mission make intuitive sense, while transformative understandings appear naive, bizarre, and even threatening. Although the new arrivals often assert the value of an organizationally diverse organic sector, they also take the legitimacy of expansionary understandings and organizational arrangements for granted and reinforce the dominance of these arrangements through their actions.

Along with these new arrivals, consumer advocates and environmental activists began to pay increasing attention to organic agriculture in the wake of the federal regulations. These advocacy groups contest the prioritization of market growth and reassert the importance of transformative goals and organizational arrangements in the organic sector. They advocate changes to the regulations and mobilize consumer boycotts to influence business practices. Surprisingly, the activists have incorporated elements of the expansionary logic into their campaigns. Rather than involving consumers in deliberations about the future of organic farming, they simply seek to alter consumers' shopping choices in ways that will provide leverage against large, market-oriented businesses. The strategy has been effective in addressing particular issues, but it also demonstrates the extent to which conflicts take place on a battlefield shaped by the principles of market expansion.

Logics in Action

By presenting this capsule history of the organic sector's development, I have sought to highlight the value of the institutional logics approach for understanding the organic sector. If I were to end the discussion at this point, however, my questions about how different understandings of organic production have persisted and about how they have influenced organization and interaction would be only partially answered. While the institutional logics perspective generates a rich and complex description of these cultural understandings, it also raises a new set of puzzles about what people *do* with them and about how they are woven into daily life (Hallett, Shulman, and Fine 2009; Hallett and Ventresca 2006). These puzzles are compelling since the contradictions between different understandings of organic farming—which appear in both symbolic representations and organizational characteristics—pose challenges that members of the sector must negotiate on a regular basis. As Binder (2007,

568) has put it, "logics are not purely top-down: real people, in real contexts, with consequential past experiences of their own, play with them, question them, combine them with institutional logics from other domains, take what they can from them, and make them fit their needs." Logics should not be seen as a deus ex machina device for resolving the complexities of social life, but rather as a means for highlighting cultural resources that people use to construct strategies of action and to understand the world in which they operate (McPherson and Sauder 2013; Swidler 1986; Zilber 2002).

The chapters to come engage with these puzzles by exploring how participants in the organic sector draw on and elaborate transformative and expansionary understandings as they reflect on the work that they do. This sort of reflexive sensemaking is one way that people use institutional logics—these logics "provide people with vocabularies of motive and a sense of self" (Friedland and Alford 1991, 251; Mills 1940; Weick 1995). Through examinations of newly arrived professionals and activists involved in oppositional campaigns, I show that many sector members construct professional identities and evaluate the organic sector's trajectory of development mainly in the terms offered by either the transformative or the expansionary logics. However, I also demonstrate that some sector members find ways to combine elements of the two understandings. For example, the leaders of organic foods cooperative stores, countercultural businesses that now compete closely with mainstream supermarket retailers, have developed identities and evaluations that grant legitimacy to both understandings through a process that I call ambivalent sensemaking.

I also consider the collective, interactive use of transformative and expansionary understandings during episodes of conflict and compromise in the organic sector. Conflict and compromise are fundamental interactive processes that help to drive the formation and maintenance of organized fields of activity, like the organic sector (Fligstein and McAdam 2012). Because of their dramatic nature and the important role that they play in generating change and innovation, processes of conflict have received the lion's share of attention from social scientists (Collins 1975; Oberschall 1978). Compromise processes, while they are studied less frequently, are no less important. In fact, they are integral to the creation of "field settlements," or agreements that ensure the predictability and stability of markets and other social arenas over time

(McAdam and Fligstein 2011). By focusing attention on processes of conflict and compromise, I aim to demonstrate that the organic sector offers a useful empirical case for making theoretical sense of mechanisms that connect over-arching cultural understandings with particular social outcomes.

Empirical examinations of conflict and compromise appear in a variety of ways in the following chapters. Here, I set the stage for these examinations by unpacking two social processes involved in these modes of interaction: inter-pretive framing and organizational and institutional work. I summarize these processes, and develop the argument through my analysis of empirical data in later chapters.

INTERPRETIVE FRAMING

The study of conflict processes has been the bread and butter of much of the scholarship about social movements that has developed in the United States (McAdam, Tarrow, and Tilly 2001). Scholars in this field have directed a great deal of attention to how participants in social movements "frame" their ar-guments for audiences of supporters, opponents, and fellow activists (Capek 1993; McVeigh, Myers, and Sikkink 2004; Snow et al. 1986). Framing is a stra-tegic cultural activity that involves "assign[ing] meaning to and interpret[ing] relevant events and conditions in ways that are intended to mobilize poten-tial adherents and constituents, to garner bystander support, and to demobi-lize antagonists" (Snow and Benford 1988, 198). Typically, social movement framing involves the creation of cultural accounts that emphasize the threat-ening and unjust nature of problematic conditions, while also emphasizing the moral virtue of social movement activity (Gamson 1992). When it is ap-plied to the organic sector, the idea of framing suggests that contradictory cultural understandings of organic farming do not alone generate conflict. Rather, members of the sector make use of elements of the cultural visions to develop effective and compelling frames.

In the organic sector, the role of framing processes in driving conflict became especially apparent during the development of the federal organic regulations and during the period of market growth that followed their im-plementation. Participants in the organic sector who were critical of these developments emphasized contradictions between the expansionary and the transformative visions and argued that organizational arrangements and practices that reflect expansionary understandings of organic farming's mission threaten the small-scale farms and relational food systems that are central to the transformative vision. Conflict is not a one-sided phenomenon, though. Although challenger groups engage in the most overt and attention-grabbing forms of conflict, their opponents also develop frames to defend the principles of market expansion and the organizational forms that are based on those principles. These "counter action frames" (Haydu 1999) invert the logic of challengers' arguments: they assert that market growth is a virtuous activity that is threatened by the challengers' campaigns, and they describe the boundaries of the organic sector in such a way that growth-oriented firms are included as legitimate participants, but activist groups are outsiders whose behavior is irresponsible and potentially destructive (Lamont and Molnár 2002).

Just as activists may create frames that emphasize contradiction and threat in an effort to mobilize cycles of conflict, so too may peacemakers offer alternative frames that encourage cooperation and compromise (Fligstein 2001b). Various participants in the organic sector have minimized the tensions between the different cultural understandings of organic farming through the development of compromise-oriented frames. Their efforts appeared in the sector's early years, when pioneering organic boosters advocated both for market growth and for the transformation of food production systems while ignoring the possibility that tensions might exist between these goals. Compromise-oriented framing also took place during the development of the NOP. Those who favored federal regulation tried to build support by arguing that it would permit market growth, while also enabling existing members of the organic sector to retain control over what the term "organic" meant, and even potentially bring organic principles into the federal bureaucracy. More recently, members of the sector have promoted compromise by arguing that market growth permits diversity in the organic sector by providing opportunities for some businesses to focus on converting increasing amounts of farmland to organic production while allowing others to develop community-oriented farms. Just as was the case with conflict-oriented frames, compromise frames demonstrate the ways in which people work with the symbolic elements of institutional logics. Members of the organic sector create compromise frames by emphasizing compatible and overlapping parts of the two cultural visions and by moving others to the background.

ORGANIZATIONAL AND INSTITUTIONAL WORK

While frames may initiate patterns of conflict or compromise, the creation of organizations and institutions that coordinate action can lock these patterns into place (Lawrence and Suddaby 2006; McInerney 2014). In the organic sector, conflicts persist in part because critics of market growth have organized groups that regularly challenge the increasing presence of mainstream food businesses. These groups deploy conflict-oriented frames to mobilize consumers in boycott campaigns against businesses that champion market expansion and in "buycott" campaigns to reward those that continue to embrace transformative goals (Micheletti, Føllesdal, and Stolle 2004). Challenger groups also push for regulatory changes that they believe would more clearly differentiate the organic sector from the mainstream food industry. For their part, members of the sector who favor market expansion support institutional arrangements that limit the influence of challenger groups. For example, they defend the relatively narrow and technical nature of federal organic regulations. The character of these regulations makes it difficult for activist groups to bring issues of farm size, community relationships, and social ethics into regulatory discussions.

These conflicts sometimes conceal the extent to which members of the sector have also worked deliberately—and to a certain extent successfully—to build compromises into regulatory and organizational arrangements. In the regulatory arena, one early and enduring effort at compromise was the creation of a stakeholder group called the National Organic Standards Board (NOSB), which advises the Department of Agriculture and has partial veto power over new regulations. The NOSB has offered a way for the sector's participants to exercise a degree of democratic control over the regulations and has provided a forum for the discussion of different understandings of the mission of organic farming. Additionally, organizational structures and practices are often themselves "pragmatic compromises" among different cultural understandings (McInerney 2014, 19). These compromises appear clearly in hybrid organizational arrangements, which emerge when organizations face contradictory external demands, when organizational members feel compelled to act in ways that run counter to their notions of the organization's identity, and when organizational leaders are themselves ambivalent about the proper path forward (Ashcraft 2001; Battilana and Dorado 2010; D'Aunno, Sutton, and Price 1991). In the contemporary organic sector, cooperative food stores offer some of the clearest examples of these hybrid compromise arrangements. Today, these co-ops face enormous competitive pressures from retailers that take market growth much more seriously than social and cultural transformation, and many co-op leaders are themselves unsure about the sort of balance that they would like to see between growth and transformation in the organic sector. In response, these leaders have developed a variety of organizational arrangements that enable their stores to pursue both market-oriented and transformative goals.

SIMULTANEITY, INEQUALITY, AND STRATEGIC ACTION

Several final clarifications are in order. First, in the analysis that follows, I treat conflict and compromise as processes that occur simultaneously. That is, at any given point in the organic sector's history, it is possible to find some members engaged in conflict-oriented activities and others engaged in compromise-oriented ones. Even particular individuals and organizations may be involved simultaneously in patterns of conflict and patterns of compromise. Emphasizing the simultaneity of conflict and compromise fits contemporary theoretical arguments that markets and other organizational fields are places that display ongoing amounts of "low-level contention" as well as collective efforts to constrain and manage the disruptive consequences of that contention (Fligstein and McAdam 2012, 12). Second, the persistence of conflict and compromise within the organic sector does not mean that the two cultural understandings of organic foods production that I have identified—transformative and expansionary—occupy a relatively equal status within the sector. As I have emphasized, one of this book's core arguments is that expansionary understandings have achieved a dominant position. Not only do many new arrivals to the sector articulate these understandings, but the businesses that produce and sell the lion's share of organic products are also modeled along expansionary lines. Institutionally, the federal organic foods regulations also encourage members of the sector to think about the virtue of organic foods production in terms of market growth rather than in terms of systemic transformation. Equality between cultural understandings is not a prerequisite for conflict or compromise, but the relevance of cultural understandings is. This means that key questions to consider are how and why members of the sector mobilize peripheral transformative understandings in processes of conflict, and how and why members of the sector accommodate these understandings in processes of compromise.

Finally, conflict and compromise are strategic activities, in that members of the organic sector participate in them as they pursue particular goals. These goals, which range from the maintenance of individual careers to the survival of businesses to influencing the direction of the organic sector as a whole, are shaped both by the local market contexts in which people operate and by their social and economic position within the organic sector. This does not mean that people in the sector engage in conflict and compromise in a purely dispassionate and calculative way, though. The outcomes of particular episodes of conflict and compromise are usually somewhat uncertain, and strategy consists of flexible and improvisational interactions, rather than the execution of long-range plans (Beckert 1998; Fligstein 2001b). Additionally, cultural pluralism in the organic sector produces "sociological ambivalence" for many of the sector's members (Merton 1976). Conflict and compromise represent ways of navigating this ambivalence as much as they do strategies for achieving long-term goals.

Case Analysis and Theory Building

The qualitative case analysis approach that I employ here is particularly effective for mapping out complicated social processes and yielding insights into the complex ways that people experience and respond to the social and cultural environments in which they act (Maxwell 2005). This book leverages these strengths to advance theoretical understandings of cultural pluralism in market and organizational settings. I discuss these contributions more fully in the final chapter, but summarize them here. First, I highlight the moral and affective dimensions of institutional logics, in addition to the conceptual and cognitive dimensions, which generates a more holistic picture of what logics are and how they shape action and experience. Second, I reveal ways in which individuals draw from different cultural understandings to construct professional identities and strategies of action. I also offer insights into the complexity and ambiguities of acting in plural and contradictory cultural environments. Third, I show how individual and collective actions mediate between contradictory cultural understandings and social processes of conflict and compromise. The concepts of framing and organization provide a way to make sense of how cultural pluralism in certain organizational fields may evolve into widespread contention, as well as how, in other situations, this contention is contained.

The Plan of the Book

This book uses both historical (tracing the sector's pathway over time) and cross-sectional (examining different contemporary patterns of organization) analysis to make sense of the development and effects of the transformative and expansionary understandings in the organic sector. The two chapters that follow this introduction are mainly historical. Chapter 1 focuses on the early years of the organic sector in order to unpack factors that produced different understandings of organic farming. It situates early organic advocacy in the context of movements for alternative agriculture, natural foods, and (after the 1960s) anti-hierarchical and ecologically harmonious living. The chapter also examines how one of these advocates, the influential J. I. Rodale, and his followers combined these transformative understandings with efforts to advance market growth. While the two understandings coexisted in a relatively egalitarian and peaceful way in the sector's early years, the development of federal organic regulations during the 1990s established market growth as a priority and ushered in an episode of sector-wide conflict. This is the subject of Chapter 2, which describes the passage of OFPA and the period of rulemaking that followed. I pay particular attention to the work of sector members to institutionalize a compromise between the principles of market growth and those of democratic participation, and I explain why these efforts had limited success. I also discuss the role of framing and organization in the protests that surrounded the release of the first draft of the regulations in 1997.

The next three chapters examine patterns of conflict and compromise within the contemporary organic sector. Chapter 3 describes convergence between the mainstream food industry and the organic sector, which took place during and after the implementation of federal regulations. These changes in the industry's structure, I argue, have increased the number of sector members with training and experience in mainstream businesses. These individuals draw on and elaborate expansionary understandings as they talk about their professional goals and the meaning of their participation in the organic sector.

As they make a moral case for rapid expansion of the organic market, new arrivals to the sector develop accounts that position profit-oriented businesses as the sector's most important players, that relegate smaller businesses and consumers to the sector's periphery, and that deny legitimate membership to activist groups that advance transformative understandings. Chapter 4, on the other hand, looks at contemporary activists who assert that the organic sector should differ structurally and culturally from the conventional food industry. Activists confront the dominance of expansionary understandings in several ways: the sector's regulatory institutions create barriers to their efforts, many sector members view their work as destructive, and the campaigns that they organize must often sacrifice deliberative, democratic principles in order to be effective. This chapter also more briefly describes the decision by some organic farmers to respond to the dominance of expansionary understandings by creating new, locally based food systems that go "beyond organic."

Chapter 5 examines organic foods co-op stores, which straddle the contradictions between expansionary and transformative understandings. As individuals, leaders of co-ops often acknowledge the legitimacy of both sorts of understandings. Organizationally, co-ops combine activities that pursue market growth with activities oriented toward changing the food system. As I explained above, these businesses offer an important example of how organizational compromises can resolve tensions between contradictory cultural understandings. The book's final chapter reviews the major points of the analysis and discusses its contributions to organizational theory at greater length. It also speculates on the future of the organic sector, and considers the sector's importance not only to organic farmers and consumers but also to people concerned with the role of democratic deliberation in food systems and other bureaucratic and industrialized arenas of modern society.

CHAPTER 1

Breaking Ground for a New Agriculture

Transformation and Expansion during the Organic Sector's Early Years

MANY PEOPLE ASSUME that the organic sector's origins lie in the efforts of idealistic farmers to transform agricultural systems, but ideas and practices that centered on business activities and market growth also have a long history in the organic sector. During the sector's early years, expansionary ideas appeared in the pages of organic farming periodicals, and farmers' groups and organic retail stores embraced practices that aimed to grow markets for organic foods, as well as ones that aimed to change relationships among farmers, consumers, and the land. One of the more striking features of the sector's early years was the relatively peaceful coexistence of these two ways of thinking and organizing. In the young, small, and decentralized organic sector, the contradictions between the two visions did not spark the widespread conflicts that emerged in the sector's later years.

The relative calm of the early organic sector, despite the presence of contradictory cultural understandings, differs from the contention that characterizes many emerging markets. Early markets and other sorts of organizational fields are usually "unsettled" in the sense that dominant understandings and modes of acting have not yet come into being, and they are often marked by struggles between participants who espouse different understandings and approaches (Fligstein and McAdam 2012). Two factors were particularly important in limiting conflicts during the organic sector's early years. The first had to do with the decentralized organization of the sector as a whole. In the absence of overarching rules and regulations, members of the sector were able to practice organic farming in different ways. Markets were limited in size, and farmers typically sold to geographically proximate consumers, which enabled different regional styles of organic farming to emerge. The sector's fragmented character and the lack of a sizable national market for organic foods reduced the chances that different regional understandings would produce widespread conflicts.

Second, leading members of the sector downplayed tensions that existed between different understandings of organic farming. They did so by articulating visions of the organic sector that included both transformative and expansionary principles, as well as by ignoring ways in which organizing the sector for the purpose of market growth might be incompatible with the objective of systemic change. They told stories that implied that organic agriculture could be a lucrative business opportunity as well as an activity that produced social and cultural changes (Lounsbury and Glynn 2001). The statements of organic advocates during this period offer an early example of how people may frame organic farming in ways that seek compromise between different cultural logics. To illustrate this compromise-oriented framing, I discuss the work of J. I. Rodale and other writers for the magazine *Organic Gardening and Farming (OGF)*, which Rodale created. Rodale was not the only mid-twentieth-century advocate of organic farming in the United States, but his prolific writings on the topic made him a central figure in the emerging organic field.[1] For its part, *OGF* helped to synthesize transformative ideas from the alternative agriculture and countercultural movements with a vision of the organic sector's market growth. It also created some of the first institutions that were intended to support the national organic trade.

I begin by placing organic farming advocacy in the context of the development of modern agriculture and food production systems during the late nineteenth and the twentieth centuries. I then examine Rodale's writing, as well as that of other advocates whose work appeared in *OGF*. I show how Rodale and his followers blended expansionary and transformative ideas as they engaged with an audience shaped first by post–World War II concerns about chemically intensive farming and industrial food processing and later by an influx of radical activists from the 1960s New Left and counterculture. I also discuss initiatives that the magazine launched during the late 1960s that aimed to grow the organic market. Finally, I examine the decentralized and regionally oriented character of the sector during the 1970s, which facilitated the existence of diverse understandings of organic production. Here, I focus on organic farmers' groups and on small-scale retailers that specialized in organic foods.

Industrialization and Resistance in the Food System

As the historian Philip Conford puts it, "Organic *methods* have existed for centuries, [but] the organic *movement* could begin only once an alternative to them existed" (Conford 2001, 17). Advocacy for organic farming emerged in the context of industrialized agriculture and mass-market food processing and built on the work of critics who called for a food system organized according to the principles of decentralized and locally oriented farms and markets. In the United States, the rise to dominance of modern (or, as it is usually referred to in organic farming circles, "conventional") agriculture was closely associated with the development of an industrial economy during the late nineteenth and early twentieth centuries. Large enterprises and mass production enabled the widespread use of labor-saving agricultural implements and machinery. These technologies allowed farmers to bring new areas of the country into cultivation and to increase the size of the acreages that they worked. The extension of railways also lowered transportation costs and encouraged the formation of national markets for agricultural commodities, which contributed to increases in the size of farms and to geographical specialization in agricultural production (Cronon 1992). Finally, the movement of people from rural areas to cities created new centers of demand for farm commodities and contributed to the growing emphasis on efficiency and productivity in agriculture.

The federal government, in an effort to ensure the food security of an increasingly urban population, subsidized the expansion of the railroad infrastructure and helped to provide access to land and credit (necessary for investments in new technologies) to farmers (Conkin 2008). Agricultural policymakers also explicitly sought to foster technical innovations through the creation of land-grant agricultural colleges and through systems of agricultural extension agents, who had a mandate to disseminate new technologies from the laboratory to farmers in the field (Henke 2008). The colleges and extension services employed agricultural economists who advocated for models of farm management that copied those in the manufacturing sector and that focused in particular on the use of standardized techniques and capital investment to increase crop yields (Lyson 2004). Later, federal research funding contributed to the widespread availability of synthetic fertilizers and pesticides, which appeared on the market in unprecedented quantities after World War II. Synthetic inputs enabled farms to increase crop yields per acre of cultivated land and reduced the pest and disease risks faced by operations that cultivated only one or two major crops (Stoll 1998). These new tools allowed a relatively small number of farmers to feed an expanding population, although the costs associated with modern farming also contributed to the consolidation of farms into larger units of production and resulted in the bankruptcy of mid-sized farms, particularly during periods in which the production of agricultural commodities exceeded demand (Kirschenmann et al. 2008).

Alongside these on-farm developments, the industrial processing and mass-market distribution of food products increased during the late nineteenth and early twentieth centuries. Giant food processing companies, such as Armour and Swift in the beef industry and Nabisco and Heinz in the packaged foods sector, were well established by the turn of the century. These companies took advantage of new transportation technologies to sell products in distant markets. Swift, for example, pioneered the use of telegraphic ordering and refrigerated railway cars to build an interregional distribution system centered on Chicago (Fields 2003). These national food corporations also helped to spur the creation of modern grocery stores through advancements in food processing and preservation. The new retailers brought lower prices to consumers by stockpiling massive quantities of dry and canned goods, as well as by introducing self-service shopping (Mayo 1993). Food companies also launched lavish advertising strategies to build customer loyalty and increase demand for their branded goods. The Heinz company (now known for its ketchup) erected a six-story illuminated sign shaped like a pickle (then the company's flagship product) at the intersection of Fifth Avenue and Twenty-Third Street in New York City and built the Heinz Pier in Atlantic City, where vacationers could munch on free samples while taking in views of the ocean and of artworks on display (Levenstein 2003b).

By the beginning of the 1950s, the United States had entered what food historian Harvey Levenstein labels "the golden age of food processing" (Levenstein 2003a, 101). Economic growth after World War II increased the household income of many American families, who purchased brand-name convenience foods and the appliances with which to store and prepare them. Large food corporations invested heavily in these value-added products, hiring food chemists, who set to work creating additives to improve the flavor, appearance, nutrition, and shelf life of processed foods, and advertisers, who developed eye-catching packages and brand identities for the new products. Marketed in particular to women in terms evocative of the postwar cult of domesticity, advertisements for frozen, canned, dehydrated, and other convenience foods promised that they would satisfy demanding husbands and children while freeing time for "bridge, canasta, garden club, and other perhaps more soul-satisfying pursuits" (Levenstein 2003a, 106).[2] The explosion of the food processing industry even shaped decision making on the farm, as fruit and vegetable growers shifted to varieties that were more able to withstand the rigors of processing, although the gains in hardiness were often offset by the loss of flavor (Goodman and Redclift 1991).

This modern American food system did not escape criticism. Throughout the twentieth century, dissident farmers, consumers, and agricultural thinkers found reasons for skepticism about the changes in farming and food processing (Beeman and Pritchard 2001; Goodman, DuPuis, and Goodman 2011). Critics drew attention to the environmental consequences of modern farming, arguing that intensive cultivation contributed to the erosion of topsoil and the depletion of soil-based nutrients. Early in the twentieth century, for example, the American soil scientist Franklin H. King completed a study of Asian peasant agriculture titled *Farmers of Forty Centuries*. The book contrasted the use of machinery and manufactured inputs in Western agriculture with Chinese, Japanese, and Korean practices of composting biological wastes and planting cover crops to reduce soil erosion. King argued that the latter techniques were more efficient and, as the title of his book implied, more sustainable over the long term. In the wake of the Dust Bowl crisis of the 1930s, other agricultural reformers such as Hugh Bennett, Paul Sears, and Henry Wallace produced lengthy analyses that linked soil erosion to the possibility of famines and social and economic crises. As Bennett noted in 1935, "History has shown time and again that no large nation can long endure the continuous mismanagement of its soil resources. The world is strewn with the ruins of once-flourishing civilizations, destroyed by erosion" (quoted in Beeman and Pritchard 2001, 14).

New critical voices began to emerge as American agriculture leaned more heavily on synthetic herbicides and pesticides in the years that followed World War II. In the early 1960s, Rachel Carson's influential book *Silent Spring* exposed the hazardous nature of these widely used chemicals. Carson took particular aim at chlorinated hydrocarbons and organophosphates, two common families of synthetic pesticides, arguing that these substances and their by-products had permeated the soil on farms, leached into groundwater supplies, and created dangers for humans and animals alike. She documented cases of acute pesticide poisoning and examined connections between chronic, low-level exposure to pesticides and the development of cancer and other degenerative illnesses. Like earlier environmental critics, Carson also raised the specter of ecological collapse, although her work focused on the loss of beneficial organisms and the development of chemical resistance among pests rather than on soil erosion (Carson [1962] 2002).

The growing food processing industry also fell under the scrutiny of critics. Some of the earliest commentary of this sort came from "natural foods" advocates like Sylvester Graham in the 1830s and his successor John Harvey Kellogg at the end of the nineteenth century. Graham and Kellogg advocated diets of limited variety, with special restrictions on red meat and spicy foods, in the interest of physical and mental health, but they also linked the industrial processing of milk and flour to a decline in public health and argued that the consumption of processed foods created an unnatural state of excitement in the body that contributed to physical illness and moral degeneracy (Gusfield 1992). Later in the twentieth century, food purity critics targeted the widespread use of synthetic additives and preservatives in processed foods. In the 1930s, the consumer advocates Arthur Kallett and F. J. Schlink (1932) published the widely read book *100,000,000 Guinea Pigs*, which argued that the indiscriminate use of these substances exposed the public to unknown but significant health risks. Several decades later, Ralph Nader and his protégés took up the campaign, focusing on the use of monosodium glutamate in baby food and on the potentially carcinogenic sweetener cyclamate (Peters 1979). These critics and others contended (with some justification) that industrial processing robbed food of nutrients that were needed for good health and a long life. The enormously popular nutritionist Adelle Davis, for example, encouraged consumers to turn to natural, minimally processed foods and to use vitamin supplements to make up for the nutritional deficiencies of processed foods (Fromartz 2006).

Skeptics of mainstream agriculture and food processing did not limit their critiques to agricultural technologies and ingredients. Many also challenged what they saw as a distinctively American attention to short-term profits, as well as agricultural policies and scientific institutions that encouraged market-oriented "big farming" at the expense of environmental quality, rural communities, and public health. The problems of modern agriculture, for many of these writers, were symptoms of a more extensive alienation of industrial society from the natural world and from the principles of social and environmental responsibility. Some agricultural critics produced "soil jeremiads" (Beeman and Pritchard 2001) that linked farmland erosion to the vacuous moral character of industrial society. Drawing from agrarian political thought, which had its clearest American expression in the Jeffersonian idea that widely distributed land ownership was necessary for political freedom and social order, they argued that reinvigorating small-scale, family-run farms as the foundation of agricultural production would improve soil management and realign the country's moral compass (Guthman 2004a). The food processing industry's challengers made similar arguments. Natural foods advocates from Sylvester Graham to Adelle Davis lamented the fact that industrially manufactured products had displaced home gardening and cooking, which they described as bastions of physical and mental health. Like agrarian writers, they suggested that as people became more distant from stable communities and direct experience with food production, they were more likely to fall prey to superficial temptations and to lose a sense of moral focus (Gusfield 1992).

Agricultural and consumer activists also linked problems of food purity and healthiness to the dominance of large corporations in the food industry and raised concerns about the accountability of these corporations to the interest and welfare of the public. In *100,000,000 Guinea Pigs*, Kallett and Schlink contended that food corporations' political connections enabled them to obstruct meaningful product safety legislation.[3] Similarly, Nader's group criticized the ability of lobbyists employed by the food industry to shape public dialogue and policy related to food additives and food quality (Turner and Nader 1970). Their arguments paralleled those of Carson, who attributed the overuse of synthetic pesticides to the influence of the chemical industry and to a political system that privileged economic growth over the public interest. In their focus on agrarianism and in their challenges to concentrated economic power, these critics tied the goal of food system reform to a vision of broader social and cultural change.

The Beginnings of Organic Farming Advocacy

These critiques of mainstream agriculture formed a backdrop for the emergence of organic farming advocacy in the 1940s. One of the earliest and probably the most energetic of these advocates was the magazine publisher Jerome Irving (J.I.) Rodale, who founded the magazine *Organic Gardening and Farming* (*OGF*) in 1942.[4] Organizations researchers and economic sociologists have highlighted the important role that discourse plays in the creation of new sorts of organizations and new fields of activity (Phillips, Lawrence, and Hardy 2004; Rao 1998). Pioneers in new fields win support for innovations by constructing stories and accounts that identify problems with existing arrangements and that justify alternative structures and practices (Greenwood, Suddaby, and Hinings 2002; Lounsbury and Glynn 2001; McInerney 2014). Rodale occupied a central position in the emerging organic field largely because of his ability to produce and disseminate copious amounts of talk about organic farming, although he acted more as a conduit for the ideas of others than as a cultural innovator in his own right (Peters 1979). He relied heavily on the work of the British soil scientist Albert Howard, who had developed a compost-based approach to farming while studying agricultural practices in colonial India, as well as on German philosophers of biodynamic agriculture and on a variety of critics of the food processing industry (Conford 2001). Rodale's effectiveness as an advocate for the organic approach had much more to do with his tenacity and his ability to frame the virtues of organic farming in compelling ways to an American audience than with the novelty of his ideas.[5] His work engaged with the critics of mainstream agriculture, although he asserted that organic foods production represented a healthy business opportunity as well as a movement for positive social and cultural change.

Rodale's advocacy operated on several levels. First, he was a pragmatic writer who offered instructions to his readers about how to succeed at organic farming. Articles in *OGF* discussed techniques for solving everyday problems encountered by organic gardeners. His book *Pay Dirt* ([1945] 1959) included a lengthy chapter that explained how to construct and maintain a compost pile that could be worked into the soil as an organic fertilizer, to which he appended a list of "36 reasons why compost farming is superior to farming or gardening with artificial fertilizers" (83). Rodale also emphasized the health benefits of eating a diet of fresh, organically grown foods. For example, *Pay*

Dirt compared the synthetic fertilizers used in conventional farming to human-ingested drugs that produced a temporary boost in vigor but created long-term problems and argued that "the low status of American health is directly related to the condition of the soil in which we raise our food" (153). The book engaged with the critiques of food contamination that were developed by consumer advocates in the 1930s. At one point, for example, Rodale encouraged his readers to "read *100,000,000 Guinea Pigs* by Kallett and Schlink and you will be absolutely convinced that [pesticide residues] do incalculable harm to the human system" (180).

Rodale also positioned organic farming as a populist political movement that aimed to break the control of industry and a scientific elite over farmers. He argued that "the average farmer who uses chemicals . . . has been led to believe that this is the height of scientific farming . . . You can't blame him because he has been systematically propagandized to and has come to believe that it is the only thing to do" ([1945] 1959, 99, 168). The blame, according to Rodale, lay with agricultural scientists and with the chemical and fertilizer companies that funded their research. These claims earned him no love from the scientific establishment, who tended to view his techniques as amateurish quackery at best and as a threat to the American food supply at worst (Peters 1979). Rodale replied in kind by attacking what he saw as the tendency of laboratory science to eliminate farmers' intimate knowledge of the land. "Farming has been too much reduced to a chemical formula by unimaginative, doctrinaire men," he wrote. "The good farmers of bygone centuries in every continent were no more aware of *why* humus, crop rotation, and manure were valuable in keeping land fertile; they knew it from use and observation and experiment, just as the Egyptian knows that the silt of the flooding Nile fertilizes his acres" (129).

The populist elements of Rodale's writing resonated with agrarian concerns about the alienation of people from land ownership and food production. As he noted in terms that may have been drawn directly from one of the early twentieth-century soil jeremiads, "civilizations that get too far from the land are bound to decay. Nations, like Antaeus of old, need to renew their strength by contact with the earth . . . If not, society and civilization decay through ignorance, antagonism, exploitation, and the artificiality that is their product" ([1945] 1959, 237). But agrarian ideas also appeared in Rodale's justification of the organic approach in economic terms. He asserted that organic techniques would enable small-scale landowners with little formal training in agricultural science to make a living from food production. In *Pay Dirt*, he addressed veterans returning from the fronts in Europe and Asia who, in his view, "wanted, many thousands of them, to become farmers" and who would benefit from knowing that "there is a way of farming that is, on the whole, pleasant and rewarding, one that does not require a long course of chemical study by way of preparation" (235). He coupled this down-to-earth appeal with a critique of the educational and capital investments necessary for a novice to begin to farm in the "scientific way," suggesting that the latter would lead to indebtedness, lack of autonomy, and quite possibly, business failure. These entrepreneurial arguments reflected his personal experiences and beliefs, as well as his sense of the concerns of potential adherents to the organic project. An entrepreneur who funded his publications with a small fortune made in electronics manufacturing, Rodale was hardly a critic of the market. He dreamed of a wholesale shift in American farming methods, but he "wanted no confrontation with capitalism" that had enabled his own success (Peters 1979, 114).

In sum, Rodale offered a compromise between a vision of organic farming as a business opportunity and as a program for social change. Economic motivations might draw people into the organic fold, and the satisfactions of farming on a small scale unbeholden to the chemical industry and agricultural scientists might keep them there, but collectively, the organic movement would change the structure and the culture of food production in the United States. The possibility that organic farming might someday be subjected to the same organizational principles that guided the mainstream food industry did not enter Rodale's writing.

Encounters with the Counterculture

During the 1950s and most of the 1960s, Rodale's advocacy for the organic approach mainly reached an audience of home gardeners and a sliver of commercial farmers. In the early 1970s, though, subscriptions to *OGF* soared because of a new interest from a younger generation of readers. Many of the new subscribers were attracted by the affinities that they perceived between organic farming and the countercultural and progressive political ideas that circulated in American society in the wake of the 1960s. They found that the contrast between organic farming and "chemical" food production offered a way to talk about different social visions and values: while choosing to eat organic foods spoke of authenticity, independence, and social and environmental consciousness, the "plastic" foods available in supermarkets "suggested the false, saccharine, stagnant life of the much-despised Organization Man, a spineless bureaucrat molded into accommodating shapes by the lever pullers above" (Belasco 1989, 37). Some of these youthful food critics went beyond consuming natural, minimally processed foods to experiment with growing crops on communal farms. Influenced by survivalist publications such as the *Whole Earth Catalog* and by environmentally minded magazines like *Mother Earth News*, they also turned to *OGF* for inspiration and advice.

While countercultural ideas overlapped with Rodale's critiques to a certain extent, the new organic gardeners also brought into the organic sector a deeper questioning of hierarchical organization, technocratic expertise, and economic systems based on private ownership (Breines 1989; Roszak 1969). One of the earliest groups to make food into a political issue, the Diggers in San Francisco, embraced anarchism as an organizational principle. Members of the group disavowed formal leadership and distributed food for free at open-air "Digger feeds," explaining to passers-by that the food was "free because it's yours" (Alkon 2012). Similarly, participants in cooperative stores and communal farms rotated responsibilities and made decisions collectively in an explicit rejection of the bureaucratic principles that dominated organizational life in the United States (Rothschild-Whitt 1979). The organic ideal of growing food in harmony with natural processes spoke to the vision of cooperative and egalitarian social relationships that lay behind these organizational experiments, although longtime *OGF* subscribers sometimes looked askance at these practices. In turn, the magazine's editors hastened to reassure traditional subscribers that they had much in common with the new organic gardeners. In one article, J. I. Rodale's son, Robert, who had assumed the magazine's editorship in the 1960s, explained that despite some of the new arrivals' propensity to "try drugs, nudity, communal living, free love, and anarchism," those who had an interest in organic foods "pick essentially the same items of diet as you and I, and probably their reasons for wanting to eat organically are actually similar to ours. They just want simple food that isn't messed up and refined in factories, and that isn't contaminated by chemicals or devitalized by synthetic fertilizers" (Rodale 1969, 21–22). Projecting an attitude of amused tolerance, the younger Rodale encouraged his readers to give the "hippies" a patient hearing and to bear in mind that they would probably grow out of their more eccentric practices as the years wore on.

In fact, it was the magazine's advocacy of organic foods that shifted to incorporate some of the ideas that countercultural organic gardeners brought into the organic sector.[6] In particular, concerns about widespread environmental degradation, which also appeared in ecological writings that were popular in the counterculture, became more prominent and more closely linked to the themes of cultural disintegration and social conflict. Robert Rodale and his staff quickly caught on to the resonance of these ideas with their readership—which after all were not so greatly different from the critiques of industrial specialization and agricultural science that appeared in *Pay Dirt* and in J. I. Rodale's other works—and the younger Rodale discussed his fears about an imminent, technologically induced ecological collapse (which organic techniques and the organic mentality could help to prevent) on several occasions. In 1970, for example, he argued that

> [technology] is a powerful force that is out of control in our modern society, almost a Frankenstein's monster. No one person or group of people have [*sic*] the power to prevent the technological expansion which is making pollution worse . . . The need for mental adjustment for everyone is going to be greater than perhaps even you and I realize now. Some of our most cherished goals may have to be shunted aside . . . [and] replaced by a scheme of living which recognizes the limits of our world and its resources. (Rodale 1970c, 32–33)

In addition, the magazine emphasized that organic farmers offered a vision for the organization of agriculture in the United States that resonated with the decentralized, communalist orientations of many of the new adherents. One article by writer Jerome Goldstein called for a "new American Revolution" in agriculture, based on organic principles (Goldstein 1976). Clusters of small organic farms would surround cities, the author explained, since organic products were much better suited to local distribution than long-distance transportation systems. These farms would help to compost urban waste and would provide employment opportunities to urban residents. Even more importantly, food consumers would interact directly with the farmers, which would enable trust and goodwill to filter into economic transactions. Once again, these ideas were not wholly new for the magazine's editors. After all, *Pay Dirt* frequently brought up questions of scale in its critiques of industrial food production and in its assertion that compost-based farming was more suited to small farms than large ones, as well as in its positioning of organic farming as a lucrative entrepreneurial opportunity. For new adherents steeped in the ideals of participatory democracy and the practices of communal living, though, the notions of reorienting agriculture toward communities and of placing relationships ahead of profits had particular significance.

It is important not to exaggerate the affinities between the Rodales' vision of organic agriculture and the more radical ideas of countercultural activists in the 1970s. *OGF* took for granted the value of private ownership of farms and businesses, and certainly did not throw its weight behind the principles of collective ownership and egalitarian decision making. However, the magazine remained relevant by shifting with the times. As countercultural and environmental activists became interested in organic foods production, *OGF* became a conduit through which their ideas and concerns spilled over into the organic sector (Meyer and Whittier 1994). The presence of these ideas helped to elaborate the notion that organic farming was a program for social and cultural change, as well as a healthier and more environmentally sustainable way to grow food. As one staff writer explained, "All of us together are trying to create a new change in the philosophy of American agriculture . . . There is a certain subtlety about the organic idea that requires reflection, time, and compost-making (both in the garden and in the head) to comprehend. It's a very simple idea—but not enough Americans now grasp the direct line between food and garbage, between welfare and agriculture, between campus unrest and 'plasticized' living" (Olds 1970b, 51).[7]

Making the Organic Sector Ready for Business

The increased interest in organic farming that occurred at the beginning of the 1970s also translated into growing consumer demand. The notion of seeking out and eating organically grown foods began to make inroads into the minds of consumers as the result of increasing concern about health risks associated with pesticide residues on foods. In 1970, one reporter answered the question "Why the trend toward organic foods?" by noting that "Rachel Carson's book *Silent Spring*, published in 1962, and countless articles since, alerted the public to the dangers of some pesticides and other harmful substances that had found their way into the nation's food supplies" (Hewitt 1970). A year later, a second writer remarked that "a few years ago, the market for [organic] products was fed by a scattering of faddists . . . but that was before the back-to-nature spirit roused the young, and the rest of the nation was shaken by the cranberry scare, the mercury-in-tuna scare, and the cyclamate scare" (*Time* 1971). *OGF* also noted the surge in consumer demand in an article that bore the provocative title "Ordinary Housewives Flocking to Health Food Stores? There Must Be a Reason—Maybe It's DDT!" (Rodale 1970b). As one executive at Rodale Press put it, "I've been in this business for 16 years, and nothing happened for the first 13. Since then, it's been phenomenal" (*Time* 1971).

Even as *OGF* writers incorporated ideas from the counterculture into the magazine, they also sought to ride the wave of growing consumer demand and to usher rationalized market structures into the organic sector. Writers lamented the lack of efficiency and standardization in the organic marketplace, pined for consistency in organic foods prices and definitions, and criticized the haphazard distribution systems that resulted in limited and unpredictable supplies of organic products to consumers. One exasperated contributor commented that "organic food marketing today has many of the same qualities as an adolescent female—inconsistent, sometimes sublime, sometimes ridiculous, often expensive, frustrating, and full of promise" (Olds 1969c, 66). In a separate article, Olds also presaged the success of contemporary organic foods retail chains like Whole Foods Market by proposing the creation of a national network of "market centers" that would sell a wide range of organic foods and act as "clearinghouses for information that pertains to the organic way of life" (Olds 1969b, 68).

It appears surprising from a contemporary vantage point that these writers saw few contradictions between their calls to create a rationalized infrastructure for growing the organic market and the critiques of mainstream farming and technocratic culture that also appeared in the magazine. As I will discuss below, writers sometimes noted that consumer demand for organic products might attract the interest of unscrupulous farmers who did not grow organically but had no qualms about advertising their products as organic in order to gain access to the market. However, there appears little other evidence of concern among the magazine's writers that growth and rationalization might be *inherently* antagonistic to the ambitions of some organic advocates to usher in social and cultural change. Instead, authors of expansionary articles tended to assume that making organic foods available to an increasing number of consumers would draw more small-scale farmers into organic production, rather than encouraging existing organic farmers to adopt the commodity-oriented strategies of their conventional counterparts. While they may have been nervous about fraud, they (like J. I. Rodale in previous decades) stopped short of considering the possibility that organic techniques might be adopted by mainstream producers without corresponding changes in farming systems.[8]

These writers' longings for efficiency, consistency, and growth within the organic sector also revealed the influence of mainstream understandings of how markets *should* function within this emerging field of activity. As the consumer trade in organic foods increased and as markets for organic products became more established, members of the organic sector referred to criteria used to evaluate success in other markets and industries. The fact that they did so without questioning the appropriateness of these criteria for the organic trade suggests that at least some members of the sector took the legitimacy of these broader commercial logics for granted. As Jepperson (1991, 147) explains, the notion of the "taken-for-grantedness" of institutional logics, which appears frequently in the literature on organizational institutionalism, is actually fairly complex because "taken-for-grantedness is distinct from conscious awareness: one may take for granted some pattern because one does not perceive it or think about it; alternatively, one may subject the pattern to substantial scrutiny, but still take it for granted—if in a quite different fashion—as an external constraint." The ease with which *OGF* writers deployed these ideas indicates that their taken-for-grantedness was of the former variety.

In addition to publishing articles that called for rationalized organic foods marketing and distribution, *OGF* also launched two initiatives that aimed to grow sales of organic foods—or at least the sales of people who fit the magazine's definition of "real" organic farmers. The first of these initiatives targeted consumers, while the second was aimed at farmers. In 1969, the magazine announced "a major effort to increase the sale of organic foods throughout the United States" through the publication of the annual Organic Foods Directory and a new Organic Food Shopper section (Olds 1969a, 39). The directory would help to guide customers who wanted to buy organic foods to local stores that sold them, while the Organic Food Shopper section would demystify the world of organic foods retailing by profiling organic businesses "from California supermarkets to New York shoppes" (Olds 1969b, 56). The focus on the purchase and consumption of organic foods represented a departure from the magazine's traditional emphasis on gardening and farming, and an acknowledgment that increasing numbers of people who were interested in organic foods found the details of compost-making less than stimulating. Nevertheless, the magazine continually reassured its readers that farmers would also benefit from market growth, and it suggested, in fact, that consumers who were not willing or able to grow their own organic foods had a responsibility to support farmers who were. As the editor of the Organic Foods Shopper section explained to these readers, "Only you as part of the American Consumer Market can help farmers become organic—and stay organic. They have shown that they don't need sprays, or high nitrates, or super phosphates. But they do need you to purchase their produce [and] maybe go out of your way a bit to find a store that carries their harvest" (Olds 1970a, 89).

The second initiative aimed to increase the consistency of the practices used by organic farmers. As Robert Rodale noted in 1970,

> The phrase "organic food" means different things to different people. When you are growing organic food for yourself, your personal definition is all that counts. But when you represent to the public that a food is organically grown, there must be a standardized meaning so that people know what they are getting. The lack of a standard definition of "organic" and a means to enforce that definition has held back the marketing of [organic] food. (Rodale 1970a, 30)

Rodale and others at *OGF* saw several obstacles to this sort of standardization of organic farming practices. Commercial organic farmers had organized themselves regionally into associations and cooperative groups in many parts of the country, but there was little communication across the different regions. Additionally, increased consumer demand for organically grown foods raised new possibilities for fraudulent marketing. In 1971, Rodale warned his readers that "some money-oriented farmers are prepared to accept a loose definition of what organic means [and] the money in organic foods selling is causing marketing people to get hungry for a slice of the profits they see waiting to be harvested, and some of these marketers have shown a willingness to stretch the truth" (Rodale 1971, 73).

In order to fend off these "money-oriented farmers" and unscrupulous marketers, *OGF* developed an independent certification program for organic foods producers. This program established a baseline definition of organic farming, created procedures for farm inspection and certification, and offered certified organic farmers the opportunity to use a specially designed label to "identify themselves for the benefit of organic food buyers" (Allen 1971, 80). The program's rules were straightforward and, by contemporary standards, quite flexible: farmers had to work toward improving soil through the use of compost (the program stipulated that certified farms either possess or achieve within five years a minimum 3 percent humus content in soil), while avoiding synthetic fertilizers, herbicides, and insecticides. Inspection procedures were likewise informal. As one inspector explained, "When I visit a farm I look for evidence that there is a commitment to basic organic farming methods. How are weeds controlled; can I see weeds where there should be weeds? I look for birds and insects and other evidence that there has been no recent spraying or dusting with toxic insecticides" (Allen 1971, 80). The program was launched in California in 1971. Despite the obvious fact that the inspection procedures were not foolproof, the magazine optimistically predicted growth in the number of certified farmers and in the sales of certified organic products and the eventual national expansion of the program.

Decentralized Organization in the Organic Sector

Although interest in organic farming continued to grow, *OGF*'s certification program lasted only a few years. In 1973, the magazine explained that it had learned that "certification programs are best developed by organic farmers and by persons directly associated with distribution and consumption of their harvest, on a *grass-roots, regional basis*" (emphasis in original) and announced that it would shift its efforts to helping organic farming groups that wanted to develop their own certification programs (Foote and Goldstein 1973, 89). This change reflected both the sector's decentralized character and the fact that not all farmers were equally inspired by the goal of creating a standardized, expanding market for organic foods. Regional variations in organic farming practices existed, and farmers' groups in various parts of the country created different sorts of collective and organizational identities that combined commercial work with visions of social and cultural change (Albert and Whetten 1985; Polletta and Jasper 2001). Similarly diverse orientations existed in organic foods retailing. Many of the sector's participants appreciated the lack of overarching definitions and valued the freedom to work out ways to "do organic" at a more local level. The sector's decentralized character thus hampered initiatives aimed at standardization and efficiency, but it also reduced the extent to which widespread conflicts developed around different visions of organic production.

FARMERS' GROUPS

The number of regional organic farmers' groups that existed in the United States increased during the 1970s. By the middle of the decade, the upper Midwest, California, Oregon, Texas, New England, and the southeastern states all hosted active communities of organic farmers. Some of these farmers' groups focused narrowly on promoting organic crops to consumers. For example, one article in *OGF* described the work of Malcolm Beck, a Texas organic farmer, who along with other growers organized a cooperative marketing and certification program to increase sales of organic produce at local stores (Rodale 1970a). For other groups, sales growth was a secondary concern. Organized by novice farmers, these groups operated as sources of social support and as places to exchange knowledge about organic cultivation techniques. They were also settings where these new organic farmers could discuss the social and environmental concerns that drew them away from mainstream careers, and where they could escape the hostility that they often encountered from more-established agricultural institutions. Members of these groups were invested in preserving the organizational and ideological distinctiveness of the organic sector and they displayed various levels of engagement in the sorts of market-building activities that *OGF* promoted.

An examination of groups in two of these regions—New England and California—helps to illustrate the variations that existed among farmers' groups. In New England, organic farmers were led by a former chemist turned yogurt entrepreneur named Samuel Kaymen to form the Natural Organic Farmers Association (NOFA) in 1971. NOFA's organizational bases during the 1970s were in Vermont and New Hampshire, although farmers founded additional chapters in Massachusetts and New York during the early 1980s. The group also sponsored free-flowing summer conferences about organic ideas and methods that drew attendees from around the region and from Canada. These conferences were philosophical as well as technical—for example, they included discussions about connections between organic foods production, alternative energy, and cooperative organization—and they provided opportunities for organic homesteaders to meet others with similar countercultural leanings.

Many of NOFA's members turned to organic farming as a result of their involvement with other social movement communities. For example, one early member described herself as a "New York City girl" who "really began to focus on environmental issues around the time of the first Earth Day," in 1970.[9] She moved to Montreal after that event, where she worked at a food cooperative, read back issues of *OGF*, and became acquainted with the work of the ecological anarchist Murray Bookchin. Several years later, she moved to Vermont and helped to create a number of community food projects, including a farmers' market and a cooperative cannery. It was through this work that she connected with NOFA organizers. A second member, who had grown up "in a suburban environment with no interest in agriculture whatsoever" discovered the work of ecological philosophers while in college. He left the suburbs after graduation and moved to a small town, where he taught high school courses in ancient history and comparative cosmologies and read the work of ecological poet Gary Snyder and Stewart Brand's *Whole Earth Catalog* in the evenings. He began to attend NOFA conferences after purchasing an "off-the-grid" farm in a community populated by "other organic minded people."[10]

The group's events were important for these individuals and for other former urbanites who had little experience with agriculture, but NOFA provided more than instruction in organic techniques. The group also reassured its members that their goals were not foolish and their work was not futile, countered the hostility that novice organic farmers experienced in more conventional agricultural settings, and helped to build collective identity among farmers in the region (Polletta and Jasper 2001). As a third member of the group explained,

> When I started farming . . . I called up the [university] cooperative extension office and I asked if they had any information about growing raspberries organically and the extension person just laughed at me. He said that's not possible so I didn't call back for a long time . . . There wasn't very

much encouragement about what I was doing except among a wonderful community of people who were homesteading or doing some small-scale farming around the Northeast who I got to know through NOFA.[11]

Many of the organizers of California Certified Organic Farmers (CCOF), one of the leading West Coast organic farming groups, also lacked agricultural training or experience. Barney Bricmont, who led the group's formation in 1973, had little farming experience outside of summer work on the orchard of an aunt who was an avid reader of Rodale's magazines and who refused to treat her apple trees with pesticides. He was an energetic organizer, though, and helped to launch farmers' markets, cooperative food distributors, and a recycling center before turning his attention to organic farming. Like NOFA, CCOF possessed a prominent "countercultural element" and also organized annual meetings, which group members referred to as "tribal gatherings" (Guthman 2004a, 112). Members of the group received practical advice in organic techniques, moral support, and a sense of community that aided inexperienced farmers who found little encouragement from other sources. Janet Brians, an early participant who had purchased a ranch with her husband as a way to escape the smog and congestion of San Francisco, recalled that "it was so wonderful to meet people with the same philosophy, who . . . were concerned about feeding the earthworms, feeding the soil, these kinds of things. It was very reinforcing of what we believed in."[12] As was the case in the Northeast, conventional agricultural organizations were of little help to these organic pioneers. Russell Wolter, another early CCOF member, remarked that "they used to make fun of me over at the Salinas 4-H office, [saying] "over there is Wolter's weed patch because he won't use anything to kill his weeds.""[13]

Despite these similarities, CCOF became active in the inspection and certification of organic farms much earlier than NOFA did, partly because CCOF emerged in the wake of the Rodale certification effort and involved some of the same farmers that had supported the earlier program. The greater attention that CCOF devoted to certification also had to do with the more extensive organic foods market that existed in California and with growers' sense that consumer demand for organic foods had attracted the attention of larger, commercially oriented farms that would use organic labels without buying into organic practices. Inspections involved visits to a farmer from other group members, who would look for evidence of chemical use and other blatant violations of organic practices, but who were often just as interested in gleaning tips about organic techniques from another practitioner. Farms that passed inspection—and most did—were permitted to use a label bearing the CCOF logo to market their products.

NOFA's certification procedures, by contrast, developed later and occupied less of the group's energy. Efforts to develop a certification program began in Vermont in the late 1970s after one member ran a newspaper ad seeking a volunteer organizer to take on the work. Some years later, the Massachusetts chapter secured a small federal grant that provided for the hire of a part-time certification coordinator. NOFA members used a variety of strategies to create formal definitions and rules for organic certification: they surveyed members' techniques, analyzed existing programs such as the one designed by CCOF, and convened meetings between farmers and consumers. The demand for certification services was quite low, though, since few members sold their crops at a great distance from their farms. One individual involved in the Vermont program recalled that "until 1984 there were probably no more than five certified organic growers in any given year."[14]

CCOF's role as a gatekeeper to the organic market also politicized the organization in ways that did not occur in NOFA. Commercial growers, frustrated by the group's clubby, "hippie" atmosphere, gained positions on the CCOF board and pushed the organization to become more similar to the conventional trade associations and growers' groups with which they were familiar (Guthman 2004a, 119). These new arrivals also played an important part in making sure that organic certification did not include consideration of factors like farm size and labor standards, despite the efforts of more activist members to promote them. Of course, there were limits to the group's co-optation by market-oriented actors—CCOF continued to discourage "mixed" (organic and conventional) operations and to insist that certified farms compost their wastes—but the organization was marked by continual struggles between more and less commercial visions of organic production.

DISTRIBUTION AND RETAILING

Just as organic farming groups and certification programs differed across regions, so were distribution and retailing arrangements similarly fragmented. The organic and natural foods supermarket chains that figure so prominently in today's retailing landscape did not exist in the 1970s. Moreover, commercial considerations were secondary for a number of the participants in the early organic foods retailing world.

A significant amount of organic foods on the market moved through direct sales from farmers to the public. These markets took several forms. In California, open air farmers' markets began to appear after the loosening of state laws that prohibited growers from selling their products off their property. Organic farmers gathered at schools, at churches, and in downtown areas to sell produce directly to consumers. In Michigan, farmers developed markets for their crops by advertising in local newspapers. *OGF* profiled one such farmer, who reported that selling to customers in nearby areas enabled her to arrange visits to her garden, which reassured buyers about the quality of her crop and gave her the chance to educate the public about organic gardening techniques (Franz 1970). However, not all direct sales were local. Producers of dry goods and products that could be frozen, like meat, shipped products by ground and air freight to customers around the country.

Direct marketing most closely resembled Rodale's vision of an organic foods system organized around small-scale farms and regional markets. Making a living through direct sales was no easy task, though. Farmers not only had to persuade people to pay more for organically produced foods, but they also had to find ways to encourage them to forgo the convenience of supermarket shopping. This sort of marketing doubled the work of enterprising farmers. For example, *OGF* reported on one "virile" Virginia rancher who raised organic beef cattle, developed a local base of customers, and opened an independent health foods store, while "lecturing widely" about the health benefits of organic foods and the rise in degenerative diseases that followed the industrialization of agriculture in the United States (Goldman 1969, 36). Relationships with customers had to be managed on an individual basis, and arrangements such as farmers' markets offered little economic security. What was a farmer to do if customers stayed home because of a rainstorm on market day? Most fresh organic crops needed to be sold right away and would not keep until the next market day rolled around.

Given these challenges, the natural foods stores that also began to proliferate in the 1970s became an important channel for the distribution of organic products. These stores consolidated produce from a number of organic farmers and food producers, and offered a relatively convenient location for customers to shop. Many of these stores operated as collectively owned and democratically run cooperatives. Store members certainly cared about eating organic foods, but they also brought a variety of other ethical and political concerns into their organizations (Zwerdling 1979). Their democratic decision-making procedures also led to long and tortuous meetings about store policies and priorities. One former member of a co-op recalled her initiation into the organic sector at one of these organizations:

> I came out [to California] in a hippie van and went to work at a place . . . that was a collective, collectively owned. Everybody that worked there was an owner, and we had an equal vote. There was nobody that had any more power than the other person. There were a lot of radically different ideas about what our agenda was. Was it to have healthy food, or were we doing political things, or were we changing the environment? Were we giving work to minorities and women? All different agendas.[15]

Other natural foods stores were more typical small businesses, with single owners, hierarchical management structures, and a focus on meeting market demand. These stores were more efficient in a commercial sense, but they also faced challenges. One of the greatest of these was ensuring that the foods that they sold were actually grown organically. Store owners and managers relied on certification programs when they were available, but they also did their own research and cultivated relationships with farmers and other suppliers that they knew to be committed to organic production. This meant that supply chains were often local or regional in nature, particularly in states, such as California, that had relatively large communities of organic foods producers. Maintaining consistency and quality in supplies of organic products was also a challenge for some natural foods stores, especially those that worked with small-scale organic producers. Store owners and managers developed a number of creative responses to this problem. One Pennsylvania store owner created "contract agreements" with local organic farmers, in which he provided them with seeds and pre-purchased their crops at the beginning of the growing season (Goldman 1970). A store owner in Chicago opened a processing center to freeze organic produce shipped in from California, which he then sold to area retailers. Other store owners grew their own organic fruits and vegetables, which placed them in the same frustrating position as farmers engaged in direct-sale distribution (Wyndham 1969).

When combined with limited demand for organic foods, the challenges of authenticity and consistency were enough to keep most mainstream supermarkets out of the organic foods business. Exceptions were unusual enough to draw considerable attention. One article in the early 1970s described a Colorado-based supermarket company as a "chain store that dared" to carry a limited selection of organic produce (Sirota 1970). The twenty or so organic items available at its Denver-area stores were flown in from growers in California and sold once each week at a full-service counter to health-conscious elderly customers. The company's produce manager explained that these customers "like the idea of service" and appreciated the chance to "discuss the fine points of organic foods (as well as their personal problems) among themselves and our sympathetic produce clerks." The company also installed a self-service organic foods section in a downtown store that was visited mainly by students who were "well-versed in the ecology movement" (67). The company reported considerable success from this experiment, but by and large, mainstream supermarkets ignored or avoided products that came with organic claims.

Conclusion

In both discourse and practice, the early organic sector nurtured multiple understandings of the nature and purpose of organic farming. Ideas about efficiency, consistency, and growth filtered into the sector from the business world, and some participants accepted the legitimacy of these principles without question. On the other hand, the notion that organic farming aimed to bring about broad social and cultural changes also had a robust existence in the sector. These ideas were rooted in long-running critiques of mainstream systems of food production and of industrially manufactured foods that existed in the United States, but they also drew from the rich symbolism of the countercultural and environmental movements of the 1960s and 1970s. As these movements converged with the organic sector in the early 1970s, their critiques of mainstream society spilled over into the stories that the sector's leaders told about the purpose of organic agriculture (Meyer and Whittier 1994).

Multiple cultural understandings often exist in emerging markets, and it is easy to assume that contradictory visions of purpose and organization will make these fields into arenas of struggle and conflict (Fligstein and McAdam 2012). In the organic sector, however, this was not the case. Localized conflicts existed, such as those that split CCOF between market-oriented growers and countercultural farmers, but the sector as a whole was a fairly tranquil place in which diverse visions existed in different regions with a limited amount of friction. The sector's relative lack of contention had much to do with the fragmented and decentralized character of organic production and organic foods markets at this time. With no overarching legal framework that forced members of the sector to produce or market organic foods in particular ways and with the trade in organics organized mainly at a local or regional level, the sector's members did not have compelling reasons to interpret their peers' ideological and organizational differences as threatening.

In addition, leading advocates for organic farming developed accounts that downplayed the potential contradictions between activities oriented toward market expansion and those oriented toward systemic change. This sort of compromise-oriented cultural framing characterized the advocacy of J. I. Rodale during the 1940s and 1950s, and it continued to appear in the pages of *OGF* in subsequent years. Rodale and the magazine's other writers asserted the complementarity of market growth and systemic change by suggesting that increasing the number of organic farmers and consumers would help to shift the American food industry toward small-scale, owner-operated farms. They largely ignored the possibility that mainstream farms and food businesses would take up organic techniques, and assumed that market growth could occur with little or no change in the organic sector's organizational patterns. These ways of framing the organic project, as well as the decentralized, fragmented character of the organic sector itself, encouraged tolerance of different understandings of organic farming.

In Chapter 2, I explain how the development of a national market for organic products and the creation of federal organic regulations introduced widespread conflicts between expansionary and transformative understandings of organic farming within the sector. The law that authorized federal regulations spelled the end of the ability of organic farmers in different regions to craft their own styles of organic production. It forced members of the sector to accept a single set of rules for organic farming, and in doing so, it made them confront more directly the contradictions between these cultural understandings. Members of the sector who supported the federal regulations argued that this change would not interfere with the ability of organic farming to transform the food system, and in fact, they worked to bring transformative organizational principles into the regulatory environment. Increasingly, though, advocates for the organic sector's growth confronted cultural frames that emphasized contradictions between market expansion and systemic change.

CHAPTER 2

Stabilizing the Market, Dividing the Field

Federal Regulation, Field Settlement, and the Emergence of Conflict

THE PASSAGE OF the Organic Foods Production Act (OFPA) by the U.S. Congress in 1990 marked the beginning of federal regulation in the organic sector. This law directed the Department of Agriculture (USDA) to create rules for organic foods production and mechanisms to ensure the credibility of organic marketing claims. One member of the sector, thinking of the hostility with which mainstream agricultural institutions had treated organic farming and the scope of the changes that the law promised to bring to the sector, described OFPA's passage as a "legislative miracle" (Forster 1990). Indeed, it would be difficult to overestimate the law's significance. Instead of the decentralized, regionally oriented, and voluntary patterns of organization that I described in Chapter 1, OFPA paved the way for a uniform set of national regulations with which all organic farmers and food producers would have to comply. Whether they loved it or loathed it, the law would change the rules of the organic game in ways that sector members could not ignore.

State regulation is often essential for achieving settlement in emerging fields of activity, which are characterized by consensus about the rules that govern the field's activities and by a resulting "generalized sense of order and certainty" (Fligstein 2001a; Fligstein and McAdam 2012, 22). In the organic sector, though, the impact of federal regulation was somewhat paradoxical. In the first place, regulation stabilized the national organic marketplace and contributed to unprecedented growth in sales of organic foods. This was OFPA's goal, and in this respect, the law was successful. However, OFPA and the regulations that it created also sparked greater amounts of conflict within the sector as a whole by enshrining market growth as a priority and by pushing transformative ideas and practices to the sector's margins. Conflict was inevitable in some ways: since compromises between different under-standings during the sector's early years relied on decentralized organization and regional diversity, a uniform regulatory framework could not help but inflame tensions. But divisions occurred despite the best attempts of individuals involved in the regulatory process to build compromises into the law and into the rulemaking process that followed its passage. The circumstances involved in the law's passage and the processes by which it was implemented limited their efforts and also contributed to conflict.

This chapter examines the efforts to institutionalize compromises between expansionary and transformative understandings in the federal regulations and traces the history of the law and the trajectory of the ensuing regulatory process to account for the emergence of widespread conflict in the organic sector. I begin with an analysis of the economic and political factors that led to OFPA's passage, which illustrates how field-level governance institutions may come into existence through a combination of efforts to solve long-term problems and responses to unexpected, disruptive events. The first two sections of the chapter make the case that the form that OFPA took was not wholly determined by the needs of a growing market, but rather resulted from the strategic work of sector participants in fluid, unpredictable circumstances. In particular, sector participants worked to ensure that OFPA included a guarantee of democratic participation in rulemaking, which they saw as essential for the law's legitimacy within the organic sector.

Next, I turn to an examination of interactions between organic advocates and federal bureaucrats within the Department of Agriculture after OFPA's passage. While the law created a basic framework for the National Organic Program (NOP), the details of the regulation were hashed out on the unfamiliar (at least for organic advocates) terrain of the federal bureaucracy. This posed another challenge: although OFPA had mandated public participation in rulemaking, organic advocates needed to transform the law on paper into institutional practice in ways that would satisfy skeptics within the organic sector. They responded with the sorts of activities that organizational theorists have labeled "institutional work" (Lawrence and Suddaby 2006; Lawrence, Suddaby, and Leca 2009). This concept shifts attention from the formal characteristics of laws and regulatory institutions to the actions that participants in these institutional settings take to advance their interests and influence.

Among other things, institutional work involves the strategic and creative manipulation of meanings, rules, and procedures in order to achieve desired ends, although these efforts occur within the limits defined by institutional settings (Maguire, Hardy, and Lawrence 2004; Rojas 2010). Organic advocates engaged in two sorts of institutional work. First, they tried to frame the rulemaking process in ways that minimized contradictions between transformative organizational principles, the market-oriented character of OFPA, and the routines of the USDA bureaucracy. Second, they surprised USDA staff by bringing unexpected levels of public participation to bear in rulemaking through the mechanism of a stakeholder advisory group called the National Organic Standards Board (NOSB).

Despite these efforts, skepticism about the federal regulations persisted in the organic sector. As the NOP moved toward completion, members of the sector who opposed federal regulation became convinced that USDA oversight would erode alternative farming structures within the organic sector. They were (reasonably) concerned, as three members of the sector put it, that the process was reducing organic farming "to materials lists and environmental benevolence [by excluding from consideration] notions of whole systems, let alone fair prices and environmental justice" (Kirschenmann, Kahn, and Ferguson 1993, 19). Critics framed regulation in ways that emphasized fundamental contradictions between the USDA's priorities and the essential features of organic agriculture. These conflict frames helped to fuel public protests against a draft version of the regulations that the USDA released in 1997, although I will make the argument that supporters of the regulatory process also played a key role in these protests and used conflict frames strategically to defend the NOSB's role in rulemaking, rather than to undermine federal regulation as a whole. The episode of protest highlights the role that political contestation plays in shaping governance institutions in fields that contain contrasting institutional logics (Bartley 2007), and it also hints at ways that field settlements can lock in ongoing patterns of contention.

Preparing the Ground for Federal Regulation

Institutional economists and economic sociologists have demonstrated that participants in markets rely on formal laws and informal rules to moderate competition, resolve disputes, establish standards of exchange and product design, and control market entry (Fligstein 1996; Williamson 1981). In the absence of the order and predictability that these governance structures provide, it is difficult for markets to persist over time. But where do governance structures come from? On the one hand, they stem from efforts by market participants to ensure their own welfare by solving collective problems of uncertainty and instability. Since organizational survival ranks high on participants' list of priorities, they usually have ample incentive to engage with others to negotiate rules that will limit destructive forms of competition (Fligstein 2001a). On the other, disruptive events that unsettle existing understandings and relationships may lead participants to perceive new opportunities to advance their interests or pose urgent threats to which members of a market feel that they must respond (Clemens and Cook 1999; Fligstein and McAdam 2012). In these cases, trajectories of negotiation may be redirected toward the creation of types of governance institutions that differ from those that were previously envisioned. Unexpected disruptions also propel "socially skilled" individuals into pivotal positions. These individuals are able to "take what the system will give" (Fligstein 2001b, 113) and organize cooperative action around new possibilities. Thus, governance structures are often an amalgam of consensual arrangements that have accrued over time and improvised responses to unexpected events that are ushered in by particular individuals who often leave a personal stamp on the process.

The history of OFPA provides an illustration of this general process, although it also includes an interesting variation. As the national market for organic foods grew, participants faced destabilizing instances of fraud and frustrating complexities in interstate trade. They sought to resolve these problems by creating sector-wide rules and frameworks for production and exchange. It is common for participants in growing markets to turn to the state for assistance in stabilizing markets, usually "by approaching the government to legislate to promote 'fair' competition" (Fligstein 2001a, 27–28). However, the position of organic farming vis-à-vis the agricultural policy establishment initially made many sector members reluctant to involve the federal government in market governance. Most organic farmers had experienced or heard of hostile treatment from policymakers and bureaucrats, which contributed to widespread skepticism about whether federal involvement was desirable or even possible. Instead, they invested much of their energy in creating private-sector governance institutions, with more or less success (Obach 2015). A wholesale (but somewhat reluctant) switch to a federal legislative strategy occurred after a national scare about the effects of the agricultural chemical Alar disrupted these efforts and revealed serious problems in organic foods supply chains.

During the 1980s, markets for organically grown products expanded at a modest but steady rate. Certain areas of the country became hot spots of organic production and consumption. In Northern California, market-oriented growers like Ted Koons of TKO and Myra and Drew Goodman of Earthbound Farms began to supply networks of restaurants and shops with organically grown lettuces and other vegetables (Fromartz 2006). Health and body image concerns fueled the demand for organic products, as did the desire of upwardly mobile and highly educated consumers to spend their money to support what they perceived to be environmentally and socially enlightened forms of food production (Guthman 2003). Elsewhere, chains of natural and organic foods retail stores emerged. Whole Foods Market, which is currently a leader in the organic foods retail market and is the sole surviving chain of substantial size from that era, was founded in Austin in 1980 and had expanded to other locations in Texas and Louisiana by the mid-1980s.[1] Bread & Circus, a northeastern chain, and Mrs. Gooch's, a Southern California one, played the same role in other parts of the country. These chains did not replace the direct-to-consumer marketing arrangements and independent stores that had come into existence during the previous decade, but they did bring a new way of doing business into the organic sector. Chain retailers sourced organic goods from a variety of farms, some of which were quite a bit larger than the pioneering organic farms of the 1970s, and they were more likely to rely on suppliers that were distant from the retail locations themselves. National markets for organic products expanded through these retailers' activities, and the sector's economic balance of power began to shift in the direction of larger businesses (Klonsky 2000).

As organic foods markets expanded, members of the sector who were involved in the national trade began to argue that the voluntary, decentralized organic certification system that had developed during the 1970s was ill-equipped to support a growing market (Ingram and Ingram 2005). Members of the sector relied on certification programs developed by organic farming groups, as well as a small number of programs created by state agriculture departments (Bones 1992).[2] These groups inspected farms that marketed organically grown products and provided a guarantee to retailers and customers, in the form of a label affixed to a product's packaging, that the farmer had followed the program's rules for organic production. Since these groups established rules through investigation of the practices of their farmer-members, variations existed in program requirements and definitions. For example, California Certified Organic Farmers (CCOF) required that farmland be managed organically for only one year before crops could be marketed as organic, but other certification groups required two or three years of transition time. Also, since some of these groups combined certification with technical and marketing assistance for farmers who were experimenting with organic production, they offered some flexibility in the certification process. Even farms that did not meet all of their requirements could gain certification if they demonstrated that they were working to conform to organic principles (Fetter and Caswell 2002).[3]

Since consumers could not tell by the characteristics of a product whether it had been grown organically, confidence in certifier labels was essential for market growth. The problem was that private certifiers had a limited ability to challenge fraudulent marketing claims. Even in the few states with organic laws on the books, enforcement was often spotty or simply nonexistent. Fraud became a serious problem as demand for organically grown foods increased and as retailers faced greater pressure to find supplies of organic products, and simultaneously, the growing distance and anonymity in organic supply chains made fraud difficult to detect. Even when certifiers discovered fraud, they often had to go to extraordinary lengths to protect their labels. One well-known case that occurred in the spring of 1988 involved a California produce distribution company named Pacific Organics, which was providing conventionally grown carrots that been labeled falsely as organic to stores in California, Oregon, and Washington. Retailers became suspicious of the product only when they realized that other West Coast organic foods distributors were facing a seasonal shortage of organic carrots and other vegetables. Working with an employee from one of these other distribution companies, members of CCOF organized an undercover operation to photograph workers at Pacific Organics who were putting bundles of conventionally grown carrots in bags with CCOF's organic label. The organization sent the photos to a reporter at the *San Jose Mercury News*, and the newspaper ran them on the front page with an accompanying article about the investigation (Benson 1988).[4]

Lack of equivalence between certification programs posed a second problem for the growing organic foods market. The challenge here was that the labels of different certifiers were recognized in different regions of the country, so that farmers who wanted to sell their products across state or regional lines found themselves needing to obtain multiple, expensive certifications from different groups. Retailers and manufacturers who sourced organic products from different areas of the country also had a difficult time keeping abreast of the variations that existed in the requirements of different certifiers and explaining these variations to their customers. Certifiers were sympathetic to this problem and some of them worked to harmonize their rules and requirements, but since these groups also competed with one another, harmonization was a partial solution at best (Guthman 1998). As one former organic farmer explained, "[California Certified Organic Farmers] said that it had the highest standards and wouldn't accept certifications from the Organic Growers and Buyers Association, which said that it had the highest standards, and Oregon Tilth, which said that they had the highest."[5] Another farmer recalled a particularly acrimonious meeting between certification groups in which a participant from the East Coast (where farmland was required to be managed organically for three years before organic certification could be obtained) remarked to his California counterparts (who required only one year of organic management), "You can sell your crap [i.e., food certified to the California standard] in California but you whores can't bring your crap to my coast!"[6]

Taken together, the problems of fraud and certifier equivalency created uncertainty in the organic market and increased the costs associated with the organic trade.[7] In an effort to solve these problems, some members of the sector developed certification programs with a national scope. One important example was the Organic Crop Improvement Association (OCIA), which was created in 1984 by Tom Harding, an organic farming consultant, and Joseph Dunsmore, the owner of an organic foods wholesale and distribution company. Dunsmore's company purchased organic crops from a number of different farmers, and while he was concerned that his suppliers all follow similar organic cultivation practices, he did not want to take responsibility for investigating each farm.[8] OCIA stepped into this gap as a third-party certifier: it developed national rules for organic farming and relied on state-level chapters to carry out farm inspections and certifications (Guthman 2004a).

Farm Verified Organic (FVO), an organization launched by North Dakota organic farmer Frederick Kirschenmann and trader Michael Marcolla, played a similar role. The difference was that FVO certified crops mainly for clients in the European market, which at the time had higher levels of demand and a different set of standards and expectations than American buyers.

The Organic Foods Production Association of North America (OFPANA), a trade group that came into existence after a meeting of organic farmers and manufacturers in 1984, introduced a somewhat different strategy. The OFPANA participants' original intent was to create a North American chapter of the International Federation of Organic Agriculture Movements (IFOAM), a Europe-based organization that had helped to convene the 1984 meeting, but participants decided instead to create an independent accreditation program for certifiers in the United States. The program's concept was simple: certifiers that adopted a common baseline set of requirements would be accredited by the organization and could use an "OFPANA Mark" in their labeling. Manufacturers and retailers, in turn, would be able to treat products that bore the label of an accredited certifier as equivalent to one another. As the organization's executive director explained several years later, the initiative was inspired by accreditation organizations that existed in other fields, such as higher education.[9] The challenge lay in getting certification groups to agree on a shared set of baseline standards. OFPANA spent much of the late 1980s gathering information from regional certifiers and consulting with international organic farming organizations in order to develop this program. While the organization did eventually settle on a definition and set of standards for organic production, efforts to create a national accreditation program failed to bear fruit and eventually dissipated in the chaos surrounding the Alar scare, described below.

Although talk about federal legislation also began to appear in the sector during the 1980s, many organic advocates and businesspeople doubted the possibility of federal involvement during this period. The skeptics pointed out that efforts to win federal support for organic farming had already been rebuffed several times. One window of opportunity had seemed to open up when President Carter's secretary of agriculture, Bob Bergland, released a report in the summer of 1980 that provided cautious endorsement of organic farming practices (Papendick et al. 1980). This window slammed shut the following year, though, when the incoming Reagan administration disbanded the research team that had produced the document and allegedly destroyed all the copies that remained in storage at the Department of Agriculture.[10] Several years later, an organic farming bill proposed by Oregon congressman Jim Weaver died in committee (Youngberg, Schaller, and Merrigan 1993). Skeptics also noted that large food corporations had a great deal of political influence and wondered whether a federal law would end up defining "organic" in terms that were un-recognizable to most organic farmers. It seemed reckless for organic farmers to relinquish their control over the meaning of the adjective just as organic foods were beginning to command a premium in the marketplace.

It is also important to note that not every member of the sector viewed national private-sector certification and accreditation programs as worthwhile or legitimate endeavors. Indeed, the organic market's growth increased the distance between people who identified themselves as members of an organic foods movement organized around principles of regional food production, community empowerment, and cooperative organization, and those who affili-ated with the goal of expanding the organic trade (Ingram and Ingram 2005). However, the relatively small size of the organic sector and the fact that par-ticipation in these programs was voluntary, rather than mandatory, helped to smooth relationships between these groups. Movement-oriented farmers could sell their products in local and regional markets and rely on movement-affiliated organizations for certification, while market-oriented farmers and businesses could make use of national programs to facilitate long-distance trade.

The Alar Event and the Move Toward Federal Legislation

Efforts to develop national private-sector regulations were interrupted in 1989, when the Natural Resources Defense Council (an environmental advocacy organization that was not affiliated with the organic sector) released a report titled *Intolerable Risk: Pesticides in Our Children's Food*.[11] The report argued that loopholes in the government's regulation of agriculture had led to farm chemical residues on a range of fresh fruits and vegetables. It also asserted that children faced particular risks of developing cancer and other medical complications as the result of exposure to these residues. The report singled out daminozide, a growth regulator used in apple production that went by the trade name Alar, as the most dangerous offender (Sewell and Whyatt 1989).

Intolerable Risk took the organic sector by storm. One respondent recalled that "the Alar report, because it linked pesticides so clearly to health, personal health in this case of infants and children, created a visceral or emotional response that you could never get away from."[12] The price of apples and other fresh fruits and vegetables labeled as organically grown soared as shoppers sought to calm their anxieties about contaminated food by purchasing organic options (Shapiro 1989). Members of the organic sector who experienced the Alar report and the resulting spike in consumer demand remember the event as a turning point for many people's understanding of the challenges of creating a national market for organic foods. One policy activist explained to me:

> When the Alar story broke, you had school systems panicking to not feed their children apples that were contaminated with Alar [and] they turned to this very nascent organic community and said, "we'll buy your organic apples." Well, the quality of our organic apples at that time was really bad and I think in some ways we were harmed because I think people were thinking, "oh my God, if this is what we have to eat!" . . . We had a good tasting apple but, you know, people don't want any apples that have blotches on them and smut and all kinds of things like that. So I mean that was a wake-up call for us in realizing how much more work we had to do to come up with the quality to really compete in the marketplace.[13]

Even more seriously, fraudulent marketing of organic products increased in the wake of the Alar report. An individual who worked as a certifier at the time remarked that "all these apples came out of nowhere that were 'organic' . . . They were contaminated not only with Alar but they were also contaminated with organic phosphate insecticides [and] with a number of fungicides."[14]

Organic advocates also found that environmental and consumer interest groups paid greater attention to the sector in the wake of the Alar report, but that these organizations were less interested than many organic farmers and businesspeople in building a *private* certification system (Obach 2015). Instead, they targeted federal policymakers by circulating petitions and collecting signatures in support of *public* organic regulation.[15] It was strange and a little unsettling for some advocates of organic farming and food production, after years of laboring to police the industry with little outside support or interest, to find themselves as one part of a larger coalition pushing to define organic farming in federal law. Indeed, some members of the sector engaged in the process reluctantly. A member of OFPANA explained that

> when the Alar report was published . . . consumer groups, Center for Science in the Public Interest, in particular, and some of the environmental groups like the National Coalition Against the Misuse of Pesticides . . . [and] the Natural Resources Defense Council, which are the ones who did the Alar report, became interested in organic because they recognized it as a way to achieve some of the things that were in their goals and objectives. They didn't like the idea of the industry regulating itself . . . Eventually [we] saw that the consumer groups and the environmental groups were hot on this idea and it was sort of like, the tide's going in one direction and we'd better go with it because we can't build enough support for what we've got and we don't ever want to have the environmental and consumer groups saying that whatever we set up is brash and getting people not to purchase the product.[16]

The alarming nature—at least from the perspective of organic farmers—of several of the legislative proposals that appeared in the wake of the Alar report offered additional incentives to participate in the policymaking process. Wyche Fowler, a senator from Georgia who had few prior connections to the organic sector, put forward one proposal; Congressman Gary Condit of California began to work on another. According to one individual who participated in these debates, Fowler's proposal raised the hackles of organic farming groups because it granted the U.S. Department of Agriculture "carte blanche to set the organic standards" and ignored the existing infrastructure of farmer-run inspection and certification organizations.[17] Essentially, Fowler's bill would have eliminated the ability of farmer organizations to determine the sorts of practices and materials that could be used in the production of foods marketed as organic. Condit's approach, on the other hand, responded to consumers' concerns by requiring that foods labeled as organic be completely free of chemical residues of any kind. This sort of "safe content" approach ignored the fact that existing certification programs allowed organic farmers to use a limited array of synthetic fertilizers and pesticides, and also that organic products might be exposed to additional substances through drift from nearby conventional fields or during their transport to market. The concern, as expressed in one organic farming magazine, was that Condit's bill "would put organic farming, as we know it today, out of business" (Forster 1990). In addition to these national efforts, a number of states passed or strengthened organic laws and certification programs in 1989 and 1990 (Lee 2009).

As a result of these factors, members of the organic sector began to spend less time questioning whether federal regulation should exist and became more concerned about whether or not the impending legislation would take a form that they could live with. Their concerns focused the attention of many sector members on a third legislative initiative, which came from the offices of Senator Patrick Leahy, of Vermont, and Congressman Peter DiFazio, of Oregon. Leahy had a reputation in the Senate as a champion of alternative agriculture and environmental issues, and his region of the country hosted a number of small-scale organic farmers and one of the oldest farmer-run certification groups, the Natural Organic Farmers Association. DiFazio, for his part, had worked on former Oregon congressman Jim Weaver's ill-fated organic foods bill in the early 1980s and had a reputation for being an ally of organic agriculture. Although the exact origins of the Leahy-DiFazio initiative are difficult to determine, Mark Lipson, a well-known organic farmer and policy advocate from California, remembers placing a call to Senate Agriculture Committee staffer Kathleen Merrigan while attending a conference of anti-pesticide activists in Washington, D.C. Merrigan, who worked closely with Leahy, listened to Lipson's concerns about the Fowler proposal and his ideas about a national certification program that incorporated the work of existing farmers' groups and state certification programs. In Lipson's telling, at least, this call was the catalyst for OFPA's development.[18]

The organic farmers and advocates who gravitated to Leahy and DiFazio helped to frame the structure of the bill and participated in its development throughout the legislative process. Merrigan continued to meet with other organic advocates and reviewed existing certification programs as she drafted the initial legislation. An early version of the bill, which made federal and state departments of agriculture entirely responsible for organic regulation and certification, ran into opposition from organic farming groups in several locations around the country. One participant in these meetings noted that members of these groups were "tremendously upset" with any approach that would eliminate the control of organic farmers over certification standards.[19] These groups had formed a coalition called the Organic Farmers Associations Council (OFAC), which emphasized the history of decentralized governance in the organic sector and called for grassroots input into the national standards. OFAC's democratic vision won support from other organizations that supported the legislation, such as OFPANA and the Center for Science in the Public Interest. Partly as a result of these critiques, the final version of the bill provided for the creation of the NOSB as a mechanism to guarantee the influence of farmers and other stakeholders in the national regulation (Forster 1990). It also established guidelines for regulation that focused on farming practices rather than on the characteristics of organic foods products (as Condit sought to do).

In its final version, then, OFPA sought to legislate a compromise between the goals of market stability and growth and the organic sector's history of decentralized organization and governance. The path to this compromise was created both by sector members' efforts to resolve long-term problems in the national organic trade and by their strategic work to ward off the threats and to make the best of the political opportunities that appeared in the wake of the Alar scare. These events opened up new possibilities for advocates, while also raising the very real prospect that control of the sector would shift away from established organic farmers and toward consumer and environmental groups or federal and state bureaucracies. In this uncertain and rapidly changing environment, sector members tried to ensure that the legislation preserved the ability of members of the sector to influence the content of federal regulations. They saw democratic influence not only as a necessary component of the sector's practical survival—after all, what would a bunch of bureaucrats know about how to develop workable organic regulations?—but also as an essential part of what it meant to produce food organically. Additionally, they viewed mechanisms for participation as necessary to secure the legitimacy of federal regulations within the sector itself.

From Legislation to Implementation

Soon after OFPA's passage in 1990, the law's main author, Kathleen Merrigan, published an editorial in an organic farming magazine in which she explained that "the organic industry has a long way to go to ensure that this legislation is implemented in a reasonable and caring way by the federal government" (Merrigan 1991, 4). Implementation would occur under the supervision of the secretary of agriculture, whom the law had charged with creating rules and standards for the production and handling of products marketed as organic. The law had left it up to USDA employees, working with the members of the NOSB, to hash out the details of these regulations. For organic advocates, this meant that the work of bringing grassroots influence into the national regulations needed to shift from the legislative arena to the complicated terrain of the federal bureaucracy. This work promised to be challenging for a number of reasons.

One of these reasons was that despite the creation of the NOSB, OFPA itself positioned market growth as the overriding goal and justification of the federal organic regulations. Explaining the law to his colleagues, Leahy noted that OFPA set "one tough national standard [and] only foods meeting this standard will be stamped with the 'organically produced' label . . . Supermarkets, able to trust the 'organically produced' label, will be more willing to carry organic food, generating increased consumer demand, thus contributing to more profitable farming."[20] The law's key elements reflected this priority by establishing the distinction between natural and synthetic substances as the foundation of the regulation. According to this "origin of materials" approach, the regulations would allow organic farmers to use fertilizers, pest control applications, and other substances only if they had been derived from natural sources such as animals, plants, and mined minerals. Certain synthetically produced substances could be reviewed for approval if they had been demonstrated not to pose hazards to human health and the quality of the environment and if no natural alternatives to these substances existed, but the intention was to limit synthetic inputs in organic farming. A key part of the Department of Agriculture's work, then, was to construct and maintain a list of these approved synthetic materials. The list would also identify natural substances that, for environmental or health reasons, had been prohibited for use in organic foods production.

Most private certification groups used some version of the origin-of-materials approach before OFPA's passage, but the framework remained controversial within the organic sector. Skeptics claimed that a rival approach, known as "agronomic responsibility," offered more support for the goal of changing systems of food production. According to those who supported the latter position, certification of organic farms should be based on a holistic evaluation of agricultural "practices and materials in light of their effect on soil life, water and environmental quality, non-renewable resource use, livestock health, and nutritional value and safety of the foods produced" (Meyer 1990, 20). Some supporters also extended these criteria to include social responsibilities, including payment of hired workers and relationships with local communities (Gershuny and Forster 1992). Advocates for the origin-of-materials approach, in contrast, emphasized the pragmatic challenges of developing a market. In addition to making certification decisions more complex, they argued, agronomic responsibility would confuse consumers. Shoppers by and large thought of organic products as ones that had not been exposed to synthetic chemicals and "the practical, economic survival of organic farming requires that this consumer expectation be met" (Meyer 1990, 20). As one interviewee who had supported the agronomic responsibility position characterized this argument, "We need something that can fit on a bumper sticker was usually the thing."[21]

In making the origin-of-materials approach into the core principle for organic farming regulations, OFPA centered the market growth concerns associated with this framework and pushed the concerns associated with agronomic responsibility to the margins (Guthman 2004a). For their part, the USDA employees tasked with implementing the law also hesitated to bring larger, systemic issues into discussions about the regulations. They sought to minimize tensions with constituents in the much larger conventional food industry, who often took a dim view of organic farming. In addition, they were concerned about the logistical difficulties involved in monitoring and enforcing compliance with the regulations and were wary of exposing themselves to liability if fraudulent marketing or contamination of organic products were to be discovered. Finally, they faced political pressure to limit costs associated with creating a new program and doubted lawmakers' willingness to allocate funds to support the rulemaking process (Schwartz 1991). In their view, successful rulemaking would require limits on democratic control, a focus on efficiency and uniformity that appeared absent in the existing system of certification, and an opening up of the organic sector to participation by conventional farmers and mainstream food businesses.

Reflecting on these challenges, most of the organic sector members who had participated in OFPA's development were in complete agreement with Merrigan's belief that "the organic industry ha[d] a long way to go" to create regulations that would be acceptable to members of the sector and that would incorporate at least some of the sector's transformative practices and ideas. Although they had been able to secure a guarantee of participation in rulemaking through the creation of the NOSB, they had yet to test whether this guarantee would be enough to win widespread support for the process and whether participation would be able to make a meaningful impact on the character of the final regulations. Simply put, they had to bring the promise of regulators' accountability to the organic sector, which existed on paper in the law, to life in the rulemaking process. Many in the organic sector were skeptical that this would happen. As the farmer Elizabeth Henderson noted, "We are dealing with the vast, creaky, unoiled machinery of the federal bureaucracy and the USDA, in particular, an agency that is not too thrilled with the job it has been handed of regulating organic farming and processing" (Henderson 1991, 20).

The concept of institutional work, which reorients attention from formal characteristics of rules and institutions to the ways that people who are "embedded" in institutional environments try to achieve particular goals, offers a useful guide for understanding how organic advocates who participated in the rulemaking process responded to these challenges (Battilana 2006; Seo and Creed 2002). Institutional work consists of "the purposive action of individuals and organizations aimed at creating, maintaining, [or] disrupting" the formal rules and informal routines and expectations that guide action in organized social settings (Lawrence and Suddaby 2006, 215). The key insight offered by this concept is that, rather than straitjacketing action into immutable patterns, institutions offer material and cultural resources that enable people to pursue individual and collective interests in creative and strategic ways. Institutional work appears in new institutional settings because both opportunities and stakes are high: rules and procedures are ambiguous and underspecified, which creates openings for people to mobilize around innovative interpretations, while patterns of action established during an institution's infancy may lock in inequalities of power and influence (Maguire, Hardy, and Lawrence 2004; Rojas 2010).

Organic advocates sought to achieve at least two goals in the rulemaking process. They wanted to shore up the legitimacy of federal regulations within the organic sector while also increasing their own ability to shape the content of the regulations. They engaged in two sorts of institutional work to achieve these goals. First, they encouraged organic sector members to invest in the rulemaking process by framing the federal regulations in ways that emphasized their compatibility with organic agriculture. Second, they seized on procedural ambiguities to free the NOSB from the control of USDA staff members and to increase its influence in rulemaking. These activities unfolded simultaneously throughout the empanelment and meetings of the first NOSB. Advocates were successful in some ways, but they also faced limits imposed by legal requirements and bureaucratic actions.

Since the NOSB offered the clearest avenue for democratic participation in the rulemaking process, it became the focus of sector members' attention soon after OFPA's passage. According to law, the NOSB would be a fifteen-member advisory group comprising members of the organic sector and of the consumer and environmental groups that had helped to lobby for OFPA's passage. The NOSB's task was to collect information about existing organic standards and practices and to make recommendations about the law's implementation to the Department of Agriculture. While the secretary of agriculture had the authority to appoint NOSB members, the law granted an unusual amount of power to the board by prohibiting the USDA from authorizing synthetic substances for use in organic foods production without the board's approval. The National Organic Program staff could choose to prohibit materials recommended for use by the NOSB, but they could not admit materials for use in organic farming that the NOSB had rejected. At the beginning of the rulemaking process, the groups from the organic sector that had worked on the legislation formed a joint committee to select and nominate a slate of candidates for these seats. The committee solicited recommendations from regional organic farming organizations and from the environmentalist and consumer groups that had participated in OFPA's passage, and also reviewed résumés and statements from possible candidates. In the middle of 1991, the committee sent a slate of thirty-seven nominees to the Department of Agriculture, along with suggestions about the criteria that the agency should use in making its choices (Gershuny 1991).

The high stakes of the NOSB's work produced a sense of outrage within the organic sector in January 1992, when the Department of Agriculture made public its appointments to the board. Of the fourteen available seats, only three had been allocated to candidates nominated by organic sector groups.[22]

As Table 2.1 shows, a number of the initial appointees also worked for large food companies or for organizations such as the American Farm Bureau Federation or the American Meat Science Association that were closely associated with mainstream, conventional agriculture. Many sector members—and even some board appointees—viewed the NOSB appointments as evidence that the USDA sought to sabotage the implementation process and suggested that the national standards should be abandoned altogether (Gershuny 1993). One initial appointee recalled another board member who "on one occasion put into words, better than I think anyone else could, the antagonism of the original organic community to the establishment of the USDA, which has done everything, it seemed to these people, to kill organic. She said, we don't want the USDA to be involved in any of this program!"[23] Another well-known organic farmer from California, "Amigo" Bob Cantisano, wrote an open letter to organic farming organizations to register "concern and disgust in regards

TABLE 2.1: Appointees to the Initial National Organic Standards Board

Scientist
Esper K. Chandler, cattle farmer and member of the American Farm Bureau Federation

Handlers
Eugene Kahn, founder of Cascadian Farms (organic foods manufacturer)*
Richard C. Theuer, vice president of Beechnut (baby food manufacturer)

Farmers
Leroy D. Eppley, owner of mixed organic-conventional farm
Gary D. Osweiler, veterinarian and owner of mixed organic-conventional farm
Robert Quinn, owner of OCIA-certified organic farm
Nancy A. Taylor, part owner of uncertified organic farm

Environmentalists
William J. Friedman, attorney and member of the New Mexico Organic Commodity Commission
Thomas A Stoneback, vice president of Rodale Books publishing company
Craig V. Weakley, director of organic production at Muir Glen (organic foods manufacturer)*

Consumer Advocates
Merrill A. Clark, owner of OCIA-certified organic farm and organic foods retail store
Donald M. Kinsman, former president of the American Meat Science Association and professor emeritus of animal science
James Michael Sligh, organic inspector and director of the Rural Advancement Foundation, International*

Retailer
Margaret A. Clark, manager at an organic foods retail store

* Appeared on the slate of candidates sent to the secretary of agriculture by OFPANA and other groups in the organic sector
SOURCE: Data from Henderson and LeCompte 1992, 23.

to the USDA's appointments to the NOSB." Cantisano urged a recall of the board members and suggested that the supporters of federal legislation had been "duped by the political process" (Cantisano, Kahn, and Clark 1992, 16).

Whether the NOSB appointments actually reflected a deliberate effort to sabotage the organic regulations is debatable. The USDA had received 112 nominations of candidates for board seats—far more than the 37 submitted by organic groups—and selections were likely made with an eye to winning support (or at least moderating resistance) from the mainstream food industry. Regardless of the agency's intent, the tension about the initial appointments put members of the sector who supported federal regulation—particularly those who occupied seats on the NOSB—in a difficult position. It was unlikely that board members would be recalled or the regulations scrapped, as some of the skeptics wished. More importantly, if large portions of the organic sector turned their backs on the rulemaking process, organic advocates would lose much of their ability to influence the content of the federal regulations. Since NOSB members were meant to represent constituencies within the organic sector, evidence that these constituencies did not care about the content of the rules would erode their bargaining power vis-à-vis USDA staff. While organic advocates needed to rein in the NOSB's drift away from organic agriculture's grassroots in order to preserve support for the rulemaking process within the organic sector, they also needed to develop an effective working relationship with the "outsider" board members and the USDA staff.

Supporters of the regulations tried to minimize the significance of the initial appointments by pointing out that Secretary of Agriculture Edward Madigan had made public statements in support of organic regulation. One attendee at an early NOSB meeting also noted in a widely read organic farming periodical that she was "both impressed and relieved" by her interactions with the Board members, including the "unknowns" (Schwartz 1992). Additionally, those NOSB members who had been nominated by organic sector organizations worked to free the board from the control of USDA staff members and to tilt its balance of power back toward the organic sector. Michael Sligh, the first board chair and an organic sector nominee, emphasized the accountability of the NOSB to organic farmers by organizing public meetings of the board at different locations throughout the country during its initial years of work. His strategy was not only to build legitimacy for the board's work within the organic sector, but also to force board members from the conventional food industry to learn about the expectations that members of the sector had for them. This approach also surprised the staff at the Department of Agriculture, who were not used to the degree of public attention that the organic rulemaking process received. Sligh explained,

> We spent about five years crisscrossing the country trying to build national consensus, and I will say the USDA was not so keen on that, either. They had the idea that we would just go to Washington, locked away in the Jefferson Room, and we would kind of do it in isolation. It was really our impetus to say, no, this is the way we do it in this community. We want to go out, we want to have open meetings, we want to hear from everybody, we want to go visit farms, we want to poke around . . . We had people from serious agribusiness on that original board who were not from the organic community . . . It was a bit stacked against us and partly our strategy was to go expose these people to what was going on, on the ground. That was the other reason we wanted to go out of USDA, to show these people what [organic farming] was.[24]

Sligh's effort to secure public participation in the rulemaking process reflected the vision of organic farming as a different—more democratic, less centralized—system of food production and the impulse to use OFPA as a lever to bring these principles into the USDA. He took advantage of ambiguities in the formal procedures related to the NOSB's activities. Although USDA staff had assumed that board members would meet in the Department of Agriculture's building, safely insulated from the strong opinions of the organic grassroots, OFPA itself was silent on this issue. Sligh raised money outside of regular congressional appropriations to fund these meetings and recalled that he "did do a fair amount of going down the halls at USDA with my hat in my hand and finding that there are kind of little pots of money in USDA where they do have some flexibility."[25] Others within the organic sector also contributed to these efforts. For example, the Rodale Institute in Emmaus, Pennsylvania, hosted one round of NOSB meetings when previously arranged funding fell through.

The public comment period became an important feature of NOSB meetings and provided opportunities for advocates to argue for the legitimacy of the rulemaking process. Minutes of these meetings show that a wide range of stakeholders contributed their ideas. Organic farmers testified about the philosophy of organic production, consumer representatives called for tests of the purity of organic products, certifiers explained the origin and logic of their programs. Grace Gershuny, a longtime organic advocate who was hired by the USDA to assist with implementation, was one sector member who framed these developments in ways that emphasized the compatibility between federal regulation and social change goals associated with organic farming. In an open letter to the organic community, she noted that "one unspoken purpose of this [National Organic] Program is the conscious creation of an organic field within the federal government which will represent a model of how administrative, regulatory processes can be designed which are compatible with the principles of organiculture."[26] In Gershuny's eyes, regulation did not represent the end of the organic sector's distinctive vision, but rather offered an opportunity to democratize the workings of the federal bureaucracy!

The efforts of Sligh and others were successful in opening NOSB meetings to wider public participation and in preserving the engagement of significant portions of the organic sector in rulemaking. However, this history also shows how formal rules may limit the impact of institutional work. Organic advocates found that public participation had a limited ability to expand the regulations to include systemic concerns. Although one of the first NOSB meetings ended with a determination "that the Board needs to develop a process for assessing the following broad issues of concern: biotechnology, environmental impact, humane treatment of animals, social justice, and cost of certification," the majority of the board's time was spent on technical issues, such as setting allowances for synthetic pesticide residues, determining the status of organic farmland that had been subjected to emergency pest extermination programs, and evaluating substances proposed for use in organic farming.[27] This allocation of time was the result of OFPA's placement of materials at the center of organic farming regulations. Board members might well acknowledge the importance of systemic issues to the spirit of organic farming, but they had little ability to bring these concerns into the final regulations. In the area of materials, the board had the statutory authority to shape the regulations by prohibiting certain substances. In other areas, the board could offer suggestions, but the USDA was free to disregard them.

Mobilization outside the Bureaucracy

In part because of the limits that OFPA placed on the NOSB's work, efforts to advocate for organic farming as an alternative system of food production, and not just one that avoided synthetic chemicals, continued to occur
in the sector at large. For example, members of OFAC, which merged with a
larger organization called the National Campaign for Sustainable Agriculture
(NCSA) after OFPA's passage, considered whether organic farms should be
limited in size and whether organic regulations should cover the treatment
of farm labor, and also discussed the relationship between organic agriculture and larger movements for social and environmental change. The plenary
address of OFAC's second meeting, "Creating an Alternative Food System,"
suggested that focusing only on acceptable and prohibited materials would
limit the organic sector's ability to "participate in the world-wide movement
for ecological survival" and called for the creation of new marketing strategies that connected consumers directly with organic farmers. The organization also produced a vision statement for organic agriculture that called for
"production, processing, trading, and consumption rooted in communities
. . . where more people have access to land and capital and are producing food
closer to where it is consumed . . . [and where] farmers will be held in respect
and receive fair and real return for what they grow, giving them more freedom
to farm with care for the land and the surrounding community" (Knox and
Henderson 1992, 34).

Frustration with the rulemaking process grew as it became apparent that
the elements of this vision would play a limited role in federal regulations.
One issue that crystallized this frustration had to do with the status of private
certification organizations. The law had established the USDA as the sole ac-
creditor of organic certifiers, which meant that while the agency would not
itself inspect organic farms and food operations and certify their compliance
with the federal organic rule, it alone would be able to grant organizations
like CCOF and NOFA the authority to do so. The accreditation program's
challenge lay in the fact that many of these certification organizations—particularly those that had been established and were run by farmers—had considerable symbolic importance within the organic sector, and concerns that
the USDA would try to control or change these programs quickly raised the
hackles of their members. They were, as the organization theorist Philip Sel-

znick put it, "infused with value" that exceeded the technical requirements of certification (Selznick 1957, 17). In 1992, a rumor began to circulate that the USDA was contemplating doing away with private certification programs or making them into bureaucratic extensions of the agency. In response, members of these organizations testified before the NOSB that autonomous private certifiers played an essential role in the preservation of the community-oriented, grassroots spirit of the organic sector.[28] Elizabeth Henderson, then a member of the New York chapter of NOFA, pointed out that her organization aimed for goals that were quite different from those sought by the USDA:

> The NOFAs and MOFGA [Maine Organic Farmers and Gardeners Association] . . . saw the certification programs as a way of helping farmers to improve their farming. Regular inspections by a knowledgeable inspector and membership in the network could help farmers learn more every year . . . The impulse for the OFPA came from people who wanted to "help" organic farming become real agri-business. That is a very different conception of our mission than that held by most of the people who are farming or running the small certification programs. We are trying to build a regional, sustainable food system. We have to stay in business to survive, but we would prefer our businesses to be ethical and personal rather than competitive and aggressively expanding.[29]

This tension between the accreditation requirement and the autonomy of private certifiers also colored discussions of how organic products would be labeled after the implementation of OFPA. The law had indicated that certified producers would be able to use a "USDA Organic" seal when marketing their products, but the agency also needed to determine the fate of the seals of the private certification programs that were currently in use. This was an important issue because the certification standards of some programs included additional criteria that went beyond those of the USDA program. For example, OCIA required that certified farms work toward full organic management, while OFPA made allowances for split (organic and conventional) farm management systems. If these groups were allowed to certify both to the USDA's criteria and to their own, more stringent standards, it would make sense to also allow them to place their own labels on packages. On the other hand, Michael Hankin, a USDA staff member who participated in the board's meetings, argued that "the more seals that we allow to define the word organic, the more we get away from the intent of the law and confuse the consumer."[30] The "intent of the law," according to Hankin, was to lay the foundation for the rapid growth of the organic trade.

Over the course of these debates, USDA rulemakers offered some concessions to advocates of certifier autonomy. They agreed that packages of organic products could display certifier seals, as long as they also showed the "USDA Organic" seal, and they supported an exemption that allowed organic farmers whose annual sales totaled less than $5,000 and who were not engaged in interstate trade to use the term "organic" in product marketing without securing certification. On larger issues, though, their positions countered those of sector members who defended the autonomy of private groups: certifiers could not require additional measures beyond those established by federal regulations and could not grant additional seals to distinguish those products that went above and beyond the USDA rules. They also insisted that certifiers cease offering advice and guidance to farmers. This shifted certification away from the collaborative learning activity envisioned by Henderson and toward a more formalized, potentially adversarial interaction. In turn, the defenders of certifier autonomy continued to emphasize contradictions between the USDA's position and the fundamental goals of organic agriculture. By late 1993, frustration with the USDA led some certification organizations and farmers' groups to call for revisions to OFPA that would make accreditation of certifiers optional, rather than mandatory, and that would exempt producers that engaged only in intrastate trade and direct-to-consumer marketing from certification requirements (Gershuny 1993).

The First Proposed Rule and the Emergence of Conflict

Frustration also developed among members of the NOSB, who remained committed to creating federal regulations but became increasingly anxious about their influence in the rulemaking process. During meetings in 1994, USDA staff circulated a set of regulatory recommendations that disregarded the board's decisions about the sorts of materials that should be allowed for use in organic farming. Board members argued that the document placed the NOSB in a position that was "subservient to [the] USDA's ideas" and, over the following months, drafted and approved a resolution in response to the recommendations that reasserted the NOSB's statutory authority to determine which materials would be allowed in the production of organic foods.[31] This resolution, in turn, was viewed with skepticism by USDA staff, who questioned whether an advisory board "appointed by the Secretary [of agriculture] should be passing a resolution that insists that his advisory board has more authority than he does."[32]

These interactions set the stage for widespread conflict in the sector, which emerged when NOSB members tapped into the skepticism of groups like NCSA in order to force the USDA to take their recommendations seriously. The confrontation occurred after the agency released its "draft rule" of organic regulations for public comment in 1997, which seemed to confirm fears that the USDA had decided to define organic farming on its own terms (Ingram and Ingram 2005, Vos 2000).[33] Cissy Bowman, an organic farmer and one of the leaders in the legislative effort that led to OFPA, labeled the regulations proposed in the draft rule "deplorable."[34] NCSA members created a list of what they called the "sixty-six points of darkness" in the proposed regulations, which identified places where the regulations diverged from the recommendations of the NOSB and the preferences of organic farmers.[35] NOFA issued a press release that criticized the regulations for permitting the use of materials that the NOSB had explicitly voted to prohibit in organic farming.[36] Frederick Kirschenmann, an organic farmer who sat on the NOSB, also pointed out that the regulations sharply curtailed the autonomy of certifiers and limited the ability of farmers who chose not to undergo certification to advertise their use of organic methods. He concluded that the rule "will be a boon for the conventional food system which for years has sought to eliminate any differentiation in the marketplace that threatens their market share."[37]

There was widespread agreement within the organic sector that the USDA should withdraw the draft rule for thorough revisions, and that this process should take place in collaboration with the NOSB. The question was how to persuade the agency, which had apparently demonstrated its disregard for the NOSB's work, to do this. Since they had exhausted legislative and bureaucratic avenues of influence, NOSB members and other leaders sought to mobilize the growing frustration and skepticism that existed in the sector as a whole. Farmers' groups, organic foods retailers, consumer organizations, and allied companies provided form letters that members and customers could send to the USDA during the ninety-day public comment period, or provided information that people could use to compose their own letters. Letters of protest also arrived electronically, since the agency had recently opened an Internet portal for public comments (Zavetoski, Shulman, and Schlosberg 2006). In all, the USDA received more than 275,000 comments, mainly from consumers, which set a record for public participation in its rulemaking. According to NOSB chair Michael Sligh, the campaign caught the agency's attention in a way that the board's work had not:

> I'll never forget being called into USDA when I think we had given about 273,000 comments . . . I went to the sub-basement of USDA because I wanted to see where these things were going because we were sending in handwritten ones, we were faxing them in, you know, every way we could figure out how to get them to USDA. They had these at-risk high school kids down there actually cataloguing this stuff by hand in the sub-basement of USDA, just stacking this stuff. It was unbelievable, and they said, can you stop this? I just thought that that was the most hilarious thing I'd ever heard. I said, of course I can't stop it! I have no control over this thing. This thing has a life of its own. There's nobody in charge! You have now, you know, unleashed this thing. The only way you're going to deal with it is you're going to have to withdraw the rule and get it right.[38]

Perhaps surprisingly, many of the letters focused on a relatively minor part of the draft rule. The agency had suggested that genetically engineered seeds, food irradiation, and the use of municipal sewage sludge as fertilizer might be considered for use in producing and handling organic foods, and it had asked the organic community for comments about these issues. A request for comments could easily be seen as innocuous and in fact, one interviewee later referred to the angry rejection of the so-called Big Three as "the biggest paper tiger in the history of the organic industry."[39] Another sector member pointed out that the attention devoted to the Big Three "distract[ed] attention from problems embedded less prominently in the rest of the proposal."[40] But the fact that the USDA was open to a future in which organic products might be altered in a laboratory and zapped with radiation appalled farmers who wanted to create alternatives to industrial food production, as well as consumers who viewed organic foods as a way to avoid the possible risks of foods contamination by uncontrolled technologies. For these individuals, the Big Three offered apparent proof that the USDA, regardless of statements to the contrary, wanted to make organic agriculture into an appendage of "real agribusiness." The conflict-oriented frames driving the protest emphasized the agency's contempt for organic production, and in this light, the request for comments appeared to be a Trojan horse that would open the organic sector's gates to invaders from mainstream agriculture and the conventional food industry.[41]

Conclusion

The mobilization against the initial proposed regulations was successful, at least in part. In the wake of the protest, the USDA withdrew the regulations and began to work on revisions with the full participation of the NOSB. The agency's second draft, which was released for comment in 2000, addressed many of the issues that had raised public concerns (including the Big Three), but it also preserved OFPA's focus on market growth as the overriding goal of the regulatory program. While the decentralized character of the organic sector during the 1970s and 1980s worked against the emergence of wide-spread conflict, the final implementation of the NOP in 2002 contributed to enduring tensions between transformative and expansionary understandings of organic production. As those tensions played out during subsequent years, members of the sector elaborated the conflict-oriented frames that they had developed during the dispute over the first proposed rule. As I will explain later, they also encountered repeated challenges in connecting protests related to specific issues, like the Big Three, to the cultivation of alternative economic and organizational structures in the organic sector.

Although OFPA's passage and implementation divided the organic field, the law's history also reveals sector members' strategic efforts to create compromises between market growth and systemic change. Supporters of federal regulation developed compromise-oriented frames when they argued that OFPA enabled organic principles to filter into the centers of agricultural policymaking in the United States. This was not just talk: participants in the law's development and implementation worked to bring these principles into the text of the legislation and into the rulemaking process. The impetus for the National Organic Standards Board came from the belief that federal regulation should institutionalize the democratic, participatory forms of decision making that many sector members saw as integral to organic agriculture. NOSB members also challenged the USDA to respect these principles when they broke free from the agency's warren of conference rooms and held public meetings around the country. Even the protests against the first draft of the organic regulations were (at least in the eyes of these sector leaders) less about the so-called Big Three than they were an effort to push back against the USDA's perceived usurpation of the NOSB's authority. Although real limits existed to these efforts, they were not unimportant. This early institutional work left its stamp on the contemporary regulations, not least in the NOSB's ongoing practice of holding traveling meetings with open public comment periods, which have become an important site of engagement for contemporary activists.

Chapter 3 examines how the implementation of the rule in 2002 affected the organic sector's economic structure and further shifted the relationship between expansionary and transformative understandings of organic farming. I show how the regulations have helped to shift the sector's economic balance of power toward large firms, many of which are also players in the conventional food industry. I also describe how new arrivals to the organic sector, who work in commercially oriented business environments, have elaborated the moral virtues of market expansion.

CHAPTER 3

The Rise of Big Organic

Market Convergence and the Elaboration of the Expansionary Vision

OBSERVERS OF THE STOCK MARKET at the beginning of 2012 were caught by surprise at investors' response to the initial public offering of stock in Annie's Homegrown, a manufacturer of natural and organic pasta and snack foods. The share price of BNNY's stock—the company's abbreviation was based on its mascot, a rabbit named Bernie—climbed from $19 to nearly $36 in the first few days of trading. Responsibility for the successful IPO lay not with Annie Withey, who founded the company in 1989 by selling products door-to-door with her husband at the time, Andrew Martin, but with the venture capital firm Solera Capital LLC. Solera had made a $20 million investment in Annie's in 2002, which provided it with a majority stake in the company. Subsequently, it had expanded the Annie's product line and purchased several other natural and organic foods manufacturers. Solera chief executive Molly Ashby explained that it "was one of our points of view that this was going to make it in the mainstream" (Dezember 2012). Meanwhile, according to the company's website, Withey withdrew to operate an organic farm in Connecticut but remained "the inspiration and corporate conscience of the Annie's family of products."

The story of Annie's Homegrown provides a glimpse into changes in the organic sector that occurred along with the development of federal organic regulations in the 1990s and accelerated after the implementation of the National Organic Program (NOP) in 2002. These changes involved growth in the volume and value of organic foods sales, but just as importantly, they involved convergence between mainstream businesses and the organic sector. Convergence occurred in various ways: organic foods companies were acquired by venture capitalists that also invested in conventional foods businesses, food conglomerates launched their own lines of organic products, and organic products from both mainstream and independent companies began to appear on the shelves of mass-market retailers. These processes and others eroded economic and organizational boundaries between the organic sector and the mainstream food industry, and the independent organic foods companies that remained competed far more closely with food businesses organized along traditional lines that also made and sold organic foods. In part because of the successful institutionalization of organic foods as a distinctive category of products through law and regulation, the organic sector became more organizationally and economically similar to the mainstream food industry.

In this chapter, I examine these economic and organizational changes in the context of theoretical work about resource partitioning. I also argue that convergence has caused the elaboration of expansionary understandings of organic farming. I examine these cultural changes through interviews with a sample of organic foods professionals whom I label "new arrivals." As the name implies, these individuals launched their careers in the organic sector relatively recently, and work either for mainstream food companies that also produce or sell organic products, or for organic specialty companies that are organizationally similar to mainstream businesses. While these new arrivals might be expected to treat organic foods as a business proposition, they often offer more-complex accounts of their motivations. Many explain that they were drawn to the organic sector because of a desire to create value outside of the market by reducing the damaging social and environmental impacts of food production, and they argue that rapid market growth is the best way to accomplish these goals. That is, they link the economic project of selling increasing amounts of organic foods with the ethical projects of improved environmental quality and public safety.

The new arrivals' statements differ from those of early advocates of market growth. One key difference has to do with the question of scale: the new arrivals, unlike many early organic advocates, see little or no intrinsic value in small-scale food production. In fact, they often portray efforts to limit the size of organic farms and food businesses as naive, or even as a threat to the organic sector's ability to achieve its non-market, environmental goals. I interpret this difference by placing their accounts in a broader cultural context, explaining how the cognitive schemas provided by mainstream business training, contemporary efforts to invest business activities with moral meaning, and the practical demands of employers constitute raw materials from which the new arrivals construct understandings of the virtue of market growth. I also show that the new arrivals' perceptions lead them to construct symbolic hierarchies and boundaries (Lamont and Molnár 2002) that legitimize the position of the most efficient, competitive businesses within the organic sector but that partially or completely exclude organizations that enact transformative principles.

Finally, this chapter brings cultural understandings that are articulated by the new arrivals into dialogue with sociological ideas about the role of consumers in market settings that, like the organic sector, blend shopping with social and environmental goals. A number of sociologists have taken the emergence of these "moral markets" (Stehr 2008) as evidence of consumers' increasing ability to shape the priorities and practices of business. The new arrivals to the organic sector tell a different story. From their perspective, most consumers behave in confused, inconsistent, or self-interested ways. These professionals fear that rather than advancing the organic sector's capacity to improve the environment, consumer involvement in discussions about organic regulations and business practices may undermine it. Their expansionary understandings of the organic sector's mission ascribe a relatively limited role to consumers, who support this mission through their purchases but lack the knowledge or skills to participate in the sector's governance.

Convergence from Farm to Shelf

One way to understand the economic and organizational changes that have taken place in the organic sector is through the concept, stemming from organizational ecology, of resource partitioning. Ecological theorists refer to markets as partitioned when they support both mass-market businesses and specialist-niche players, while limiting direct competition between them (Carroll, Dobrev, and Swaminathan 2002). Generalist firms in partitioned markets tend to compete with one another for the largest and most lucrative segments, which leaves niche segments open for specialist exploitation. As generalists cluster in the market's lucrative center, a vibrant population of specialist organizations often springs up on the market's margins (Carroll 1985; Swaminathan 1995). Partitioning works in two ways: generalists may decide that peripheral segments are not worth the expense it would take to develop them, and specialists may create entry barriers by investing peripheral organizational forms with a particular value. The former process appears in media markets in which special-interest publications flourish in the niche markets left untouched by mainstream newspapers (Carroll 1985). The relationship between mainstream producers and craft brewers in the U.S. beer industry illustrates the latter process. While mainstream beer companies have been able to create their own specialty products that often match the quality of those produced by craft brewers, they have found that specialty beer consumers "balk at beverages brewed by large corporations using modern methods of mass production" (Carroll and Swaminathan 2000, 729). Craft brewers encourage consumer resistance by emphasizing their smallness, their connection to particular cities or even neighborhoods, and their use of traditional production methods.

In the sector's early years, many organic foods producers served markets that were partitioned from those of conventional foods businesses. Partitioning existed at the levels of production, distribution, and retailing. Conventional businesses—farms, food processors, grocery retailers—saw little potential and many problems with the organic trade, and the circulation of organic products took place mainly in local and regional markets. Organic sector pioneers also emphasized the importance of alternative organizational structures and invested small-scale farms, locally oriented food systems, and non-bureaucratic organizations with a particular value. During the 1990s and 2000s, the opposite pattern—convergence or "de-partitioning" (Sikavica and Pozner 2013)—became prevalent. The acquisition of independent organic foods companies like Annie's Homegrown by venture capitalists and mainstream food conglomerates was one driver of this phenomenon. During the period between 1997 and 2002, twelve of the thirty largest mainstream food processors in North America either acquired or formed strategic alliances with independent organic foods companies. A second wave of acquisitions began around the middle of the decade, as more recently launched organic start-up companies came on the market and attracted the attention of food conglomerates and venture capitalists. The result is that many iconic organic brands, such as Cascadian Farm, Santa Cruz Organic, and Stonyfield Farm, are now partially or completely owned by companies that also manufacture conventional food products (Howard 2009). Writing about this topic in 2004, an industry observer described a shift from a "roll-up strategy" in which companies that specialized in organic foods acquired their competitors, to "something really new—the acquisition of [organic] products companies by mainstream food companies" (Singerman 2004).

The food conglomerates that purchased organic companies were attracted by the double-digit growth rates in sales of organic products that occurred in the 1990s and early 2000s, as well as by a growing industry discourse about the market potential of healthy, natural foods (Schleifer and DeSoucey 2015). Even though this growth rate slowed somewhat at the end of the 2000s, it continued to outstrip sales growth in the food industry as a whole, leading to mainstream companies' continued interest in the sector (Table 3.1).

Mainstream corporations also gained knowledge of the organic sector from the experienced personnel at these firms, and some have retained high-level and line staff from their acquisitions in order to pave the way for future ventures into the sector, including the development of organic versions of mass-market brands such as Hunt's organic canned tomatoes and Kellogg's organic Rice Krispies (Kowitt 2015). Corporate buyers also gained the equity built up in the brands of pioneering organic companies, including the trust that many consumers invested in these brands. Many of these mainstream companies have attempted to cultivate "robust identities" that enable them to present their products in different ways to different audiences (Padgett and Ansell 1993; Zuckerman et al. 2003). General Mills offers a good example: while many General Mills products display the company's trademark "G" on the front panel of their packaging, Cascadian Farm and Muir Glen (two organic acquisitions) products do not (Sligh and Christman 2003). This strategy

TABLE 3.1: Growth of the Organic Market, 1998–2014

Year	1998	2002	2006	2010	2014
Organic food sales (millions of dollars)	$4,286	$8,635	$17,221	$26,708	$35,900
Annual growth rate (percent)	19.2	17.3	21.1	7.7	11.0
Organic sales as percentage of total food sales	0.9	1.6	2.9	4.0	5.0

SOURCE: Data from the Organic Trade Association (www.ota.com)

enables the company to attract customers who like the aura of independence that clings to organic brands and resembles one that mainstream companies have used to move into niche segments in other partitioned markets: in the beer industry, for example, "Miller Brewing created the fictional name Plank Road Brewery to put on its [craft beer] labels" (Carroll and Swaminathan 2000, 727). On the other hand, as the example of Annie's Homegrown suggests, mainstream companies present their acquisitions to analysts and investors in terms of the growth potential made possible through access to capital and sophisticated management.

This consolidation of organic foods processors parallels patterns of convergence—or to use terminology from agricultural political economy, "conventionalization"—that have occurred in the arena of organic farming. In the late 1990s, scholars began to document the transition of formerly conventional farms to organic production (Buck, Getz, and Guthman 1997). These conversions were particularly widespread in the high-value specialty-crop regions of California, where the number of certified organic growers more than tripled between 1987 and 1997, but they also occurred in other parts of the country.[1] Many of these new organic growers relied on crop management practices and economic structures that resembled those in mainstream agriculture. They employed input substitution (substituting fertilizers permitted under organic regulations for prohibited synthetic fertilizers) instead of more labor-intensive cultivation techniques like crop rotation and compost production, grew crops in larger quantities on greater acreages of land, and targeted long-distance consumer markets or bulk buyers instead of local markets (Guthman 2004a). Since large farms had a greater ability to set commodity prices in agricultural markets, their turn away from "deeper" organic practices also forced better-established organic growers to follow suit in order to stay in business (Guthman 2004b).

The rise to dominance of a few large organic foods distributors that serve the national marketplace has contributed to this conventionalization of organic farming. Simply put, large distributors prefer to work with large farms. As one distribution manager explained, "I can't send a truck four hundred miles to the north or south to pick up a pallet of organics. It just doesn't make sense logistically. So we try to consolidate and use those vendors who grow a lot of items for us so that we can make less stops."[2] By achieving economies of scale in this way, large distributors have been able to out-compete smaller rivals. This is seen in the case of United Natural Foods, Inc. (UNFI), which as of this writing is the leading independent natural and organic foods distributor in the United States. UNFI was created through a 1996 merger of Mountain People's Warehouse, founded in 1976 in California, and Cornucopia Natural Foods, a Rhode Island firm created in the same year. The parent companies operated as regional distributors that moved crops from small organic farms to independent retailers. After the merger, UNFI extended its role in the national market through acquisitions, focusing in particular on warehouses that serviced food co-ops and independent stores. The acquisitions of Blooming Prairie, a co-op distributor that occupied a leading position in the Midwestern region, and Northeast Cooperatives, a New England distributor in 2002 cemented the company's position as the market leader (Gutknecht 2003). It has since pursued acquisitions internationally and currently competes more closely with the distribution arms of major retail chains than with independently owned companies.

Organic products have also become more widely available to consumers in the past decade. In the late 1990s, retailers that specialized in natural and organic foods handled the bulk of organic sales, with direct-marketing efforts by farmers also constituting a substantial portion. The former category included single-store co-ops and independent retailers, as well as regional natural foods chains, while the latter comprised farmers' markets, restaurant deliveries, and mail-order sales. Only a small portion of organic sales went through mainstream supermarket chains at the time, both because the volume of organic foods on the market was not large enough to meet the chains' needs and because the chains were unsure of how to market these foods to their customers (Fromartz 2006). By the late 2000s, a greater portion of sales in the natural foods channel went through "supernaturals," or grocery chains that specialized in natural and organic foods but displayed the economies of scale and competitive orientation that characterized mainstream supermarket companies (Dimitri and Richman 2000). The most successful of the "supernaturals" was Whole Foods Market (WFM); second-rung players included Wild Oats Market, Henry's (a California grocery chain owned by Wild Oats), and (to an extent) Trader Joe's. In addition, sales of organic foods through mainstream supermarkets had edged out the natural foods channel by a narrow margin, which was the product of decisions by even larger grocers, like Safeway and Albertsons, to increase the range of their organic merchandise. While direct sales remained an important channel for organic foods, they made up only 10 percent of the market in the late 2000s (Table 3.2).

Competitive dynamics within the grocery industry, as well as consumer demand, help to explain the interest of traditional supermarkets in organic foods (Guptill and Wilkins 2002; Schwartz and Lyson 2007). The "supernaturals"—WFM in particular—succeeded during the 2000s not only because they sold organic foods but also because they created an approach to retailing that emphasized novelty, authenticity, and the aesthetic pleasures (appearance, flavor, freshness) offered by their products (Shapin 2006). The company has also promoted an atmosphere of "ethical consumerism," with store initiatives to advance microloans to small businesses, promote wind and solar power, and create animal welfare standards for its meat and dairy suppliers (Johnston 2008). Organic foods are part of this larger aesthetic and ethical experience, albeit in a form that produces cognitive dissonance for some older members of the sector. One of my earliest interviewees, a man who had farmed organically for much of his adult life, wryly compared his insect-marked vegetables with those at his local WFM store, noting that "everything there is just beautiful and I wonder if it is really organically grown."[3] Nevertheless, WFM has come to define expectations about organic products for many consumers and has offered a language for talking about the virtue and purpose of organic agriculture.

In designing this marketing strategy, WFM built on the legacy of upscale restaurants like Berkeley's Chez Panisse, which positioned organic foods as "yuppie chow" for upwardly mobile and culturally sophisticated consumers during the 1980s (Guthman 2003). WFM's approach has not gone uncon-

TABLE 3.2: Sales Channels for Organic Foods, 1991–2006

Year	1991	1998	2006
Natural foods retailers (percentage of total sales)	68	63	44
Direct marketing (percentage of total sales)	25	6	10
Mainstream retailers (percentage of total sales)	7	31	46

SOURCE: Data from Dimitri and Oberholtzer 2009, 6.

tested; indeed, its prominence has made it into a target for activists who assert that the transformation of agricultural systems is central to the organic sector's mission. In 2006, best-selling author Michael Pollan challenged the company to increase the organic *and locally grown* (i.e., in the vicinity of its stores) produce and meats that it sold. While Pollan was not seeking a repartitioning of the organic market—that is, he did not call on WFM to break its contracts with larger organic suppliers—he argued that if the chain did not prioritize the sale of foods from small-scale, nearby producers, it would be "throw[ing] its lot in with the industrialization, globalization, and dilution of organic agriculture" (Pollan 2006b). The company agreed (at least publicly) with the spirit of Pollan's argument and launched a purchasing program targeting local providers—a strategy that, not coincidentally, increased its ability to present a "robust identity" to consumers.

For their part, traditional supermarkets have found themselves squeezed between WFM, with its exciting character and high profit margins, and discount retail companies like Wal-Mart, which offer mainstream food items at rock-bottom prices. As one interviewee who worked for a traditional supermarket put it, "We've become very stale over the years. When you look at a traditional grocery store . . . you come in, you buy your groceries, you go home. Little excitement, kind of a pain in the butt to go grocery shopping."[4] Some supermarkets responded to this perception by expanding their range of merchandise to include a greater variety of organic items, while others launched entirely new store formats that mimicked the WFM experience. An example of the former strategy was a $1.6 billion campaign by Safeway, the country's third-largest grocery chain, to remodel its stores and reorganize its merchandise. In addition to increasing the number of products in its "O" organic private label line, the company added hardwood floors and earth-toned walls to its stores. The goal, explained one marketing consultant, was "to make sure that when you walk into the store it gives you a natural, abundant, fresh feeling" (Hibbard 2006). H-E-B, a Texas-based grocery chain, took the latter approach by creating a new line of stores, Central Market, which emphasized fresh produce, natural and organic foods, and a shopping atmosphere that resembled a wholesale food market.

Convergence between WFM and mainstream supermarkets became very clear in 2007, when the company proposed to buy the Boulder, Colorado–

based Wild Oats Market. Although acquisitions of other "supernaturals" played an important role in the company's expansion during the 1990s and 2000s, the Federal Trade Commission (FTC) sued to block the merger on the grounds that Wild Oats was the only remaining natural and organic foods chain besides Whole Foods that had a national network of stores. From the FTC's perspective, the merger would create a monopoly situation, which could allow WFM to charge higher prices for its products. WFM responded to the lawsuit by arguing that a distinctive natural foods retailing category was a thing of the past and that, rather than dominating other "supernaturals," it competed directly with much larger mainstream supermarkets that sold a similar range of organic products (Martin 2008). Despite a scandal involving anonymous stock tips posted by company co-founder John Mackey, WFM and the FTC settled for an agreement in 2009 that would allow the merger to go forward, provided that the company sold off a number of Wild Oats stores to other operators.[5]

At the other end of the retailing spectrum, discount stores have also entered the organic foods market, albeit in a somewhat uneven way. Wal-Mart, which is the world's largest grocer in terms of sales volume, announced plans in 2006 to offer organic products at its American stores, priced at 10 percent above similar conventional products. This news promised not only to increase the amount of organic foods sold, but also to bring Wal-Mart's well-known efficiencies to organic supply chains and potentially to drive the price of organic products down in other retail locations (Pollan 2006a). At the time, Wal-Mart's venture was limited to relatively few organic items and focused mainly on organic versions of the mass-market brands that it already sold. As of this writing, the company still has not developed its own private-label line of organic items, although it announced a partnership with the Wild Oats brand of organic packaged products in 2014 that enabled it to become the brand's sole national retailer (Wohl 2014). Target, on the other hand, included a number of organic options in its Archer Farms private-label brand and released a second private-label line, Simply Balanced, at the end of 2013 that emphasized organic products. The decision was generally interpreted as an effort by the company to enhance the appeal of its private-label products to upscale consumers (Mullen 2013).

The increasing availability of organic foods at the retail level has also put the squeeze on the independent organic foods stores and co-ops that pioneered the sale of organic products in the 1970s. Small independent stores are disadvantaged in the market because they cannot exploit economies of scale in supply and distribution chains. Whereas large retailers often rely on in-house distribution centers and truck fleets, independent stores typically use separate suppliers, to whom a fee must be paid. These stores also find it difficult to create the atmosphere that some customers, conditioned by the WFM experience, have come to expect. One particularly frustrated store manager remarked on the superficiality of some customers who compared her store to a WFM location several miles away, noting, "We're not glitzy, we don't have beautiful fixtures, and we don't have somebody standing out there sampling this and that all day long . . . there's other values that go into the decisions that we make."[6] The challenge that these stores face is transforming these values into a basis for survival in an increasingly competitive market. This is apparently a one-way competition. Independent stores struggle to keep their customers from migrating to WFM, but as the debate with the FTC suggests, the company views other retail chains, not independent stores, as its competition.[7]

Expansionary Understandings and New Arrivals to the Organic Sector

Market growth and convergence have also brought a flood of new participants into the organic sector. Mainstream manufacturers have hired marketing professionals to manage their organic product lines, retailers employ skilled business administrators to assess sales performance and develop national competitive strategies, and distributors rely on specialist category managers to guide their organic operations. The new arrivals are more closely connected with the routines and culture of mainstream business than were many of the pioneers in the organic sector. Many of them are business school graduates, and most interact regularly with colleagues and supervisors who do not work with organic foods. Even those individuals who are employed by companies that focus mainly on organic foods, such as WFM, face pressure from supervisors and shareholders to meet quarterly earnings goals. Their experiences affect the ways in which the new arrivals interpret the goals of organic agriculture and, in particular, lead them to embrace and elaborate on expansionary understandings of organic farming's mission.

The concept of cultural schemas, which derives from cognitive science but has been developed by sociologists and organizational theorists, provides a key to understanding this process (DiMaggio 1997; Powell and DiMaggio 1991). Schemas are "learned, organized cognitive structures that shape attention, construal, inference and problem-solving" (Thornton, Ocasio, and Lounsbury 2012, 88). The schemas that people incorporate into analysis and decision making derive from cultural influences and are often reinforced in daily life. For example, important schematic elements provided by contemporary business training include an emphasis on quantitative reasoning as the foundation of rational decision making, a reliance on abstract concepts that may be applied across different organizational and industrial settings, and an assumption that individual freedom and market competition are sources of innovation and economic growth (Khurana 2007). These cognitive tools become "common sense" because of their reciprocal relationship with action in business environments: while schemas provide individuals with frameworks for interpreting information and evaluating options for action, the ensuing decisions and behaviors affirm the overarching schemas and embed them more deeply in their respective institutional domains (Friedland and Alford 1991; Thornton and Ocasio 2008).

People rely on cultural schemas when they navigate familiar social settings, but they also carry them into new arenas of activity through a process of transposition (Scott 2007). That is, people deploy schemas in a wide range of situations that seem to them to be analogous or similar (Sewell 1992). The idea of transposition captures, in part, what the new arrivals have done in the organic sector. In contrast to earlier participants, the new arrivals apply principles and procedures to the organic trade that are widely used in conventional marketing, retailing, and business administration.[8] However, many of the new arrivals also treat work in the organic sector as more than a business proposition. In interviews, they emphasized that they had chosen to work with organic foods (and for many, it was a choice) because they wanted to accomplish larger social and environmental goals—although they continued to rely on modes of reasoning that are typical in the business world to make sense of the extra-market values produced by their labor.

Their thinking on this score echoes that of business leaders who have tried to reformulate accounts of business purpose and strategy to include considerations of human and environmental welfare (Hawken, Lovins, and Lovins 1999; Mackey and Sisodia 2013). A key feature of their advocacy is the assertion that modern business forms can generate social and environmental values as well as economic ones, provided that business leaders incorporate these criteria into their decision making. By framing the social and environmental "mission" of business in terms of the cultural schemas that dominate the business world, advocates contend that economic growth, social welfare, and environmental sustainability are naturally aligned (Russo 2010). In their defense of "conscious capitalism," for example, WFM co-founder John Mackey and marketing professor Raj Sisodia assert the natural tendency of businesses to accomplish socially beneficial ends by describing increases in average per capita income and life expectancy and decreases in rates of global poverty and hunger during the era of industrial capitalism, although they also argue that the contemporary "myth that business is and must be about maximization of profits . . . has robbed most businesses of the ability to engage and connect with people at their deepest levels" (Mackey and Sisodia 2013, 15). These arguments not only provide a moral justification for business growth but also suggest that businesses can incorporate social and environmental goals into their strategies without damaging their economic performance.[9]

Following similar lines, many of the new arrivals cast the organic sector as an enlightened marketplace in which businesses and consumers, pursuing the ends of competitive growth and personal satisfaction, generate larger social and environmental gains. Similarity between the new arrivals' statements and these ethical business arguments is understandable. The latter arguments emerged in the business world during the 1990s and 2000s, a period when many of the new arrivals were in business school or beginning their careers, and it is likely that they encountered these arguments during their training or at organic industry events (Utting 2005).[10] Moreover, many ethical business advocates themselves lead organic foods businesses or companies that sell similar environmentally friendly products. Their reasoning is compelling because it provides a way to articulate the moral virtue of organic sector work without disrupting the schemas that the new arrivals use to navigate the professional imperatives of sales growth and business profitability. It is also useful because it provides a moral justification for mainstream business practices and for efforts to develop organic versions of mainstream products. As has occurred in other settings where market builders have encountered resistance, the existence of a moral justification for growth has helped to disarm and contain critics who question the legitimacy of these practices and products in the organic sector (Quinn 2008; Zelizer 1978).

The blending of business schemas and ethical ends appeared in new arrivals' accounts of their work in the organic sector. For example, consider the story of one marketing professional that I interviewed. She attended business school at a public university during the late 1990s, and while in the program, she secured an internship with a major food company that had recently purchased several successful organic foods brands. The internship combined interest and opportunity: she explained that she had a personal affinity for organic farming for environmental and health reasons, but also noted that organics were a "hot" area for growth within the food industry. She returned to work in the company's organic foods division after completing her MBA but found that her career track would eventually lead her to "enter the [company's] whole food system and become a line marketer," promoting conventional products as well as organic ones. She left this employer to become a national marketing director for a much smaller business that cans organic fruits and vegetables for the consumer market and also sells organic ingredients to other food processors. The move was not without risk, and when I asked her to explain the decision, she emphasized the ethical satisfaction offered by her new job:

> I only want to do work where there is a net positive happening for people and the planet because of the work that I do. The organic food industry absolutely fulfills that in my way of thinking. The more of this stuff that I find a market for, at the end of the day, there is farmland being improved . . . I'd say the most satisfying [part of my job] is actually being able to make things happen on a significant scale on both the supply and demand side. Being able to ask for a million more pounds of organic [vegetables], knowing that acreage is being farmed organically, and then going out there and creating a marketplace for that product. And just seeing that fulfilled again and again.[11]

The notion that work is meaningful when it creates social and environmental values outside of the market figures prominently in this woman's account. Whether or not this conviction was the deciding factor in her departure from her first employer, it organizes the retrospective explanation that she offers to make sense of her career path.[12] The phrase that she uses to flag this motivation—"net positive"—is a revealing one because it implies that quantitative measurement offers a reliable way to evaluate her contributions toward this goal and, by extension, to assess the ethical character of the organic foods sector as a whole. She also uses quantitative metrics to equate the goals of market growth and social and environmental improvement (Espeland and Stevens 1998). The more organic food she sells, the more farmland is improved through organic management, and her greatest satisfaction is her ability "to make things happen on a significant scale."

Evidence that new arrivals view the ethical value of their work as synonymous with market growth measured in quantitative terms appeared in other interviews that I conducted as well. For example, one supermarket category manager who worked at a "supernatural" described the virtues of market growth by noting that "when food is produced responsibly and farms grow fruits and vegetables more cleanly, and the two come together in a packaged good that there is a demand for, *it just increases the acreage where the pesticides are taken out and every aspect of the food supply chain from farmer to people's dinner plate is made better*" (emphasis added).[13] Similarly, a consultant who helped conventional farmers transition their land to organic management explained that she "always felt good about [her work] because at the end of the day *what we were doing was promoting something that had a huge impact on the environment*" (emphasis added).[14] Perhaps most forcefully, an organic foods distributor and former certifier exclaimed, "I'm interested in supporting the Iowa corn grower and the Montana wheat farmer and getting them to stop using poisons and if that means that they make Twinkies out of it and sell it in Walmart, you know, great!"[15] He continued by pointing out that Wal-Mart's sales volume is so large that the success of organic products at this retailer would pull an ever-increasing number of acres into organic production.

The prominent place of quantitative reasoning in these accounts reflects the new arrivals' professional preparation as well as their everyday experiences. Many in the new generation of organic professionals found their way into the sector through business education programs that emphasized quantitative analytic skills, and this professional training shapes the cultural schemas that they use to interpret the world (Khurana 2007). Additionally, the new arrivals work in organizational settings that charge them with constant monitoring of quantitative performance metrics. Retailers review the turnover rates of products on store shelves; marketers develop sales projections after evaluating the strength of market demand; distributors set pricing schedules according to the size of customers' orders. Since quantitative assessment is a taken-for-granted feature of the organizational worlds within which the new arrivals operate, it seems entirely natural to them as a measurement of the social and environmental significance of their work as well (Jepperson 1991).

I do not want to paint the new arrivals with overly broad brushstrokes. After all, other observers of the organic sector have suggested that entrants from the mainstream food industry find the notion that organic farming's mission exceeds the generation of economic value less than compelling (Jaffee and Howard 2010; Obach 2015). A few of the individuals that I interviewed described their work in the organic sector simply as a business opportunity or as an assignment from their supervisors. One individual employed by a wholesale company that handled conventional and organic products memorably remarked that while he agreed that organic farming was better for the environment, he was "interested in the organic business as long and as much as I can put some money to the bottom line of this company."[16] Given the sector's size and the range of the new arrivals' experiences and backgrounds, there are surely many more people who share his sentiments. In my interviews, though, these sentiments were the exception. Instead, people emphasized that they worked in the organic sector because they wanted their efforts to have some meaning besides economic gain.

BOUNDARY WORK: MARKET GROWTH, COMPETITIVENESS, AND ETHICAL INTEGRITY

Reasoning that combines business schemas and ethical ends also guides the symbolic boundaries that the new arrivals construct to distinguish which individuals and organizations have a legitimate place in the organic sector. Symbolic boundaries "are conceptual distinctions made by social actors to categorize objects, people, places, even space and time" (Lamont and Molnár 2002,

168). The contours of the symbolic boundaries that members of particular social groups create—the way they "cut up the world and create meaningful entities"—reflect the shared cultural resources that they have at their disposal (Zerubavel 1991, 3). Symbolic boundaries may also reinforce social boundaries, as when members of a profession or socioeconomic group exclude individuals that they perceive to be inadequate or unworthy of membership (Gieryn 1983; Lamont 1992). Economic sociologists have shown that members of markets create these sorts of boundaries when they distinguish valuable, legitimate, and morally appropriate forms of market behavior from others that are worthless, illegitimate, or corrupt (Abolafia 1996; Hirsch 1986).

When they engaged in this latter sort of symbolic boundary work in the organic sector, the new arrivals combined their belief that the benefits of organic farming are linked to the sector's market growth with a faith in the virtue of free-market competition. These principles led them to argue that mainstream food businesses have a core place in the organic sector, except in cases in which these businesses seek profits from organic sales without displaying a related commitment to growing the organic market as a whole. In contrast, they treated older, countercultural businesses as marginal players and denied a legitimate place to critics of the organic sector's rapid growth and convergence with the mainstream. These new arrivals reversed the criteria used by earlier sector participants who were more committed to transformative understandings of organic production. For many pioneers, businesses were legitimate if they limited their size, concentrated on local markets, and incorporated efforts to effect social and cultural change in their operations. For the new arrivals, questions of size and political activism distracted from the mission of the organic sector, while efficient, expanding businesses made the greatest contribution to converting farmland to organic production.

This boundary work is not always readily evident. Regardless of whether they worked for organic divisions of mainstream food businesses or smaller companies that specialized in organic products, most of the new arrivals initially emphasized that the organic sector should be a wide-open field in which companies of all sorts might innovate and compete. As one individual remarked, "I believe in diversity . . . It gives more richness and vitality to any movement. When you become exclusionary or restrictive, it almost becomes fanatical."[17] Another interviewee agreed, saying: "I think that the dichotomy of really large companies in organic . . . [and] another extreme of a very small, local organic farm that feels like they are the gold standard of what organic should be, and these people not having a whole lot of common ground is in general a healthy thing."[18] The marketing director that I introduced above went further, explaining, "I don't see the entry of large players as a threat, because they are bringing [organic] products to a much wider audience at a lower price . . . I think it's un-American, actually, to tether companies in a way where we say, you've sold out if you're going to go after that segment of the market!"[19] Their openness flowed more from the assumption that increased sales of organic foods translate into social and environmental benefits than it did from direct personal interest (i.e., none of the people quoted in this paragraph worked for one of the "really large companies" in question). As the first speaker put it, "If everyone agrees that all agricultural production should be organic . . . we're going to have to embrace a lot of economic structures, a lot of different types of ownership structures."[20]

Although they celebrated diversity, the new arrivals were generally in agreement that all members of the sector, whatever their size, should act in business-like ways. They had little sympathy for those who placed ideals over operational efficiency or customer satisfaction. The marketing director made this point in reference to co-op retailers, which have a reputation (not entirely deserved, as I will explain in Chapter 5) for putting political activism before business acumen:

> What's happening now is that many hard-core co-ops have dug in and decided, we are who we are. We're reflecting the real cost of food here. If you can't get it here we have good reasons why. There are a lot of independent co-ops that have done that, that have drawn their line in the sand, and I think that those are the ones that are going to have the hardest time . . . It's not going to fly in five years, because Whole Foods will come in and have a beautiful store that makes people feel great while they are shopping and they won't have to have given up so much to shop there.[21]

She was willing, in the case of co-ops and other small businesses, to let market competition run its course. That those who clung too tightly to their ideals might be destined to disappear was too bad, but it did not represent a great concern. After all, WFM and other large retailers would contribute to the goal of converting farmland to organic management even as they made their customers "feel great while they are shopping." The principle that market competition is legitimate, natural, and a good thing is certainly part of the culture of American business, and it shaped the symbolic boundary that this woman drew with regard to co-ops and other small businesses (Khurana 2007). While she did not explicitly argue for their exclusion, neither did she suggest that they had some particular value that would make them worth saving. In fact, given their smaller market share, their worth might be somewhat less than that of competitors who sold more organic foods (and thus supported more acres of organic farmland).

The only critiques of large companies that I encountered from the new arrivals focused on those companies that sought to profit from consumers' interest in organic foods without displaying a commitment to growing the size of the organic industry as a means of environmental improvement. One example appeared in a story that a public relations consultant for businesses in the organic sector offered about a British convenience store chain named Iceland. She explained that in the early 2000s, the company had publicly announced its plans to incorporate organic ingredients into the entire line of products that it sold under its own brand name.

> They hired a very dedicated staff to literally fly around the world looking for enough supply and they hired my firm to conduct an international media tour for them, to take journalists from the UK to the United States as well as to Guatemala to see the source of the foods. There was a broccoli farm in Guatemala where they were getting a lot of their supply. They started with organic frozen vegetables. They had [the product] in stores for exactly one month, right before the Christmas holiday season, and then decided to pull the plug on the whole thing. Poor timing, poor execution, probably never intended to actually do it. Their stock had risen during the whole positive press around their commitment to changing over to organics . . . It was truly an insider job, probably planned in advance, that hurt a great number of people in the process.[22]

The point of the story, for this individual, was to sound a note of caution about the commitment of mainstream food companies to the growth of the organic sector. In fact, she extended her concern to Wal-Mart, which at the time of the interview had recently announced plans to increase the number of organic products available in its stores. She pointed out that "if they don't honor their commitment to their organic suppliers, the industry could really, really be hurt by that . . . That is my fear with Wal-Mart because they have never made a commitment of time. They have never said, we'll give this five years to work and then we'll see. If Wal-Mart tomorrow said, "yeah, this didn't work for us," I can't even begin to imagine how many organic suppliers would be put into bankruptcy."[23]

The new arrivals drew the clearest boundaries against activist groups that organize consumer campaigns around the goal of influencing organic regulations and limiting the entry of mainstream companies into the organic sector. These groups deserve their own chapter (which follows this one), if only because descriptions that the new arrivals provide of them are so negative. For example, the public relations consultant criticized one of these groups, the Cornucopia Institute, which challenged the way that Wal-Mart advertised organic products in its stores;

> I think that the Cornucopia Institute, from my dealings with them, are utopian organic, in that camp. The last thing that they want to see is Wal-Mart selling organic groceries, produce, or products. And unfortunately for them . . . the train left the station a long time ago. We're already well past the utopian organic world. It's long, long past. Ten, twelve, fifteen years ago past. And you can't get it back. And for them to think that a Walmart [store] is not going to have organic products is not realistic.[24]

While she described Cornucopia as "utopian" and "not realistic," others argued that it and similar activist groups were irresponsible and possibly unethical, since their tactics threatened to slow the organic sector's growth. One interviewee commented that the group's members were "known to be very big advocates of strong standards, but also very loud in an unpleasant way. They pick up the megaphone . . . [and] it's not good even for the people that they are purportedly trying to protect because the consumers are even more confused."[25] Another respondent noted that these groups' protests against large organic dairies might cause the organic milk industry to "become a niche again where you get it delivered in your milk box on Monday morning by the milk man. And I think that is what Cornucopia wants."[26] Confused consumers and old-fashioned milk deliveries would hardly help to increase sales—and by extension, the social and environmental benefits—of organic products.

CONSUMERS' ROLES AND THE PERILS OF PARTICIPATION

A final theme that appeared in my interviews with new arrivals concerned the role of consumers in the developing organic sector. Once again, the new arrivals' accounts of consumer behavior, as well as the distinctions that they made between legitimate consumer roles and problematic ones, reflected widely shared understandings in the mainstream business world. Before considering their accounts, it is worth taking a quick detour through sociological ideas about the development of markets that, like the market for organic foods, blend the pursuit of profits with efforts to advance ethical goals. While sociologists often argue that these markets offer new roles to consumers as knowledgeable partners in governance, my respondents offered a far more circumscribed portrayal of consumers' behaviors and position.

A number of sociologists have suggested that moral markets, or markets in which ethically marked social and environmental goals "become inscribed in products and services . . . as well as in the rules and regulations that govern market relations," demonstrate a change in the nature of consumers' participation in the economic sphere (Stehr 2008, ix). In an important book about the subject, Stehr argues that the moralization of markets is occurring because of increases in consumer wealth and "knowledgeability," which he defines as consumers' confidence and ability to intervene in market processes due to a newfound understanding of the destructive impacts of many market activities on communities and the natural environment. Similarly, Stolle and Micheletti describe political consumerism, or "consumers' use of the market as an arena for politics in order to change institutional or market practices found to be ethically, environmentally, or politically objectionable," as a form of civic action that is on the rise as a result of governments' perceived inability to hold transnational corporations accountable to public welfare (Stolle and Micheletti 2013, 39). While Stolle and Micheletti offer a more circumspect view of the potential of political consumerism to affect markets (Micheletti, Føllesdal, and Stolle 2004, ch. 5), they agree with Stehr that consumers are becoming more knowledgeable about social and environmental problems produced by the global economy.[27]

The question that I take up here concerns how new arrivals to the organic sector conceive of consumers' knowledge and motivations and define their place in deliberations about organic farming practices and in the ongoing development of organic regulations. This question is important because these professionals set the terms on which many consumers encounter organic products. If they believe that consumers have the capacity to contribute to discussions about how organic farming can achieve environmental goals, they can design shopping spaces, product displays, and public relations materials in ways that encourage them to do so. If they believe that consumers' roles should be more limited, they can also make consumer engagement in sector-level deliberations more difficult. In other words, these professionals can help to make the organic sector into a place where consumers think reflexively about values and responsibilities while shopping or into a place where they focus mainly on individual concerns and satisfactions (DuPuis 2000; Johnston 2008).

In general, the new arrivals that I interviewed articulated understandings of consumer behavior that favored the latter orientation. They argued that most consumers buy organic products for individualistic (and idiosyncratic) reasons.[28] In my interviews, these professionals often pointed to health concerns, flavor, and status-seeking behavior as reasons for consumers' purchases of organic foods—as one individual put it, "You might buy organic foods to impress your mother-in-law!"[29] They doubted that collective concerns, such as concern about the contamination of farmland with synthetic chemicals, were strong motivators when it came to purchasing decisions. As one professional explained, "From a consumer perspective we know that the environment is not the number one driver when a consumer is right at that moment of purchase . . . It's like Maslow's hierarchy. People are going to be trying to look for something closer in, satisfying those needs first. And if it is a mother who feels protective of her children's health, that ranks a lot higher than the more abstract concept of protecting the environment."[30]

The fact that market growth depended on purchases by consumers who did not share the values and priorities of professionals did not bother the individuals that I interviewed, since they focused on the consequences of these purchases rather than their motivations. One trade association representative made this point very clearly:

Does it really matter to me or to [my organization] why somebody is choosing that [organic] product? Not really. Because whenever they choose that product, they are sending an economic message that we want farming that is done with the environment in mind. Whether the person

who buys it realizes that or not might not make that much of a difference
. . . If you buy it because it tastes good, great! If you buy it because it is
helping the environment, great! That's fine. It all ultimately ends up helping the environment.[31]

The notion that consumers' beliefs and values are irrelevant to the moral
character of the organic market contrasts with the sociological accounts of
moral markets that I described above. However, it echoes a broader pattern
of thinking in American society about the role of consumers and consumption in advancing public welfare. Cohen (2003) points out that through much
of the twentieth century, business and political leaders linked individualistic
consumption to economic growth, national prosperity, and civic responsibility, a pattern of thinking that she labels the "purchaser-consumer" model of
consumer behavior. This model asserts that high levels of personal consumption create individual and collective benefits and thus that it is ethical to consume. It also implies that the politicization of consumption, whether by individuals or groups, is suspect and problematic. Though the 1960s witnessed
a brief period of cultural support for politically engaged consumer mobilization, the purchaser-consumer model was firmly established in government,
business circles, and popular culture by the century's end.

While the new arrivals are confident that individualistic consumers can
contribute to organic agriculture's effort to improve the environment as shoppers, they are skeptical of their participation in the sector as partners in governance. In general, they preferred consumers to defer to the knowledge and
authority of sector members in regard to questions about organic farming
regulations and business practices. In the first place, they doubted that consumers clearly understood the content of the federal organic regulations. One
supermarket category manager offered the following anecdote to illustrate
what he perceived as widespread consumer ignorance:

I was traveling on the plane and talking to a woman who actually was
very well educated and sort of our demographic and yet she was unsure
of whether she could trust organic produce at a conventional retailer. And
I mean, at one level, it is kind of a nice question but on another level
it shows a misunderstanding of what organic regulations are. In other
words, she thought that there was maybe, like if she bought an organic-

stickered apple at Safeway it wasn't reliably organic the way that apple would be at Whole Foods . . . And so it shows again that even on a simple issue like whether organic certification means what it says there is still a lack of information out there and consumers, you know, don't necessarily know to trust the USDA seal.[32]

Others explained that consumers' participation could be dangerous to the long-term success of the organic sector. Since consumers had little understanding of the regulations governing organic production and the organic trade, they could easily be influenced by critics of these regulations to abandon their purchases of organic foods altogether. A weakening of consumer demand for organic foods would undermine the sector's ability to shift farmland away from chemically intensive management. From this perspective, consumer individualism and disengagement were not only benign, they were essential. One interviewee emphasized this view in response to a question about whether members of the sector should work to educate consumers about the different arguments in debates about the organic standards. She explained, "I think it is completely detrimental for consumers to try to understand [these debates]. I think that they need to be able to trust the USDA organic seal. I think that if a consumer asks, the answer [should] be that the National Organic Standards Board is working on definitions . . . but at the moment all of the [products] we sell in our store meet or exceed the guidelines set forth by the USDA."[33]

The new arrivals were often exasperated by the differences between their understandings of organic—which they viewed as the correct ones—and the expectations of consumers. As one person put it, "Consumers have a lot of wild ideas about organic that it was never meant to be. So I think that there's always going to be a gap between consumers' sort of glowy perception of what it is and what organic certification actually means. They kind of think that there should be a [picturesque] red barn, and that's not part of it!"[34] Another complained, "People don't see us as part of environmental sustainability and we're constantly battling whether or not we truly are even better for human health . . . It gets misunderstood and people think [organic is] also low calorie, you know. It's very interesting all the kinds of misunderstandings about what the organic label means."[35] These concerns have fueled several industry-wide public relations projects, of which the most significant is probably the Organic Center, a nonprofit organization founded and supported by the Organic Trade Association. The Organic Center reviews published research about organic foods and agriculture and creates accessible "fact sheets" for consumers and the media. Through this work, the center aims to respond to consumers' wide-ranging beliefs and expectations with authoritative statements and, not coincidentally, to encourage consumers to continue purchasing organic foods. One thing that the Organic Center does not do, however, is to encourage consumers to participate directly in debates about federal regulations or other governance issues within the sector.[36]

Conclusion

The developments that I have described in this chapter moved the organic sector further down the path defined by the Organic Foods Production Act and by the federal regulations. Many of the organizational and economic barriers that separated the organic sector from the conventional foods industry during the pre-OFPA period crumbled as conventional businesses purchased organic companies or launched their own organic product lines, and as organic foods specialists adopted forms and strategies that resembled those of their conventional counterparts.[37] OFPA's primary goal was to support growth in the value and volume of organic foods sales, and along with this growth has come a departitioning of the resources available to organic foods businesses (Sikavica and Pozner 2013). It is also worth noting that changes in the organic sector's structure have affected the composition of the National Organic Standards Board. While many of the seats on the initial NOSB were originally held by individuals from the mainstream food industry who had little direct experience with organic foods, the board is increasingly populated by leaders of market-oriented organic foods businesses and by individuals from the organic divisions of mainstream food companies (Jaffee and Howard 2010; Obach 2015).

One of the advantages of scholarship that focuses on institutional logics is that it emphasizes interplay and reciprocity between organizational and economic arrangements and cultural understandings (Thornton, Ocasio, and Lounsbury 2012). The elaboration of expansionary understandings of organic farming's mission, which has accompanied organizational and economic convergence between the organic sector and the mainstream food industry, illustrates this process. The new arrivals that work for market-oriented organic businesses have carried assumptions and cognitive principles from the main-stream business world into the organic sector (Scott 2007). The settings in which they work affirm these cultural schemas, and convergence has shifted understandings of organic farming's mission away from changing the struc-ture of agriculture and toward a focus on quantitatively measureable environ-mental improvements. The sector's new arrivals rank market growth as their highest priority, and look askance at changes that might reduce the efficiency and productivity of organic operations or constrain consumer demand for or-ganic foods. In this context, their boundary work may be viewed as a form of conflict-oriented framing (Lamont and Molnár 2002). While the new arrivals see value in organizational diversity within the organic sector, they also clearly position large, market-oriented businesses as its most important participants. They describe alternative businesses as idealistic or naive, and often portray them as quaint (or obsolete) relics from an earlier period in the sector's his-tory. At worst, they accuse those who criticize market growth of undermining organic agriculture's potential to deliver measurable environmental improve-ments. Their statements—particularly those directed at critics—emphasize contradictions between expansionary and transformative organizational ap-proaches and insist on the economic and ethical shortcomings of the latter.

In Chapter 4, I will examine the arguments, organization, and strategies of those groups that are targeted by the new arrivals' critiques. Environmen-tal, small-farm, and consumer-interest advocates assert that the organic sector continues to have an obligation to develop alternatives to the mainstream food industry. These advocates see the patterns of convergence that I have discussed as a threat to this mission. They have tried to influence regulations and to mobilize consumers in response to this perceived threat, but they have found that the current dominance of expansionary rules, practices, and un-derstandings in the sector impedes their efforts.

CHAPTER 4

The Politics of Organic Integrity

Reasserting Transformative Ideals from the Margins

IN 2006, a small organization located in rural Wisconsin released a report titled *Maintaining the Integrity of Organic Milk*. The Cornucopia Institute had been in existence for only a few years, but had already made a name for itself as a vocal critic of rapid market growth and corporate concentration in the organic foods sector. The report developed this theme, arguing that the organic dairy industry had been built up by small-scale farmers and consumers dedicated to supporting humane and environmentally sustainable agriculture, but that the commercial success of organic milk had attracted the attention of much larger firms that did not share these convictions. The report's authors explained that

> as more and more of these industrial-scale livestock operations come online, the potential will develop for a surplus of organic milk. Should a surplus occur, it is likely that the downward price pressure will wash many smaller, family-scale producers out of business. This will repeat the same sad story that has forced so many conventional farmers off the land—even though organics were hailed as an antidote to the effect of corporate-controlled food production and its accompanying vertical integration of farming and its application of the industrial confinement model. (Kastel 2006, 5)

More than a warning, the report was a call to action. The authors continued, "We believe that there is a *higher authority* than the USDA: the organic consumer! It is our hope that consumers and wholesale buyers . . . [will] vote in the marketplace for those organic dairy products from businesses who share their values" (5). To facilitate this voting, the report directed consumers to an Internet-based "scorecard" of organic dairy brands that they might encounter at a grocery store. Brands that supported family-owned farms that grazed cows on pasture received the highest score—five cows—while brands that relied on "factory-farm" production or that refused to disclose their management practices in response to the Cornucopia Institute's requests received only one cow or no cows at all.

The Cornucopia Institute and similar groups seek to steer the organic sector back toward transformative principles that were sidelined during the creation of federal regulations and during the subsequent market growth. These groups assert their desire to restore "organic integrity," a phrase that refers to the ability of the sector to realize values and goals that lie outside of market growth. For these critics of contemporary patterns of market growth, organic integrity depends on limiting the influence of mainstream food businesses on the organic regulations and on excluding practices that characterize conventional food production. Their arguments echo the agrarian and countercultural celebrations of small businesses, decentralized economies, and democratic participation that existed in the sector's early years, but they also reveal concerns about the concentration of corporate power and the lack of accountability in other sectors of the economy. Many contemporary critics view organic agriculture as one issue in a broader portfolio of concerns that includes the expansion of biotechnology, the industrialization of agriculture, and the rollback of consumer protections in the marketplace. The creation of a national market and a federal regulatory program for organic foods during the 1990s encouraged groups involved in these issues to define the sector as a new front in a struggle to limit the economic and political influence of large corporations. These critics both reassert transformative understandings of organic agriculture and link these understandings to a larger political and economic agenda.

In this chapter, I describe how these challenger groups have extended the conflict-oriented frames that developed during the implementation of the National Organic Program. They contest specific elements of the current regulations by connecting them to the possibility of a corporate takeover of organic farming. This "corporate takeover frame" enables challengers to link issues as disparate as the management of dairy cows, the use of synthetic ingredients in processed organic foods, and the spraying of apples with antibiotics under a single broad concern. The frame is based on a systemic understanding of environmental problems, which contrasts with the scalar understanding offered by new arrivals to the organic sector. While the new arrivals highlight the ability of large, growth-oriented food businesses to convert acres of farmland to organic management, critics draw attention to the disproportionate political influence of these businesses and the tendency of the profit motive to distance people from considerations of environmental and social welfare. In deploying these two frames, the critics and the defenders of growth in the organic sector tend to talk past each other.

I also examine the outcomes of these protests, focusing on the extent to which challenger groups can influence policy on specific issues, as well as their ability to affect the culture of the organic sector as a whole. The critics of growth have often found that the deck is stacked against them on both counts. Many of the newer, growth-oriented participants in the sector treat the challengers' arguments as naive or, worse, as destructive and unethical. The challengers' larger problem, though, is that federal organic regulations are constructed in ways that make it difficult to problematize economic concentration and the role of large businesses in the organic sector. These barriers have motivated some critics, such as the authors of the Cornucopia Institute's report, to launch consumer boycotts and aggressive publicity campaigns to increase their influence. This strategy has met with some success, but it has also increased the antagonism with which other members of the organic sector regard their activities and has the potential to undermine some of the goals to which they aspire. In addition, the rhetoric of consumer activism that the critics employ fits uneasily with the actions that they ask consumers to take. Despite their descriptions of consumers as a "higher authority," these campaigns call on consumers to make only limited changes in their purchasing habits. They generally *do not* try to draw consumers into open-ended deliberations about what the organic sector should look like. Implicit within these campaigns is a relatively restrictive model of consumer behavior, which paradoxically reinforces the assumptions about consumer individualism and disengagement that color the thinking of sector members who are more growth-oriented.

Other ways of reasserting transformative understandings also exist. At the end of this chapter, I briefly discuss efforts by groups of farmers and activists to move "beyond organic" by creating competing certification programs and distribution arrangements. "Beyond organic" efforts aim to produce new economic opportunities for small-scale organic farmers, but they also express their participants' sense that the organic regulations and the character of the organic sector as a whole have moved away from the meaningful social arrangements and goals that initially attracted them to organic farming. The new certification programs are designed to cultivate the sorts of close, rich relationships between farmers and their customers that are rarely emphasized by new arrivals to the organic sector. Participants attribute a substantive value to these relationships, arguing that they are part and parcel of what it means to farm organically. From the perspective of organizational theory, "beyond organic" efforts demonstrate how contradictory cultural understandings may lead not only to political conflict in markets but also to market "exit" and to the creation of entrepreneurial alternatives (Hirschman 1970).

Crafting the Corporate Takeover Frame

In this chapter, I return to the concept of framing that I have used to examine both compromise and conflict in the organic sector. In the social movements scholarship, framing "focuses attention on the signifying work or meaning construction engaged in by social movement activists" (Snow 2003, 821). Frames consist of guiding ideas that ascribe particular meanings to the events and conditions that concern social movement activists, that define appropriate courses of action in response to those events and conditions, and that encourage current and potential social movement members to pursue those courses of action (McAdam, McCarthy, and Zald 1996; Snow and Benford 1988). Compromise-oriented frames are those that smooth out contradictions between different understandings of organic foods production. Conflict-oriented frames do the opposite: they assert the incompatibility of different understandings and emphasize the threats that organizational and institutional arrangements based on one set of principles pose to the status of the other.

Conflict-oriented frames drove the protest against the initial organic regulations by defining the U.S. Department of Agriculture's tentative inquiries about the permissibility of genetically engineered seeds and food irradiation in organic production as evidence that the agency wanted to seize control of the organic sector. The corporate-takeover frame also emphasizes the possibility of a loss of control of the organic sector, but it identifies mainstream food businesses, rather than the USDA, as the main perpetrators. The difference is one of degree rather than of kind: the corporate takeover frame extends beyond the USDA by pointing to the growing influence of mainstream food companies in organic-sector trade associations and on the National Organic Standards Board (NOSB). One early, large-scale appearance of this frame appeared in a controversy about whether the organic regulations should allow the use of synthetic ingredients in processed, multi-ingredient organic foods.

Understanding this controversy requires taking another look at the content and implementation of the Organic Foods Production Act (OFPA). As I explained in Chapter 2, OFPA's definition of organic foods gave special weight to the materials used in the cultivation of an organic crop. The law prohibited the use of synthetic fertilizers and pesticides in organic cultivation, but allowed the use of most natural substitutes for these materials. This was known within the industry as the origin-of-materials framework: if a material derived from natural origins—that is, if it had been mined, extracted from a plant, or taken from an animal source—it was prima facie considered to be acceptable in an organic production system. If it had been synthetically produced, as were the majority of pesticides, herbicides, and fertilizers used in conventional agriculture, it was not allowed. However, the law also created a "national list" of exceptions to this rule, which included natural materials that *should not* be allowed in organic production because of the risks that they posed to the environment or to the health of farmworkers or consumers as well as synthetic materials that *should* be allowed because they did not pose these risks and because they did not have natural substitutes. The evaluation of materials thus included two steps. First, a determination needed to be made about whether a particular material was of natural or synthetic origin. Then, once that determination had been made, rulemakers needed to consider whether an exception should be granted to either allow or prohibit the material in organic farming and food production.

This work focused initially on materials used in farming, and only briefly considered the role of synthetic ingredients in processed food products. Indeed, OFPA's position on organic processing seemed clear. When the law was being drafted in 1989, there were few processed organic foods on the market, and the law's authors simply extended a stricter version of the origin-of-materials framework to define ingredients that would be permitted in processing. Only naturally derived ingredients were to be allowed in these products, and no provision was made for a list of exceptions.[1] This approach reflected the belief of many of the sector's participants that foods marketed as organic should be processed minimally, if at all. One interviewee who worked as a certifier in California during the 1990s recalled that "it was CCOF's perspective, and the perspective of many farmers, that only minimally processed and raw commodities should be sold as organic, and that processed products needed to be relegated to the lesser claim of 'made with organic ingredients,' using ingredients that were organically grown but once they hit the factory they stopped being organic."[2] During NOSB meetings in the early 1990s, though, some participants argued that it would be necessary to allow a limited number of synthetic ingredients in organic foods processing in order to create organic versions of the foods that consumers were used to buying.[3] They proposed creating a national list of approved synthetic ingredients—common, safe substances like baking soda and tocopherols (forms of vitamin E that are used to preserve freshness and extend the shelf life of products)—that would parallel the list of synthetic substances approved for use in organic agriculture. Most of the NOSB's members agreed with the proposal, and their recommendations to the USDA staff included this list.[4]

The proposal drew the ire of prominent organic foods advocates. Rather than focusing on the relatively innocuous ingredients on the proposed list, these critics argued that creating a market for organic processed foods would encourage the organic sector to develop economic structures that resembled those in the conventional food industry. Prohibitions on synthetic ingredients were needed, the challengers claimed, because their use would undermine the locally anchored, ecological nature of organic foods systems. Joan Gussow, a nutritionist, and Frederick Kirschenmann, an organic farmer and certifier, were among those who asserted this position. In an article titled "Can an Organic Twinkie Be Certified?" Gussow argued that the value of organic foods lay in their ability to build connections between eaters and growers, while "the global industrial food system has flourished on the destruction of human community" (Gussow 1997). Whole and minimally processed organic foods linked consumers to "a particular place, a particular time of year . . . and to a set of values that care for nature implies," while food processing did just the opposite. Allowing synthetic ingredients to be used in order to meet the demands of a mass market, Gussow concluded, involved a retreat from the goal of changing the food system. An organic Twinkie would not only be unhealthy, it would symbolize the loss of a distinctive vision of alternatives to the mainstream food system.[5]

Kirschenmann, in a paper written with Kate Clancy, attempted to envision an approach to food processing that would be analogous to the organic ideal of farming in ways that "mirrored the natural ecosystems in which farms were located." Synthetic materials, they argued, were used in conventional farming and food processing because they made it possible to circumvent natural processes in ways that allowed for the mass production and marketing of food products. They concluded that retaining the integrity of organic processed foods would require not only avoiding most synthetic ingredients but also adhering to a principle of "preserving its original wholeness and complexity" through the allowance of only the most basic processes, such as cooking, grinding, and pressing. Given the complex technology used throughout the food processing industry, the authors pointed out, "the number of foods expected to meet the standard is fairly small."[6] Gussow offered a similar assessment in a separate paper, arguing that the evaluation of materials for processed foods had been based on the "commercial context" (i.e., perceptions of consumer demand), rather than on notions of sustainability. She concluded, "Some of us may disagree with the NOSB's compromise—arguing that it is *not essential* that every food product that can be conceived deserves to be brought into an organic birth."[7]

Members of the NOSB who favored creating a list of permissible synthetic ingredients dismissed these critiques. In a response to Kirschenmann and Clancy's piece, for example, three NOSB members argued for a "practical" rather than an "idealistic" understanding of organic foods processing. They noted that very few certified organic farms conformed to the organic ideals proposed by Kirschenmann and Clancy, and argued that restrictive standards related to organic foods processing would be "counter productive to the goals of achieving adherence to organic production and processing practices, of creating a safer food supply, and of improving the environment." The authors encouraged their readers to put their confidence in the "thorough and comprehensive scientific review" that the NOSB and its technical advisors had conducted of the synthetic ingredients that had been included on the list. They also pointed out that consumers were largely accepting of limited synthetic ingredients in organic processed foods, provided that they were innocuous in nature: "When it is explained that some common food ingredients such as baking powder (found in *everyone's* kitchen) are synthetic, we have found that consumers agree that some synthetics are OK in processed organic foods."[8]

The participants in this debate were essentially talking past one another. Gussow and Kirschenmann anticipated the contemporary corporate take-over frame by linking the issue of food processing to a dystopian vision of an organic sector dominated by mainstream food businesses. Supporters of the list of exemptions to the synthetics prohibition highlighted the importance of synthetic ingredients for market growth and consumer satisfaction, and by extension, for the widespread improvement of farmland using organic agriculture techniques. Synthetic ingredients were not themselves the root of the issue; rather, the question of synthetics indexed larger, contrasting visions of the organic sector's future (Fromartz 2006). No one doubted that allowing certain synthetic ingredients in organic production would increase the variety of processed organic products that could be created and sold, encourage the participation of mainstream food companies in the organic sector, and support the sector's growth, but they disagreed about whether this development would be in keeping with the spirit of organic agriculture. The frames offered by participants on both sides of the debate raised the stakes by focusing on the outcome of decisions for organizational patterns in the sector as a whole, and they were powerful because they captured the attention of people who had little to gain or lose in this particular issue but cared deeply about the sector's future.

The synthetic ingredients list faced a final challenge after the implementation of the federal organic regulations in 2002. An organic farmer named Arthur Harvey filed a lawsuit that identified inconsistencies between the regulations and the Organic Foods Production Act. Harvey argued that the USDA had exceeded the authority granted to it by OFPA when it wrote the final rules and that it had included measures that violated the intent of Congress. He identified seven such violations, including the synthetic ingredients list (DuPuis and Gillon 2009). Like earlier critics, Harvey emphasized the high stakes in the battle, explaining that "if industry people succeed in stamping out this principle of [no synthetics added], there will be nothing to stop industry lobbyists as they team up with USDA to convert organic standards into nothing more than a label which takes advantage of gullible consumers" (Gilman 2006, 25). The lawsuit also attracted the support of several of the environmental and consumer interest groups that had participated in the creation of the organic regulations. The Rural Advancement Foundation International and Beyond Pesticides, two organizations whose leaders had occupied seats on the NOSB, filed one amicus curiae brief in support of Harvey's case. The Organic Consumers Association (OCA), a group that had helped to coordinate the protest against the USDA's first proposed rules, filed a second brief that was joined by other environmental and organic farming organizations.

In early 2005, the court agreed with three points in Harvey's lawsuit, including his challenge to the synthetic ingredients list. Katherine DiMatteo, the executive director of the Organic Trade Association (the OTA, formerly known as the Organic Food Producers of North America, or OFPANA), remarked in a public statement, "If [the ruling] goes through, in the worst case scenario, it could devastate the industry" (quoted in Fromartz 2006, xii). The OTA hired a prominent law firm to draft an amendment to the Organic Foods Production Act that would allow the continued use of materials and practices that the lawsuit had challenged. To the frustration of Harvey's supporters, the organization refused to make the language of the proposed amendment public until after it had been submitted to Congress (Riddle 2005). Even within Congress, the proposal received little debate, since the OTA's draft language was inserted into an agricultural appropriations bill after it came out of a conference committee. The success of the OTA's strategy meant that the court's ruling in the Harvey case had virtually no lasting impact on federal organic regulations, but it also fed the deeper conflicts about the role of mainstream food businesses in the organic sector. In the wake of the amendment's passage, OCA director Ronnie Cummins described the change as a successful "stealth attack" by the mainstream food industry on the organic sector.

Attributing the amendment of OFPA solely to an industry-led "sneak attack" was not accurate, given the extensive debate that had already occurred within the organic sector about the issue of synthetic ingredients. In addition, the OTA counted numerous small businesses and independent organic farmers among its members, and some of these organizations supported (or at least did not actively oppose) the organization's action. The OTA had also pointed out that eliminating large numbers of organic processed products from store shelves would reduce the overall demand for organic ingredients, which could create hardships for organic farmers, and had also argued that the change would make it more difficult for organic foods specialty retailers to compete with mainstream supermarkets.[9] Nevertheless, the interpretation resonated even among those who agreed with the OTA's position on the Harvey lawsuit. One interviewee, a business consultant who worked with independent organic foods retailers, commented that while he found the use of synthetic ingredients in organic foods "pretty reasonable," he thought that the process of amending the law was "pretty lousy." He was particularly offended that the OTA had hired a firm that had also done work for tobacco companies. He explained, "The folks that OTA hired to do their lobbying and their attorneys certainly weren't interested in creating a transparent process. It was, let's get this thing done on behalf of our vendors and our manufacturers as quickly as we possibly can. They're very good at what they do. That's why they were hired. And they won!"[10]

Contemporary Critics and the Politics of Materials

The Harvey lawsuit helped to focus the attention of a range of consumer and environmental groups on the participation of mainstream food businesses in the organic sector. These groups approach the organic sector from different points of view, although their members share a general concern about concentrated corporate power in American society and view their work in the sector as part of a broader struggle for political and economic democracy. For example, the OCA and the Center for Food Safety, which both submitted briefs in support of Arthur Harvey's lawsuit, are run by activists who previously worked with well-known agricultural biotechnology critic Jeremy Rifkin. These two groups combine their organic foods advocacy with criticism of biotechnology companies and with the promotion of legislation to require the labeling of genetically engineered foods. Beyond Pesticides (formerly the National Coalition Against the Misuse of Pesticides), the Union of Concerned Scientists, and Food and Water Watch have connected political work in the organic sector to a larger mission of reducing the use of toxic farm chemicals and encouraging the development of alternative approaches to pest management in agriculture. Consumers Union, which is the political advocacy wing of the Consumer Reports organization that publishes the well-known shopping guide with the same title, aims primarily to empower consumers by promoting transparency in the marketplace. This group's engagement with the organic sector stems from an effort in the late 1990s to evaluate the authenticity of various sorts of environmental labeling claims that were appearing on the market. Finally, the Cornucopia Institute defines itself mainly as an advocate for the welfare of small-scale farmers.

Members of these groups treat the organic sector as one front in a larger battle against the extension of unaccountable corporate power. Central to their activism is the perception that the American regulatory system tends to privilege economic growth above public welfare, which results in a lack of corporate accountability and public control over industrial activities. For critics, this analysis of corporate power and accountability connects disparate issues and concerns. As one activist put it,

> there's a lot of big ag[riculture] people that we're not overly fond of . . . I don't want to start naming off a whole list of who we're mad at but all of these corporations are motivated by the fact that they are legally obligated to produce profit for their shareholders and that's where we believe their human decency and common sense break down . . . That colors everything in the society in which we live at the moment because they are incredibly powerful. It can't help but color [the organic sector] . . . That's probably for the foreseeable future going to continue because I don't see the overall setup with corporations being the way that they are and business being the way that it is changing too terribly much.[11]

In their recent study of the global anti-biotechnology movement, Rachel Schurman and William Munro trace this analysis of corporate power to the radical movements of the 1960s. Just as radicals of that era connected social problems that ranged from imperialistic foreign policies to domestic poverty to corporate political influence, contemporary activists are outraged that biotechnology companies, with the consent of policymakers, are "unilaterally making decisions about technology choices that carr[y] profound implications and repercussions for the rest of society" (Schurman and Munro 2010, 74). In this context, an organic sector that is free of corporate dominance is valuable because it demonstrates that alternative principles of market organization might have a viable existence. One consumer advocate made this point by explaining:

> Organic in so many ways is the hope and I think the model for how alternative systems that are not drug-laden, chemical-laden, [and] pesticide-laden, for how these systems can really work in the marketplace. The marketplace doesn't have to be filled with huge conglomerates that we don't fully understand, or that are driving policy decisions or there aren't many regulations for them, or that can get things "generally recognized as safe" just by using them. I think that organic keeps the conventional food industry in check and I think that without it, that would be a very sad consequence for the food movement as a whole . . . I think that once those systems that have shown viability and shown feasibility go away, then it's very hard to reconstruct them.[12]

From the perspective of these activists, the imperative of protecting the organic sector from being taken over by large food corporations is the key reason for participating in the ongoing review of materials for use in organic agriculture and foods production. The corporate takeover frame that served as the interpretive device for opponents of synthetic ingredients continues to justify the contemporary critics' resistance to allowing new materials into the organic regulations, even if these materials are related to agricultural production, rather than food processing. The consumer activist quoted above emphasized this concern in a somewhat technical account of one of these materials debates:

> [Organic] integrity to me, when I use that phrase, has to do often with what the standards are. I tend to think of integrity as the standards and sort of the strength of them, making sure that they can't be pushed around and poked through . . . I think that's something that we have to tackle as a community because there's this weird circular reasoning that comes into play, which is, "In order to produce an organic version, we have to use this [material]." This issue applies to a lot of the apple and pear varieties that

we see on the market. In the Fuji apple and the Gravenstein, antibiotics [like] streptomycin and tetracycline are used to treat blight, and these farmers say that if they don't have it, then they can't fight the blight. The blight will kill the whole crop very, very quickly. And, I mean I think that's devastating and it's tragic, but is it organic? I don't think it is . . . But now, everything is coming out with the organic seal on it, and I think that's problematic . . . [NOSB meetings] are mostly filled with industry folks who are trying to get a material through, and then there are a handful of us that go twice a year to bat balls back over the fence and say what's not right given what we knew ten years ago or twenty years ago.[13]

This concern about the integrity of the organic standards is striking, since even members of the sector who are deeply convinced of the virtues of growth agree that without a strong and consistent standard, the expansion of the organic market will have little ethical value. One of the new arrivals that I interviewed for the previous chapter, who occupied a seat on the National Organic Standards Board (NOSB) as well as working for a national food processing company, asserted, "We've put rules in place that govern the way organic food is grown and processed and I am personally responsible for that for the next five years and I take it very seriously."[14] Where the champions of growth and the critics of it differ is in their willingness to give new participants in the organic sector, including mainstream food companies, the benefit of the doubt. The new arrivals generally assume that the federal regulations will lead large, profit-oriented companies to scale up organic production in ways that contribute to overall agricultural sustainability, while the critics are concerned that the economic and political power of these companies will enable them to erase the differences between organic agriculture and conventional food production. At the institutional level, the new arrivals trust in the ability of the market to promote public welfare, while the critics are skeptical of it.

Activists frequently link discussions of particular materials to larger concerns about corporate power, and the details of the materials themselves are sometimes secondary to the consequences that they might have for the sector's organization. Strategically, activists' resistance to allowing new materials into organic production represents an effort to limit the sorts of organizational forms and practices that can exist within the organic sector and to preserve its distinctiveness as an alternative system of agriculture and food production. One environmental activist explained this strategy in reference to a debate about the poultry feed additive methionine.

> Where we come from . . . this is a conversation about what style of chicken operation are we using. Is [synthetic] methionine used as a crutch to keep large numbers of chickens tightly confined indoors? We think that it is. We can have this technical argument about the biochemical processes of methionine, but it's really a proxy for a conversation about how many chickens do you keep in a house and do they get outside, and do they eat bugs, and do they live on a farm that looks like the picture on the package.[15]

Methionine is not necessary in organic poultry operations *in general*, she explained, but only in those operations that aim for large-scale production by raising chickens in crowded barns with limited outdoor access. Non-synthetic sources of methionine are also available, although they tend to be more expensive than synthetic ones. Activists thus hope to leverage opposition to particular substances into regulations that make it more difficult for mainstream production methods to take root in the organic sector. If synthetic methionine is prohibited in organic production, the strategy runs, intensive livestock-raising practices will become less feasible and mainstream farmers who wish to enter the profitable organic market will be pushed to change the size and character of their operations.[16]

Institutional Barriers to Change

Although critics of growth, in order to "bat the balls back over the fence," diligently attend NOSB meetings where new materials are discussed, the structure of organic regulations does not support their goals. The obstacles that they face exist because expansionary understandings are built into the institutions that govern the organic sector (Guthman 2004a). One key difficulty has to do with the prominent place of the origin-of-materials framework in the review of substances for use in organic agriculture. Regulators and certifiers originally embraced the origin-of-materials framework because it promised to draw a "bright line" between acceptable and nonacceptable materials and hence between organic and conventional agriculture.[17] In practice, however, many materials fall into an ambiguous gray area. Even materials that are closely associated with conventional agriculture and industrial food production can be, and sometimes are, classified as natural during materials review. Once this determination is made, it is very difficult for critics to oppose these materials.

Debates that took place in 2010 and 2011 about a substance called corn steep liquor illustrate the fuzziness of the distinction between natural and synthetic materials. Corn steep liquor is a by-product of the wet milling of corn. This industrial process separates corn kernels into the basic components of starch, germ, fiber, and protein and precedes the creation of edible corn derivatives (such as corn syrup), corn-based animal feed, and ethanol. Corn steep liquor is the liquid in which the corn kernels are soaked during wet milling, and it has been used as a crop fertilizer in organic production. Challengers to the material, including the Consumers Union and Beyond Pesticides, argued that since the wet milling process involves the addition of sulfur dioxide (a synthetic chemical compound) to the water in which the corn is steeped, the resulting material should be classified as synthetic, and should therefore be subject to an additional review focusing on its acceptability within a system of sustainable agriculture.[18] Supporters of the material countered that the sulfur dioxide was not responsible for the changes that took place in the corn kernel during the process, but that these were the result of "naturally occurring fermentation." Thus, they argued, corn steep liquor was a natural product and should not be subjected to the additional review.[19] The debate ended with a decision to classify corn steep liquor as a natural substance, although a significant minority of board members disagreed with this outcome.

Critics also find that the National List of exceptions to the prohibition on synthetic materials raises additional challenges. It is quite possible for farmers and food processors to argue that a particular synthetic material should be granted an exception, either because it is necessary for production or because there is no evidence that it causes physical or environmental harm. If a material is determined to be synthetic but passes its additional review, it is added to this list of substances that are permitted for use in organic production. Streptomycin, one of the two antibiotics used to treat blight in apple and pear orchards, is an example of a listed synthetic material. Until 2013, tetracycline was also listed. According to law, materials on the National List undergo a review every five years, which may result in their removal. The "sunset" provision was intended to encourage organic producers to find non-synthetic alternatives to listed substances, but also to allow them time to adapt to changes in production and crop management. In practice, critics argue, sunset reviews rarely result in the removal of materials from the list, and the fact that most producers know that their use of listed materials is unlikely to be challenged reduces the incentive to seek alternatives. This de facto construction of what one activist called a "perpetual list" was deeply distressing to several of the environmental and consumer group representatives that I interviewed.[20]

Removing materials from the National List became even more difficult in the summer of 2013, when the USDA issued a procedural rule that altered the sunset review process. Before this rule, sunset materials required a vote of two-thirds of the members of the NOSB to gain renewal to the National List for another five years. The procedural change altered the terms of this vote. Instead of requiring super-majority support to *stay* on the National List, materials would have to be voted down by two-thirds of NOSB members to be *removed* from the List. The National Organic Program's deputy administrator, Miles McEvoy, argued that the change would make the review process more efficient by preventing a minority of NOSB members from blocking the relisting of a material, while critics argued that it undermined the sunset provision's intent of moving organic agriculture and food processing away from dependence on synthetic materials. At the NOSB's meeting in the spring of 2014, several board members registered their opposition to the change by delaying a vote on materials that were up for sunset review until later in the year, perhaps in the hope that the USDA would reconsider its position. A small group of activists chose a more disruptive method of protest by occupying the meeting room and chanting, "Don't change sunset!" until local police handcuffed and carried away Alexis Baden-Mayer, OCA's political director and the protest's lead organizer. Despite the protest, the new rule remained in effect.[21]

But perhaps the most dismaying feature of the regulatory structure created by the National Organic Program, from the vantage point of critics, is that it provides few opportunities to explicitly discuss concerns about corporate accountability and the value of alternative business forms. The regulations themselves say nothing about the organizational characteristics that farms and businesses in the organic sector should possess, and the attention that regulators devote to reviewing materials for use in organic production tends to crowd out other concerns. As one activist put it,

> The way that the NOSB has been set up, I think it is a particularly poor place for having system-level conversations . . . They're voting on very particular things . . . but we don't have any place to decide the non-specific big things, and these little things add up and accumulatively are greater than the sum of their parts. Decision after decision after decision, a lot of us are starting to feel like they are dragging us down this road toward one system that looks pretty industrial, and lots of folks don't have any problem with that. Some of the bigger players, the bigger companies who are seeing a lot of growth potential in organic, are seeing it as parallel to their kind of conventional stream, just without the chemicals.[22]

The frustrations that these contemporary activists experience mirror those of members of the organic sector who tried to build transformative understandings into the federal regulations during an earlier period in the sector's history. In that earlier period, people who favored an organic sector that followed different organizational principles from those of the mainstream food industry found that though the regulations offered some opportunities to advance this goal, on the whole they were designed around a more mainstream vision of rapid market growth. The regulations took shape as members of the sector tried to craft a compromise between different understandings of the identity and purpose of organic agriculture. The compromise was not an equitable one then, and as activists are frequently reminded, it remains inequitable today. The practical character of the regulations, in turn, supports the dominance of expansionary understandings and the marginalization of transformative views in the sector.

From Challenging Regulations to Consumer Mobilization

The critics' frustration with the regulatory process helps to explain the appeal in the Cornucopia Institute report that I described at the beginning of this chapter to "a higher authority than the USDA: the organic consumer" (Kastel 2006, 5). The report focused on the extent to which cows that produced organic milk could be kept in confinement, rather than being allowed to graze on pasture. When the NOP went into effect in 2002, the federal rules translated OFPA's requirements that organically raised livestock be allowed to express instinctual behaviors into a somewhat vague mandate that organic dairy cattle have regular "access to pasture." This mandate was also meant to protect small-scale dairy farmers who had turned to organic production after watching their markets erode under pressure from much larger confinement operations. During the 1990s and early 2000s, though, the dairy companies Horizon Organic and Aurora Organic Dairy had experimented with large dairy operations in arid areas of Idaho, Colorado, and Texas. Although these operations had extensive open areas for grazing, the dryness of the land and the size of the herds at these locations meant that cows received much of their diet from organic hay and grains fed in open-air lots, rather than from pasture.[23] It was operations like these that the Cornucopia Institute aimed to challenge in its dairy report. As one of the architects of the campaign explained in an interview:

> If "organic" [allows] a ten thousand cow dairy farm . . . a split operation that is [both] conventional and organic in the same dairy, if that's what "organic" is, there won't be room for family-scale farmers. For those of us who are very committed because of the economic justice element of organics, what have we accomplished? For people who care about humane animal husbandry . . . what have we accomplished?[24]

Cornucopia's dairy campaign is only one of the many consumer-oriented protest campaigns launched by activist groups in the contemporary organic sector.[25] Along with the Cornucopia Institute, the OCA has also mobilized consumers in efforts to preserve the alternative organizational character of the organic sector. In 2004, the OCA launched the "Coming Clean" campaign, which focused on the rules governing the use of organic labeling on soaps, shampoos, and other cosmetic products. As one of the campaign's coordinators explained to me, mainstream manufacturers used extracts of organically grown plants to "front load" their formulas. These extracts gave the appearance that the product consisted mainly of organic ingredients, but in reality, the extracts had no functional purpose. Instead, they concealed what was "really a conventional formulation" consisting of synthetic ingredients used widely in the cosmetics industry.[26] Manufacturers were able to do this because the USDA had no legal authority to regulate cosmetics. The agency refused to act against companies that used the word "organic" in the name or advertising of a body care product that had not been certified as organic, so long as the product did not also display the "USDA Organic" seal.

OCA published on its website a list of "organic cheater" brands that it encouraged shoppers to avoid, as well as a second list of body care products that met the national rules for organically labeled products. It also published a record of retailers that had made a public commitment to stop selling brands that did not conform to the national organic standards. For consumers who preferred a more active approach, it provided a link that, when clicked, would print a sheet of stickers that read, "Panic! This product is not organic!" The OCA encouraged the use of these stickers "where necessary to alert the public to this ongoing sham." Finally, it organized protests to draw attention to products that did not meet the national rules, including one at the Natural Products Expo West, a major industry event, in which demonstrators waved five-foot-tall images of offending brands before attendees. On the legal front, the OCA, Consumers Union, and several body care companies filed petitions with the Department of Agriculture and the Federal Trade Commission to ask for enforcement of labeling regulations on body care products.[27]

Both the dairy campaign and the body care campaign resulted in significant, if not unequivocal, successes for activist groups. After some prodding, the Department of Agriculture began to discipline large organic dairies that appeared to be taking advantage of the vagueness of the pasturing regulations. In 2007, it threatened one of the largest of these dairies, Aurora Organic Dairy, with the revocation of its organic certification. In 2010, the Department of Agriculture issued new rules for organic dairy cattle management, which required that cattle graze on pasture at least 120 days during the year and that they get at least 30 percent of their food intake from grazing during this time. OCA gained the support of the NOSB in the body care campaign, but the USDA has continued to argue that it has no jurisdiction to levy penalties against companies that use the word "organic" in labels on cosmetic products but do not use the seal or claim to be in compliance with federal organic standards. The OCA has had greater success in persuading retailers, such as Whole Foods Market and numerous independent organic foods stores, to exclude these products from their shelves. By blocking access to markets, these retail policies have put pressure on product manufacturers to reformulate their products or to remove organic labeling.[28]

Scholarly interest in how social movement actors shape markets and business organizations has increased in recent years (King and Pearce 2010; Weber and King 2014; Zald, Morrill, and Rao 2005). In his book *Market Rebels*, Hayagreeva Rao argues that conventional economic scholarship has "largely neglected to understand how the *joined hands* of activists and their recruits make or break radical innovation in markets" (2009, 5; emphasis in the original). Activists can propel new products to success or doom them to failure by framing innovations in emotionally resonant terms (creating what Rao calls "hot causes") and by engaging consumers in collective activities where they "actively live meanings and values" associated with the frames (which Rao labels "cool mobilization"). The efforts of the Cornucopia Institute and OCA offer examples of the dynamics that Rao describes. Their accounts of small farms and businesses that are struggling to operate with integrity in the face of duplicitous, profit-seeking corporations aim to evoke feelings of outrage from consumers and sector members alike. They have combined these critiques of corporate infiltration with dramatic actions that capture media attention and magnify the reach of their frames. In 2014, for example, the Cornucopia Institute hired pilots to fly over and photograph fourteen large organic dairy and egg operations. The photos appeared in a *Washington Post* blog article titled "Think Your Eggs and Milk Are Organic? These Aerial Photos Will Make You Think Again." The article also quoted Cornucopia Institute director Mark Kastel, who explained, "When people buy organic milk and eggs, they are buying the story behind the label . . . [but] when they see the reality, they really feel betrayed" (Whoriskey 2014). The resonance of these frames among consumers has created ongoing pressure on regulators and members of the NOSB.

The groups' encouragement to consumers to "vote in the marketplace" by purchasing only those brands that conform to their sense of what organic farming should look like represents the "cool mobilization" side of their campaign. These boycott and "buycott" efforts walk a fine line, though. The Cornucopia Institute and OCA differ from groups that seek to "break" markets for entire categories of products, such as those that oppose the commercialization of genetically engineered seeds, but they run the risk that significant numbers of consumers will respond to their critiques of specific organic firms by losing confidence in organic products *in general*, which would be very disruptive for organic businesses of all sizes. Indeed, the fear that consumers may not distinguish between "good" and "bad" organic products but may simply treat the organic label as misleading and compromised fuels the hostility that expansion-oriented members of the sector direct toward these campaigns and has also generated a certain amount of skepticism from smaller players.[29] Activists understand their own work as a sort of brinksmanship. The possibility of market disruption adds to the leverage of their campaigns and increases the seriousness with which leaders in the organic sector (even those who are not swayed by the merits or emotional resonance of their arguments) take their concerns. On the other hand, their ultimate goal is to increase opportunities for farmers and business owners who produce organic products with "integrity," which would vanish if the organic sector as a whole collapsed.

A second, more subtle tension also exists in these consumer campaigns. Activists assert that consumers have both the right and the ethical obligation to participate in debates about the organic regulations and to hold companies accountable to high ethical standards of organic production. As one activist put it, "We feel like it is consumers' right as well as responsibility to make choices that will better their community . . . Because the government isn't regulating the things that we wish it would regulate, it is consumers' job to use their dollars to support the things that they would like to see more of."[30] This understanding of consumers' role differs from the ideal of the individualistic "purchaser-consumer" that appeared in my interviews with new arrivals to the organic sector; it resonates instead with transformative notions of the organic sector as a democratic, deliberative community (DuPuis and Gillon 2009; Goodman, DuPuis, and Goodman 2011; Hassanein 2003). In practice, though, activists focus on mobilizing consumers' purchasing power to stop practices that they view as egregious violations of organic integrity. Campaigns tend to be organized in a top-down fashion, in which activist groups select issues for protest, frame those issues in evocative terms, and suggest particular actions that consumers might take in response. The argument that activist groups offer to motivate consumers to take these actions—that the organic sector is under imminent threat of corporate takeover—tends to simplify complicated issues and foreclose other interpretations.[31] The activist groups tend not to engage consumers in deliberations about the regulations and organizational forms that *should* exist within the organic sector. This strategy has helped to make the campaigns into an effective tool for critics of market growth, but it does not encourage thoughtful reflexivity or rich civic participation.

Using the case of Whole Foods Market, Johnston has written persuasively about the rhetoric of consumer citizenship in contemporary marketing discourse (Johnston 2008). She argues that the company's marketing presents consumption as a form of civic engagement by suggesting that purchasing organic foods will enhance environmental sustainability, support the livelihoods of small-scale farmers, and reward businesses that show respect for people and the planet. However, this equation of shopping decisions with a "vote" for a better world does not push shoppers to reflect on deeper changes in business practices and consumer lifestyles that might be necessary to check global environmental degradation and rising social inequality. By reducing civic responsibility to consumer choice, consumer citizenship forestalls collective and critical deliberation about tensions between consumer-oriented capitalism and the needs of the global commons.[32]

The fact that a similar cultural framework guides many activist campaigns in the organic sector needs explanation. Essentially, activists carry out their work on a battlefield defined by the dominance of expansionary institutions and organizations. They are in a defensive position, and as challengers, they play the game according to rules established by their opponents (Fligstein and McAdam 2012). While activists might like the organic sector to be a place in which consumers engage thoughtfully in discussions about the values guiding farming and food production, the reality is that businesses and regulators are more likely to respond to economic and political pressure generated through mass mobilization (King 2008). Activists marshal that pressure through campaigns focused on changing individual shopping decisions made by large numbers of people. This strategy has been effective in influencing regulations and business behavior in certain instances, but it leaves the circumscribed role of consumers in deliberations about the sector's governance relatively untouched.

Local Markets and Alternative Certifications

Early in my research, long before I had mapped out the activist campaigns that I have just described, I sat down for an interview with the produce manager of an independent organic foods store who also operated an organic orchard with her husband. The interview had been arranged by the store's general manager, who explained that her colleague, "along with an entire group of local growers have just decided that they are not going to be certified organic anymore."[33] The produce manager explained that the group's members were experienced organic farmers, who had been raising crops organically for twenty years or more. They had obtained certification under the National Organic Program when the federal rules went into effect, but grew "increasingly weary and dissatisfied and frustrated" with the program.[34] In addition to certification costs and record-keeping requirements, the farmers were dismayed by the NOP's bureaucratic restrictions. A cultural change had accompanied the institutionalization of organic farming and the organic sector's market growth, and it was not a change that the members of this group wanted to be part of. The manager explained:

> One of the things that fell apart with the National Organic Program is that the [certification] inspector in the old days used to be like an extension agent and would provide assistance, would provide information, advice on better ways to do things, information that they had gotten from other farms on how to get rid of a certain weed or on a certain seed that is more viable in this climate. Now they are not allowed to do that. They are not allowed to give farmers any information at all . . . When we were doing it in the old days we were helping each other and it was much more of a shared environment . . . Now all of these bureaucrats have taken it over and it is not something that we can work with anymore.[35]

Her complaint echoes one of the contentious issues that emerged during the development of the federal regulations. Against the wishes of many small-scale farmers, organic inspectors and certification agents that are accredited by the National Organic Program are prohibited from providing specific technical advice and consultancy services to farmers. This rule is intended to avoid conflicts of interest between certifiers and their clients, and this manager acknowledged that a formal relationship is probably necessary for "2000 acre organic farms growing organic baby greens that [are] packaged in plastic bags and then sold 3000 miles away."[36] But for small farms like hers, which sell to local markets and value personal relationships with their customers, such formality is disconcerting. For this respondent, it speaks to an ongoing transformation of organic farming from a collaborative, relational project into a much more anonymous, market-oriented field of activity. The new rules for organic certifiers and inspectors reveal the contours of a new—and for this farmer, problematic—organic culture.

These concerns bear some similarity to those that motivate activist critics, but this farmer and other members of her group have forged a less confrontational path. Rather than seeking changes in the federal regulations or mobilizing consumers in advocacy campaigns, they have created an alternative certification and marketing system. Group members continue to use organic methods, but instead of seeking certification to NOP standards, they have arranged regular farm tours for their customers and monitoring visits to one another's operations. The group has also created a new marketing label (which does not use the word "organic") and secured assurances that local retailers and restaurants will continue to carry their products after they stop using the "USDA Organic" seal. As my respondent put it, this project is less a critique of the NOP than it is an assertion of the legitimacy and value of collaborative, trust-based food systems.

> Organics has now "grown up." There are some really good benefits to that, obviously . . . [and] the thing that we don't want to do is have a negative message about organics because that would be a really destructive thing to do and it would go against our better interest. We're not saying that it's a bad program, [that] it's a bad idea, [that] we don't want it anymore. We're just saying that it's not a good fit for us. It's a good thing but it's not something that we need . . . We want to say that there is another way and there is another type of food chain that is much smaller and we want to help people and we want to promote that.[37]

Several decades before the contemporary surge of interest in markets and social activism, the economist Albert Hirschman identified two forms of market-based protest (Hirschman 1970). The political path, which Hirschman labeled "voice," involves collective protest against market leaders. This is the path followed by the Cornucopia Institute, the Organic Consumers Association, and other advocacy groups. The alternative path, "exit," occurs when dissatisfied participants cede the market to dominant players and seek out new arenas of activity. In Hirschman's view, exit was a more individualistic and less confrontational path than voice, and it tended to occur in situations that provided people with the option to separate their own welfare from participation in the market. Although Hirschman developed his ideas about exit while thinking of the behavior of consumers who substitute one product for another, the concept is also useful for making sense of the decision of this produce manager and her companions. Indeed, her unwillingness to directly challenge the expansion and mainstreaming of the organic sector—elsewhere in the interview, she explained that she strongly disagreed with activist groups' support of Arthur Harvey's court challenge to the NOP—and her confidence about pursuing a separate path attest to the distinction that she has created between her own fortune and the fate of organics, more broadly.

However, the concept of exit needs some revision if it is to fit the experience of producers who leave established markets to create new ones. In the first place, Hirschman's argument that exit is a fundamentally individualistic behavior does not hold. As my respondent's experience suggests, creating and sustaining alternatives to organic certification is nothing if not a collective endeavor. Farmers who are involved in these efforts do not simply strike out on their own. Rather, they work with consumers, retailers, and other farmers to create alternative networks of production, distribution, and consumption, as well as new meanings and governance institutions (Goodman, DuPuis, and Goodman 2011; Weber, Heinze, and DeSoucey 2008). The cultivation of relationships plays a key role in the networks that this group is trying to create, and the viability of their project depends on practical support and a degree of shared vision from these parties.[38]

The collective dimension of exit can be seen on a grander scale in the example of Certified Naturally Grown (CNG), a farmer-run organization that offers an alternative to organic certification and that (at the time of this writing) operates in every state except Wyoming. Like the much smaller project described by my respondent, CNG aims to certify small-scale, direct-market farms that find themselves out of place in the expanding organic sector. CNG certification requirements differ from the national organic standards in ways that reflect this focus. For example, food processing operations cannot be certified and the program's livestock pasturing requirements are more extensive than those that existed at the federal level before the Cornucopia Institute dairy campaign. The organization also makes use of a participatory inspection system, in which certified farmers inspect one another's operations and add inspection results to a public online profile. As the organization explains to potential members, this approach "promotes farmer-to-farmer knowledge sharing about best practices and fosters local networks that strengthen the farming community . . . Peer-support networks that develop often help ward off challenges that might tempt someone to cheat if they get out of hand. Peer-inspectors who participate in CNG have a stake in protecting the program's integrity."[39]

To an extent, these alternative market-building projects can be seen as a variety of compromise between transformative and expansionary understandings of organic production, although their goal is not to create cultural or organizational blends of these understandings but rather to segregate them into different markets. CNG positions its certification services as a complement to USDA organic certification and emphasizes that its goal is not to replace the "USDA organic" label with the CNG seal but to provide recognition for small-scale farmers who farm organically and sell their products locally. But, *pace* Hirschman, they do not always avoid confrontation. To return to an idea that I developed in Chapter 3, CNG and similar projects represent an effort to rebuild economic partitions in the organic market by differentiating foods produced by small-scale farms from others that also bear the organic label (Sikavica and Pozner 2013). Members of the sector who favor market growth do not always appreciate these efforts. In 2014, for example, an organization called Organic Voices that included as members several large organic foods manufacturers released a video that criticized the labeling of processed food products as "natural." The video's sponsors portrayed these labels as part of a strategy by mainstream food companies to cut into the market share of organic products. The video also emphasized that the organic label was the *only* label that provided clear and reliable production guarantees to consumers—a claim that (perhaps unintentionally) questioned the credibility of CNG certification as well. Similarly, the new arrivals to the organic sector that I interviewed sometimes treated advocacy for local foods as a competitive threat. As one individual remarked during a conversation about media coverage of organic farming, "In the last month, all of the stories that have been about organic have been about, local is better, the organic fad is over . . . Hey, it's not a fad. We're not talking about a fad here. It's here to stay and it's an agricultural method and it is still as popular as it ever was, if not more . . . It is not going away but consumers are bound to be confused by all of this."[40] Despite their goal of coexistence, alternative certification advocates sometimes respond in kind. Speaking of the video produced by Organic Voices, CNG's executive director noted, "Organic is not the only game in town . . . [Like organic] Certified Naturally Grown means no genetically modified organisms, no toxic pesticides, and no growth hormones or antibiotics. And Certified Naturally Grown also means the food is produced on a local farm with direct community ties, it is real food, from the soil, not from a factory, and the food does not come from a corporate conglomerate."[41] When placed in the context of the critiques of mainstream food companies in the organic sector that I have described, her references to food produced by "a corporate conglomerate" come very close to being fighting words.[42]

Conclusion

Chapters 2 and 3 examined how the organic regulations and the organic sector's convergence with the mainstream food industry propelled expansionary ideas and practices into a dominant position. This chapter focused on the sector's insurgents, although it also made the case that challenger campaigns are best understood in the context of this shifting balance of power between the sector's two institutional logics. Just as growth-oriented newcomers to the organic sector elaborated the meanings of market expansion in new ways, so did activist challengers link older, transformative understandings to a more encompassing critique of corporate power. Since they fight on terrain that is defined largely by the logic of market expansion, though, activists find themselves struggling in institutions that are intransigent with regard to their concerns, as well as reproducing expansionary understandings when they mobilize consumers in boycott campaigns. Other organic farmers who are frustrated by the sector's rush toward market growth have tried to avoid these battles over the meaning of "organic integrity" by creating alternative certifications and food networks, but they sometimes also find themselves struggling for legitimacy.

Conflict has served as the central theme of this discussion, but in Chapter 5, I explore how some participants in the organic sector have sought compromise between expansionary and transformative orientations at the organizational level. The chapter examines how natural foods co-op stores—

a business form that emerged at the time of the organic sector's encounter with the counterculture—have responded to convergence and growth. Co-ops are examples of what sociologists label "prefigurative organizations," whose members tried to model in practice the egalitarian and participatory ways of living that they hoped to create in the larger society, but these stores now find themselves competing closely with market-oriented businesses (Breines 1989; Polletta 1999). In an uneven and ambivalent way, co-ops have crafted arrangements and practices that preserve some of their prefigurative character, while also allowing them to survive in the growing organic sector.

CHAPTER 5

Caught in the Middle

Negotiating Compromise in Organic Co-op Stores

HOUSED IN A CUSTOM-BUILT STOREFRONT in a commercial district studded with independently owned businesses, Pacific Food Co-op (PFC)[1] cheerfully broadcasts its devotion to organic foods. A large clock that adorns the outside of the structure is ringed by a friendly suggestion: "It's time to eat organic!" The doors open onto a tidy sales floor that occupies only a fraction of the space taken by the nearby Whole Foods Market but contains a variety of fresh, frozen, and packaged organic foods. Each bin in the produce section also carries a tag that indicates whether or not the contents were grown locally and often names the farm of origin. A small café on an upstairs level serves freshly made organic sweets and lunch items. In addition to shopping, visitors to the store are often invited to sign petitions that call for the regulation of genetically engineered seeds or for modifications to the USDA's organic rules. When they check out, customers are also encouraged to join the co-op by purchasing a share in the business, and members who have made this investment receive the opportunity to vote in annual elections for the store's board of directors. Along with works from local artists, photos of the current directors line the stairs leading to the café. Directors' e-mails are published in the store's newsletter, and members are also invited to attend monthly meetings to weigh in on the co-op's future. In all, the co-op offers an amalgam of commerce and activism—you can come to shop, to engage in food politics, or to do a little bit of both.

PFC, like many of the roughly 140 other food co-ops[2] in the United States, existed before the explosive growth of the organic foods market. These stores trace their history to the late 1960s and early 1970s, when co-op founders sought to build a foundation for a decentralized and democratic food system that would empower local communities and challenge what they saw as the individualistic, selfish character of American capitalism. For co-op founders, selling organic foods was more than a business proposition; it was an agenda for social change. As one co-op representative put it to me, at this time "kind of the national tag line for food co-ops, if you will, was 'Food for people, not for profit!'"[3] In this chapter, I turn to a set of interviews with the leaders of organic foods co-op stores in order to examine how their organizations have navigated the organic sector's shift in the direction of expansionary principles and market growth. I argue that the co-op experience is one that involves the management of ambivalence in an effort to create compromises between market growth and systemic change. These compromises appear in hybrid organizational arrangements within and between co-op stores, and they reflect negotiations about the identity and purpose of co-ops as much as they do strategic thinking about the stores' economic position in a changing market (Oliver 1991).

Ambivalence, Hybridity, and Compromise in Co-ops

The term "ambivalence" is often used to describe a psychological state of uncertainty or confusion, but sociologists argue that ambivalence may also be built into social relationships and arrangements that contain contradictory expectations, incentives, and belief systems (Jansen and Von Glinow 1985; McInerney 2014; Merton 1976). In this sociological sense, both organizations and individuals can be said to experience ambivalence. Individuals may feel torn between incompatible sets of values, while organizations may find themselves appealing to multiple constituencies that have very different expectations about how they should behave. Ambivalence is particularly acute in social environments—such as the organic foods sector—where people struggle over competing definitions of legitimate goals and activities. To use the terminology developed in this book, organizational fields that possess competing institutional logics are especially conducive to ambivalence (Kraatz and Block 2008).

Organizations often respond to ambivalence by developing hybrid arrangements that "combine institutional logics in unprecedented ways" (Battilana and Dorado 2010, 1419) and that enable them to both capitalize on strategic opportunities produced by complex environments and defend against the inevitable critiques that emerge in divided organizational fields

(Borys and Jemison 1989; Powell 1987). In his analysis of social enterprises that combine elements of business organization with activities oriented toward the public good, for example, McInerney (2014, 108) notes that hybridity "allows organizations to produce accounts of worth amenable to stakeholders in multiple institutional domains." McInerney (2014) and Pache and Santos (2012) both demonstrate that social enterprises strategically incorporate social welfare activities into their operations in order to advance their acceptance in the nonprofit field. Another example comes from the field of for-profit learning centers. Using ethnographic data from one of these privately owned educational facilities, Aurini (2012) documents how the organization allows tutors to interpret rules in ways that maximize both its educational legitimacy and the satisfaction of its customers.

While co-ops also display organizational hybridity, the ways in which they blend different organizational elements result as much from internal negotiations between organizational participants as from strategic efforts to meet the expectations of external audiences and secure advantages in complex fields (Fine 1984). These negotiations are in turn shaped by the belief of co-op members that cooperative practices are valuable and worth preserving whether or not they contribute to the stores' competitive position or overall legitimacy. The negotiated character of hybridity in co-ops appears clearly in several recently created innovative business arrangements that exist in these stores. In response to increasing competition from natural foods supermarkets like Whole Foods Market, for example, co-op leaders across the country pooled their buying power in the early 2000s by forming what they called a "virtual chain" of stores in order to gain discounted rates from product suppliers. At the same time, and in response to a widespread sense that the retail chain model smacked of hierarchical "Wall Street" values rather than community-oriented cooperative ones, they developed measures to protect individual store autonomy and local governance. Similarly, moves to increase efficiency in particular stores have often been accompanied by the development of charitable efforts and volunteer programs that reflected the determination of staff members that co-ops should not act simply as businesses, but should also work for the good of their communities. Co-op leaders embraced these practices because they believed that they had intrinsic value (Selznick 1957), not just because they bolstered the reputations of their organizations (although they engaged in such practices all the more enthusiastically when they believed that the result would be increased customer loyalty and satisfaction).

When it comes to responding to changes in the organic sector as a whole, co-op leaders have also struggled to find compromises between understandings and actions that are anchored in their stores' countercultural histories and ones that they believe are necessary and appropriate in an expanding market. These efforts are complicated by the fact that co-op leaders' evaluations of the sector's shift in the direction of market growth are themselves characterized by ambivalence. In interviews, these leaders raised concerns about the possible exclusion of small-scale farms and businesses from the organic sector and about the eclipse of efforts to transform American agriculture. However, their critiques of the sector's growth were tempered by their acceptance of mainstream arguments that market growth produces environmental benefits by moving increasing amounts of farmland into organic management. Their accounts echoed those of new arrivals to the organic sector on this score, and left the tensions between these different ways of envisioning the sector's future unresolved. In their store operations, the co-op leaders that I interviewed also sought to combine support for the vision of organic agriculture as a systemic alternative to mainstream food production with activities that supported the growth of their businesses and of the organic sector as a whole. For example, they promoted items from small-scale farmers and producers that they felt had the most "organic integrity," and supported efforts to construct "beyond organic" certification programs and distribution networks. They also tried to educate their customers about the virtues of local food systems and even encouraged them to engage in political activism around issues related to food regulation and policy. In all of these activities, though, the co-op leaders that I interviewed worked very hard to avoid acting in ways that might upset their customers. Their efforts reflect economic realities—these co-ops generally operate in competitive retail environments, which present customers with multiple options for organic foods shopping—but they also revealed the extent to which co-op leaders accept ideas about consumer individualism and sovereignty that I have described in previous chapters.

Through these hybrid arrangements, co-op members construct working compromises between different understandings of organic foods production at the level of organizational practice and design. The contemporary dominance of expansionary structures and understandings in the sector certainly shapes the character of these compromises. Economically, co-op leaders find that the need to compete with mainstream stores limits the sorts of democratic and change-oriented activities that they are able to pursue. At a cultural level, many co-op leaders are at least partially swayed by arguments about the legitimacy of mainstream business participation in the organic sector and about the need to respect consumers' diverse motivations for buying organic foods. However, it would be a mistake to reduce co-op operations to only considerations of economic strategy or the diffusion of new cultural ideas (DiMaggio and Powell 1983). Co-op leaders wrestle with the meaning of the organizational arrangements that exist in their stores as much as they do with the consequences of those arrangements, and their efforts to make sense of their stores' identity and mission in the rapidly changing organic sector have important implications for the way that their businesses operate. In what follows, I focus on the negotiated, interpretive character of co-ops' development to show how meaning-making at the local level is consequential for compromise as an organizational outcome (Hallett, Shulman, and Fine 2009; Hallett and Ventresca 2006).

Anti-Businesses in a Changing Market

Leaders of organic foods co-ops frequently refer to their stores as part of a "third wave" of consumer cooperative organizations. This label connects them to the community co-op stores developed by industrial workers in nineteenth-century England (the "first wave") and those that emerged during the Great Depression in the United States (the "second wave"), but it also highlights the unique character of organic foods co-ops (Knupfer 2013). Like their predecessors, organic foods co-ops are collectively owned businesses that aim to provide competitively priced goods and services to their members. Their devotion to organic foods is different, though, as is their reputation for political engagement around progressive issues and environmental causes. Both characteristics stem from these stores' origins in the 1970s, when young activists turned their attention to organic foods and farming. These activists treated organic agriculture as a template for alternative relationships and values—cooperation instead of competition, community instead of individualism—and they cast participation in the organic sector in terms of a broader effort toward social and cultural change. Co-op founders tried to make organic foods more accessible to grocery shoppers, but they also tried to promote the sorts of ideas and behaviors that they believed would create a more virtuous society. As "prefigurative" organizations, organic foods co-ops modeled the ways of living that their founders hoped to bring into American life (Breines 1989; Polletta 1999).

In keeping with this ethos, co-op founders combined the sale of natural and organic foods with distinctive practices that reflected their aspirations for social and cultural change. Observing co-ops in the late 1970s, Rothschild-Whitt argued that they illustrated a pattern of organization that she labeled collectivism (Rothschild and Russell 1986; Rothschild-Whitt 1979). Co-ops explicitly rejected the trappings of bureaucracy, including formal rules and hierarchies of authority, and embraced horizontal forms of organization that were meant to encourage democratic participation and collaborative interpersonal relationships. A distinguishing feature of many co-ops during the 1970s was the member labor requirement (Haedicke 2012). Regular co-op shoppers were expected to volunteer their time to complete activities that traditional businesses assigned to paid staff, such as cleaning, stocking shelves, and preparing food for sale. Member labor programs helped resource-poor co-ops find their feet by replacing financial assets with "sweat equity," but they also offered a way for members to experience cooperative relationships. As one store manager recalled, member labor programs reflected store founders' beliefs that "people should be able to successfully work together and be able to organize themselves around work in an organization that benefits all of them . . . When people work together on something, they really feel a connection to it that they wouldn't feel if they were not working."[4] Similarly, many co-ops made decisions democratically—voting at monthly meetings and negotiating to consensus were both popular—and rotated management responsibilities among members. One manager recalled that during her store's early years, all workers had the title "co-coordinator" (rather than "manager"), "since there was this anti-management mentality out there." In this store, "each person would do a little bit of everything."[5] Other stores asked their shoppers to weigh in on decisions that ranged from disciplinary actions against members who refused to work to the mix of products that would appear on store shelves.

Co-ops that were organized along these lines proliferated in the 1970s. One survey at the end of the decade tallied several thousand active co-ops in the United States, although this number included informal buying clubs and temporary arrangements as well as established storefronts (Zwerdling 1979). Indeed, the informal character of co-ops meant that they were easy to create. PFC's manager traced her store's origins to a group of neighborhood organizers who were frustrated by the high prices and limited selection of organic foods at a local supermarket. The organizers visited wholesale markets and local farms to buy products in bulk and met at a neighborhood park bench to distribute their purchases. In the winter, they moved their operation into a garage, and then into a rented storefront.[6] Another respondent explained that his store began as an urban commune in the late 1960s, which brought together "hippies," student activists from the local university, and volunteers from a nearby church.[7] Co-ops tended to cluster in areas with a high concentration of young, progressive residents, who supplied both the labor and the consumer demand that enabled the organizations to get off the ground. The San Francisco Bay area, Ann Arbor and surrounding communities in Michigan, and the Twin Cities of Minneapolis and St. Paul in Minnesota were hubs of co-op organizing, as were university campuses with a reputation for progressive politics (Belasco 1989; Cox 1994; McGrath 2004).

By linking urban consumers with organic growers, co-ops supported the organic sector in the 1970s and 1980s. However, democratic decision making and rotating management responsibilities also led to confusion and internal dissent in many stores, particularly when members disagreed about the products that the store should sell. A longtime member who served on the board of directors of one co-op recalled contentious meetings when factions would argue about the ethics of allowing particular items on the store's shelves. The result, he noted, was "a very inconsistent base, at least for the business world, of products going in and out."[8] Relying on co-op members to work in stores also posed problems. Volunteer workers would show up late—or not at all— to their assigned shifts. Even when they did show up regularly, one manager explained, "it was too time-consuming and there was no long-term picture of anything because everyone was just there for their day-to-day thing."[9] The sense that not all members were contributing equally to the store's success also bred conflict in some co-ops, and those that required members to work in stores often ended up unintentionally excluding potential members whose schedules or preferences made such commitments impossible.

Co-op leaders were not alone in facing these problems. Similar dilemmas appeared in other sorts of anti-hierarchical, collectivist organizations that
emerged during the same period, from free schools to rural communes to
feminist health clinics (Berger 2004; Ferree and Martin 1995; Swidler 1979).
Like members of these other organizations, co-op leaders tended to argue that
the value of collectivist practices could not be measured solely by their contributions to efficiency and organizational stability. Instead, they contended,
these practices, and the values that they expressed, were essential parts of the
social and cultural changes that co-ops were trying to produce in the larger
society. The co-op leaders tried to preserve these distinctive practices in modified form even as they adapted organizational arrangements from the mainstream business world to fit their stores. As I explained earlier, the metaphor
of organizational life as a "negotiated order" captures the quality of these developments (Strauss 1978; Strauss et al. 1963). This metaphor suggests that features of organizations are produced through micro-level negotiations between
members with different ideologies, interests, and responsibilities (Barley 2008;
Bechky 2011). That is, organizational arrangements reflect evolving compromises between different ways of understanding the organization's needs and
purpose. Most members of the co-op world agreed that co-ops should not become identical to mainstream businesses, but different groups of co-op leaders adopted different strategies to preserve organizational distinctiveness while
increasing their stores' odds of survival.

During the 1980s, for example, most co-ops moved away from member
labor requirements and hired a paid staff. This shift did not occur easily, since
co-op leaders were determined not to replicate the alienating market relationships that they perceived in the mainstream business world. The author of one
article that appeared in a national co-op trade magazine during this period
noted a tendency for co-op leaders to "regard member labor as an important
part of their mission" and as a "necessary expression of the purpose and identity of the co-op" (Henderson 1989). Many stores instituted collective ownership programs that required members to purchase a share of the business,
and they spoke about these programs in terms formerly reserved for member
labor. As one of my respondents put it, as a result of her store's collective
ownership program, "people feel that it is not one owner that is profiting
from everyone's labor and sort of a we/they dynamic, but that we're all in it

together."[10] Some stores also encouraged members to volunteer in education and outreach programs, and created employee governance mechanisms that enabled paid workers to participate in managerial decisions. Employees in one of the stores that I visited had veto power over new hires, for example, and in another, they were allowed to elect representatives to the co-op's board of directors. The fact that these adaptations took different forms in different stores reflected local community expectations and market conditions as well as distinctive histories of negotiation (Knupfer 2013).

Although consumer demand for organic products during the 1990s and 2000s increased sales at many co-ops, the arrival of rationalized, profit-oriented retail chains to the organic sector posed additional identity challenges. The retail chain model seems antithetical to cooperative organization—chains are centrally managed, accountable to distant stockholders rather than local communities, and they compete on the basis of efficiency—but the chains increasingly set the tone for organic foods retailing as a whole. Anxiety about the chain model appeared at a national gathering of co-op managers that took place soon after the implementation of the National Organic Program. At the meeting, Michael Funk, the founder and president of United Natural Foods, Inc., a natural and organic foods distribution company that had established control of the national market in part by acquiring many of the regional co-op warehouses, exhorted participants to "give up your individual store preferences and combine to create a national force . . . a chain that spreads its expertise and best practices to ensure a consistently well-run store in every community across the country [and] that is strong enough to expand financially when needed and attract future capital as desired" (Gutknecht and Funk 2003). In response to Funk's speech, a group of co-op managers staged an unanticipated mock "takeover" of the event. They paraded into the conference hall and chanted a satirical rejection of his recommendation that co-ops employ an "Attila the Hun" approach to market competition: "Funky Dumpty stood in the hall, Funky Dumpty, Attila and all. But all of that Wall Street and all of that talk can't stop our co-ops from walking our walk!" (Gutknecht and Funk 2003).

This protest notwithstanding, co-ops borrowed organizational arrangements from the retail chains during the 1990s and 2000s. Starting in the early 1990s, co-ops began to form regional associations to share information and develop standards for employee training, management, and accounting.

Later in the decade, these associations also launched a Common Cooperative Financial Statement program that consolidated the quarterly financial statements of stores across the country to facilitate comparisons and to help to identify "best practices" (Jagiello 1999). These changes culminated in the early 2000s, when the regional associations voted to merge their assets into a new National Cooperative Grocers Association (NCGA), which billed itself as a "virtual chain" of co-ops and which developed joint marketing and purchasing programs for its member stores (Schrader 2000).[11] The formalization of relationships between stores made co-ops more efficient relative to their chain store rivals, but it also produced ambivalence about the extent to which these stores were remaining true to their original mission. As the general manager of one co-op explained, "We have this new organization that can go to Imagine Foods and say, where we used to buy twenty thousand cases of Rice Dream, now we can buy two million cases of Rice Dream because we can make sure that every outlet that we represent will put it on their shelves and sell it . . . [but] we're finding our way in not becoming Bed, Bath, and Beyond."[12]

The desire not to "become Bed, Bath, and Beyond" has been evident in the NCGA's emphasis on democratic decision making and in its efforts to protect the autonomy of member stores. The association has its own president and staff, but it also has a board of directors that includes managers from member co-ops. Its programs that aim to enhance the efficiency of member stores are generally proposed on an opt-in basis. One example occurred in 2007, when the NCGA initiated a "systematic store improvement program" following a vote in which member representatives established "continuous improvement" of retail locations as a major priority. In an article about the program, NCGA regional manager Ben Nauman noted that these representatives "didn't want homogeneous stores but would like a common set of operating standards" and explained that the program, titled "Support our Success (SoS)," was designed around a set of tools that could be used to assess the strengths and challenges of member stores and information-sharing techniques to spread knowledge of "best practices" throughout the co-op sector. Nauman also emphasized that SoS "is being designed so as to avoid being prescriptive, and in most cases the support available to a member co-op will be fully voluntary" (Nauman 2007).[13]

Co-ops today are hybrid organizations that combine organizational arrangements that resemble those in mainstream stores with collectivist and democratic practices. This hybridity is the result of negotiations about the immediate needs and larger purpose of co-op stores, and it has involved both the revision of established co-op practices to meet the needs of competitive market environments and the adaptation of mainstream business structures to the co-op world. These changes enable co-op leaders to act out their stores' dedication to the goals of economic democracy and community empowerment, while also enjoying greater stability and predictability. From the perspective of organizational theory, the history of co-ops suggests that organizations' responses to ambivalent environments are shaped by reflexive consideration of core values and identity, as well as by strategic efforts to appeal to multiple audiences (Dutton and Dukerich 1991; Ravasi and Schultz 2006).

Ambivalent Sensemaking in Co-ops

The hybridization of cooperative organizational structures has a counterpart in the ambivalence with which many co-op leaders interpret and respond to the growth of the organic market and the convergence that is taking place between the organic sector and the mainstream food industry. The concept of sensemaking highlights the way that organizational "reality is an ongoing accomplishment that emerges from efforts to create order . . . [as] people try to make things rationally accountable to themselves and others" (Weick 1993, 635). People engage in sensemaking by bringing established interpretive frameworks to bear on the events that they experience in organizational settings. Much sensemaking is commonplace and routine, but it is nonetheless important to organizational life. Research about sensemaking in hospital settings, for example, shows that medical workers interpret signs of changes in patients' physical conditions by bringing both situated professional experiences and abstract medical knowledge to bear in particular cases (Benner 1994). Sensemaking also functions as a "springboard to action" because the emergent meanings guide the actions people take (Weick, Sutcliffe, and Obstfeld 2005). A medical worker's interpretation of signs of a patient's condition as "ordinary" or "alarming" shapes that worker's selection of responses, which range from uninvolved monitoring to seeking immediate intervention.

In much the same way, people identify, interpret, and respond to events that occur in the environments in which their organizations operate. However, making these events "rationally accountable" is difficult when members of organizations are situated in fields that are changing as rapidly as the contemporary organic foods sector. During times of rapid change, people often feel that they have been "thrown into an ongoing, unknowable, unpredictable streaming of experience in search of answers to the question 'what's the story?'" (Weick, Sutcliffe, and Obstfeld 2005, 410). This disorientation is common for co-op leaders who, when they peer outside of the walls of their stores and the boundaries of local markets, look into an organic sector that is increasingly populated by mainstream food business and large, profit-oriented farms. This mainstreamed organic sector is hardly what the founders of co-ops had in mind when they created businesses that were democratic rather than hierarchical, and collaborative rather than competitive. Yet co-op customers enjoy the products of these new businesses and many co-ops themselves have benefited economically from the increasing demand for organic foods that has accompanied the sector's growth.

Moreover, when co-op leaders attend trade conferences or open the pages of organic industry journals, they encounter a "story" that portrays the mainstreaming of the organic sector as a positive development. As I have explained, mainstream business leaders envision a future in which large companies, delivering organic foods to an ever-increasing pool of consumers, drive the conversion of farmland to organic management. Not only is it naive to imagine that organic agriculture could be the province of small businesses and decentralized farming networks, these new arrivals argue, but the inefficiencies of such systems would hamper the ability of the organic sector to deliver the environmental and social benefits that it is capable of producing. On the other hand, co-op leaders hear the opposite story from environmental and consumer activists, who assert that the increasing participation of conventional companies in the manufacture and sale of organic foods will undermine the "integrity" of organic regulations and the ability of small producers to survive in the organic sector. The latter story resonates with themes from co-ops' countercultural history, but the former one speaks to co-ops' success as businesses in an expanding organic market.

The efforts of co-op leaders to make sense of these competing stories and to determine the meaning of changes in the organic sector are themselves characterized by ambivalence. In their evaluations of the organic sector's convergence with the mainstream food industry, co-op leaders often give credence to both expansionary and transformative accounts. The co-op leaders that I interviewed echoed activists' concerns about the growing influence of mainstream food companies, but they usually hesitated to issue blanket condemnations of these companies. Like their counterparts in larger food businesses, these co-op leaders suggested that environmental and social benefits might result from market growth. They seemed to want to have it both ways, which led them to make confusing and self-contradictory statements. However, they usually shied away from grappling with the tensions that appeared in these accounts that they provided. For example, one co-op general manager commented:

> It's a spooky thing when Wal-Mart starts demanding organic products. I don't really believe that just because it's a large corporation or just because it's big that it's evil and that it has a bad intent. But I certainly think that it is suspect. And to have Wal-Mart basically driving the demand of organic supply is pretty frightening to me because I think that there is some concern about the standards. I mean obviously we have national standards, but with just a little bit more corruption of people, we won't be able to keep up with it in a way that preserves the integrity of the industry. It's really hard to say . . . [because] there is something kind of good about it too, provided the integrity is preserved. I'm not a person who feels that we really need to be threatened.[14]

Clearly, this manager was on the fence about whether or not the sale of organic products by Wal-Mart—and by extension the entry of mainstream food companies into the organic sector—was a good thing. Her experiences as the manager of a small business that has struggled in the face of competition from mainstream retailers informed her response to my question about the advantages and problems of the growth of the organic market. Much of what she said went beyond these immediate concerns, though, to engage with the opposing arguments that I discussed in previous chapters. On the one hand, like consumer and environmental activists, she characterized Wal-Mart as "suspect" (although not necessarily "evil") because of its political and economic power and its orientation toward profits rather than social or environmental responsibility. On the other hand, she suggested that there is "something kind of good" about Wal-Mart's demand for organic products. Presumably, this is because

Wal-Mart's sales would result in more consumption of these products, and more acres of farmland converted to organic management. In perhaps the most telling illustration of her ambivalence, this manager concluded that she does not feel "threatened" by Wal-Mart's foray into the organic sector, despite her description just a few moments earlier of this foray as "spooky" and "pretty frightening"!

This ambivalence appeared in several of the other interviews that I conducted as well, including the three excerpts that follow. According to the membership coordinator at one co-op:

> There is this one school of thought that says that co-ops in the seventies did the hard work of educating people and bringing people around to a natural, healthy lifestyle. And then these big companies came in, and they have shareholders with a lot of money, and they are able to move into markets and basically close down the food co-ops. I'm not sure. Just from my own personal feeling, I don't believe that Whole Foods is evil or anything like that . . . I think that generally what I notice across the board is that the result of Whole Foods and Wild Oats in the industry is now you can go into Wal-Mart and Kroger's and find a little organic section. In that sense I think more people are being reached by the message of, hey, organic and natural is good for you and you should eat it if you can.[15]

Similarly, one co-op founder explained:

> People say to me, aren't you worried about organics in the supermarket? . . . What I have found is that when stores do carry organics, conventional stores, it just puts organics more in the consumer's eye and it has been to my mind more of a benefit. I think that anybody in this industry should be grateful for bringing the organic idea or the organic product into the public consciousness to the extent that Whole Foods has done . . . But I know that part of the reason is the profit motive. My concern is that the industry may become influenced to too large of an extent by people who are only in it because of the profit motive and at the end of the day they don't care whether they are selling organic produce or what they're selling, be it high-chemical produce, but they're doing it for the money. If that was the case I would be concerned that at some point the industry would not have the same standards that it currently does.[16]

Finally, one co-op manager noted:

> I think organics are now widely recognized as different than conventional
> foods. It's much more mainstreamed and it's beginning to show up in con-
> ventional grocery stores, although it's limited to a few products like grapes
> and carrots. It's not considered weird anymore, so I would say that's been
> a very good thing . . . But we're just now beginning to see organic being
> used as a marketing tool. Really I think the people who were in organics
> [before] were idealists and weren't looking to create a brand to sell. I think
> there's a growing tension over who is accessing it and how fair it is.[17]

Each of these co-op professionals acknowledged potential benefits that
could result from the organic sector's expansion—increased public awareness
of the risks of "high-chemical" agriculture, a broadened access of consumers to
organically grown foods, more farmland converted to organic management—
but each questioned whether the extension of mainstream commercial principles into the organic sector would undermine its ethical character and displace
the "idealists" (among whose ranks they included themselves) with businesses
whose moral legitimacy was questionable. They struggled to bring these competing assessments, which were based on very different ideas about how the
organic sector *should* be organized in order to maximize its environmental and
social benefits, into agreement. Often they simply left the tensions unresolved.

Grappling with these competing accounts in an interview is one thing, but
determining store policy in the face of a changing organic sector is something
else entirely. Here, co-op leaders were called on to make decisions with real
consequences. Would they ride the wave of the sector's growth or swim against
the tide by supporting small-scale farms and local food networks? Surprisingly,
ambivalent sensemaking also appeared in the actions that co-op leaders took
in response to changes in the organic sector. As in the excerpts above, many
of these leaders emphasized that they saw value in small-scale organic farms
and decentralized food systems. They tried to promote those systems in their
stores, but they tended not to call the organic sector's growth into question
and often hesitated to criticize particular companies. They also arranged their
stores so that customers who did not want to engage with these issues would be
able to avoid them. Just as they granted credibility to both transformative and
expansionary understandings in their verbal accounts of the mainstreaming

of organic foods, they tried to make their stores into places that straddled the cultural and organizational divisions in the organic sector. This stance appeared in activities related to the selection and presentation of merchandise and in the ways that co-op leaders and staff interacted with customers.

All of the co-op stores that I visited carried a wide selection of organic products on their shelves. In many stores, though, the formal and informal "gatekeeping" activities related to merchandise went beyond an emphasis on organic items. Several of the stores had written policies that prohibited food items that were commonly sold at mainstream supermarkets, on the basis of health or ethical considerations. One store manager explained, "We wouldn't sell anything with additives, with any kind of unsafe additive. I mean FD&C colors and that kind of stuff. Anything with additives, that covers Coca-Cola and a lot of mainstream-type products."[18] The director of another co-op noted that he and other store buyers "definitely have a charter. If [we] bring a new product in it has to be locally-made, organic, or Fair Trade."[19] Other managers mentioned merchandising policies that barred products that contained refined sugar or non-organic items that contained genetically engineered ingredients. Several of my respondents referred to these gatekeeping activities to argue that they were more ethically responsible than chain competitors. As one manager put it,

> This is where the values thing really comes into play in that we have a hard line rule that we won't carry conventional strawberries because of the methyl bromide issue. That is because there are people in our community that work in the strawberry fields. It is a local issue and it is one that we feel strongly about. You can walk into Whole Foods and they are not averse to having a whole big display of conventional strawberries right when you walk in the door. They might have a lot of organic produce, too, but I don't see them as being as committed to it.[20]

Beyond these formal policies, store managers also described preferences and rules of thumb that guided the merchandising decisions that they and their staffs made. These informal guidelines often took account of the size and ownership structure of product manufacturers. For example, the manager of Pacific Food Co-op remarked, "We look at the company to see if they are a conglomerate or local, or at least privately owned and operated at a smaller scale . . . When we hear about a buyout, when we hear about Celestial being sold into Hain, and Hain being sold into General Foods, that shows up in our trade journals. That is usually of interest to us, and we will be looking for alternatives and actively soliciting alternatives at the trade shows."[21] Other store leaders mentioned that they made a point of stocking locally grown fruits and vegetables when they were in season, and that they tried to promote the wares of independent businesses. In practice, economic considerations and customer preferences limited the extent to which co-op managers were able to enact these merchandising commitments. Working with small, independent vendors placed additional burdens on busy store staff, and more than one manager mentioned that they had experienced problems with small companies that were unable to fill orders or, even worse, vanished without warning. One manager complained, "I can't handle all those little companies! I can't handle placing all those separate orders [and] dealing with the UPS box coming in whenever . . . especially if it is a healing salve or something else that we already have ten sources for! I feel bad telling them that . . . [but] I've gotten better at just saying no."[22]

On the other hand, managers and staff explained that they sometimes stocked products that violated store guidelines in order to meet the expectations of customers. This practice resulted in the occasionally jarring appearance of conventional, highly processed food products on co-op shelves. One interviewee explained to me that her store "absolutely will not carry products that have artificial ingredients or artificial colors or preservatives unless we feel that there is enough of a demand for that product that we can inform someone with a sign by that product that will say, we know you want this specific kind of thing for Easter or whatever, but it does contain this one kind of ingredient that's artificial."[23] A second interviewee, who managed a small chain of co-ops, was even more specific: "When we have members who want Karo light corn syrup at the holidays to make pecan pies with, even though that is nasty, evil stuff on a lot of levels, if the members want it, we put it out and make it available for them . . . I don't like using the word 'no' from a marketing standpoint. I don't want people to come into the store and see no, no, no."[24]

These considerations also influenced co-op leaders' responses to controversies within the organic foods sector. For example, three of the co-op leaders that I interviewed mentioned that they had reconsidered their decision to carry products from Horizon Organic dairy after the Cornucopia Institute released its organic dairy report, which I described in Chapter 4. The Cornucopia Institute had identified Horizon as one of the companies that took advantage of vagueness in the organic regulations to raise milk cows in confinement operations that resembled those in the conventional dairy industry. These leaders were furious at the company, which, as one interviewee explained, "was making a joke out of what organic is." Yet they also hesitated to pull Horizon products from their shelves entirely. This interviewee continued, "In terms of our dairy, we'll probably be seeing Horizon go away altogether, unless they have some unique products."[25] The hedge in his statement indicated a reluctance to restrict the options available to his store's customers, especially when it came to products for which identical substitutes were not available from other companies. The one interviewee whose store had discontinued Horizon products explained that this decision had been made only in the wake of public meetings with customers, in which staff had explained their concerns with the company and gauged customers' willingness to accept the change.[26]

Co-op leaders' hesitation to act as "strict gatekeepers" who excluded all but the purest products made by independently owned and ethically sound companies was closely related to the presence of nearby supermarket competitors, which also carried organic products but had fewer merchandise restrictions. One interviewee explained, "I think that people go to Whole Foods or they go to a store that has a pretty decent organic selection, and then they come to the co-op and maybe the delivery was late or maybe someone called in sick and we don't have a huge pool of substitute employees to pull from . . . and [they] think well, gosh, Kroger can manage to get their products on the shelves on time, why can't you guys? . . . When you're running a small business like we are, you don't necessarily have a whole lot of flexibility with things like that."[27] In this context, co-op leaders were reluctant to do anything that might evoke additional criticism from their customers. But these attitudes also reflected a broader shift toward an ethic of consumer sovereignty in co-op stores. This form of thinking suggests that as free-market agents, consumers have the right to make purchasing decisions according to their own assessments of their needs and values without facing interference from others (Slater 1997). The efforts of co-op leaders to distinguish between their own beliefs about the tainted nature of particular food products and the hands-off character of their role as professional retailers illustrate the extent to which they had internalized this ideology. They believed that making customers feel bad or guilty about their food choices was an irresponsible and unethical thing to do. They did not want to behave, as one of my interviewees put it, like "food Nazis."[28] In contrast, a store manager summarized a widespread view of what these co-op leaders *did* want to provide to their customers: "I'd like them to be greeted by a friendly, helpful staff in an impeccable store, finding the products that they want, which have the purest and best ingredients, at really great prices."[29]

In addition to product gatekeeping, co-op leaders developed strategies to satisfy consumers while also promoting regionally based, decentralized food systems. The manager of one store explained to me that he had leased a re-frigerated truck and a warehouse and had hired drivers to pick up foods from suppliers within a three-hundred-mile radius. The store had also launched an in-store marketing campaign to promote these items to customers. The campaign's ads emphasized that buying these products would help keep local farmers in business, but also pointed out that the products were available only at the co-op, and not at local competitors' stores. Another co-op participated in a private certification and distribution system that used the term "sustainable" as an alternative to "organic." While these "sustainable" farmers found that large grocery stores were reluctant to purchase their products without an organic certification, the co-op continued to put them on its shelves. The co-op's manager explained that customers trusted the store to check up on the quality of the products and the credibility of the "sustainable" certification, and that many customers also knew the farmers personally and placed more trust in them as individuals than in an impersonal organic label. She also worked to cultivate these relationships by inviting farmers into the store on a monthly basis to give presentations about their growing practices and to provide samples of their products. This placed the co-op in a stronger market position, since it was one of the few places where customers could buy products from these farms, and it also provided personal rewards to the manager and other members of the co-op staff, who cared deeply about constructing alternatives to centralized and industrial food systems.

The efforts of these two stores spoke to the interest among co-op leaders in moving "beyond organic," both as an ethical imperative and as a marketing strategy. In the first place, co-op leaders were aware of and concerned by the fact that federal organic regulations did not enable customers to distinguish between producers who were committed to organic agriculture as a way of life and those who viewed it as a marketing opportunity. As one manager explained, "You can have an organic feedlot farm, where you've got horrible animal waste run-off and soil erosion and all these things that are happening, but you can still get that organic label. So if I am a local hog farmer and I am working with like three hundred pigs, I am taking care to make sure that the water stays clean and the soil stays where it is and the waste is disposed of properly and the animals are fed what they actually like to eat that is natural, I want to be able to distinguish myself by saying I'm organic but also I'm sustainable or I'm whatever this word is going to be."[30] But also, co-op leaders viewed what one interviewee called "pushing the envelope" as an important competitive strategy. She elaborated by engaging in a mock conversation with a manager from a mainstream grocery store: "We're always going to stay ahead of the eight-ball . . . OK, you're over there? Great. Well, we're over here. Sorry, you're still playing catch-up. OK, you're over there? You're up to where we were ten years ago? Great. We're so glad you're there. But we're over here now."[31]

INTERACTING WITH CUSTOMERS

The selection of merchandise was only part of the work of co-op managers and staff members. They also had to present these products for sale and interact with the customers who came to buy them. My interviewees had no shortage of stories about the confrontational interactions between staff members and customers in their stores that had once taken place around questionable products, but they used these stories to highlight their current efforts to avoid confrontations with consumers. One manager explained that the "danger used to be that back in the old days, we attracted a lot of people who wanted to work here who were I would say more food purists . . . [and would] tend to be judgmental about other people's food choices . . . [Today] we look for people who just have a lot of respect for other people's food choices."[32] A second manager agreed. "We have our political issues, you know. So we are a little biased, but we are pretty careful. I think most people know where we stand personally, but we really try . . . to keep it out of the workplace."[33]

As was the case with product gatekeeping, my interviewees' wariness about confronting customers about the morality of their food choices in part stemmed from the competitive forces at play in local retail markets. As one interviewee put it, "You've got to be careful here. It's an extremely competitive market. There's Wild Oats and Whole Foods and Trader Joe's and Vitamin Cottage and Sunflower Markets and more coming, I'm sure, and we don't want to be dictating and we don't want to be preaching . . . That doesn't help us as we try to grow and broaden our appeal to more people."[34] This manager's reluctance also reflects the assumptions about consumers' right to make shopping decisions according to their own needs and values. He continued by explaining, "We're not here to dictate what [customers] can have and what they can't have. We're here to give them what they want and hopefully to educate them over time to where they will want better stuff."[35]

The reference to education in this manager's statement flagged a set of practices that occurred in the stores that I visited. Rather than challenging customers at the register, my interviewees invested resources in educational activities that were intended to increase customers' awareness of the social and environmental consequences of their food choices. Although co-op leaders did not use this phrase, scholars of food politics would recognize their educational activities as an effort to cultivate consumer reflexivity. This term refers to consumers' consciousness about the ways that their shopping decisions may support or challenge problematic features of food systems, as well as their ability to think critically about the claims made by food marketers and other powerful institutional actors (DuPuis 2000; Goodman, DuPuis, and Goodman 2011; Guthman 2003). From the perspective of co-op leaders, efforts to cultivate consumer reflexivity through education are attractive precisely because these efforts allow them to distribute knowledge about alternative food systems in a relatively neutral, non-confrontational way, while also respecting their customers' freedom to make the choices that suit their individual needs and values.

Educational activities often took place around products about which co-op leaders had concerns, but which they continued to sell because of consumer demand. In one store, for example, Odwalla organic juice products remained on the shelves after the company was purchased by Coca-Cola, but the staff also "put up some signs that say, 'Odwalla is a fine product of the Coca-Cola Company,' just to make people aware of that."[36] Another store, which sold organic yogurt from Stonyfield Farm (owned by Groupe Danone) and Springfield Creamery (an independent company), also put up signs that identified the corporate parentage of the former brand. In the fresh produce sections of nearly all of the co-ops that I visited, I encountered signs that distinguished locally grown organic fruits and vegetables from those that came from a greater distance. Several stores went further, such as the two that I described above, in inviting local farmers to visit and speak with customers about their operations.

Information in stores was complemented by articles about changes in the organic sector that appeared in co-op newsletters. Several stores also hosted talks, film screenings, and conferences about food and environmental issues, and organized educational activities directed toward children. PFC had created an especially impressive example of the latter sort of event by sponsoring an annual field trip for local middle school students to a nearby organic farm. By the time of my interview with the store's manager, the program had been running for several years and more than six thousand children had visited the farm. The manager explained that while the event organizers did not explicitly tell the students that they or their parents should buy locally grown organic foods rather than processed products from large corporations, she believed that it created "breakthroughs in awareness" that guided them in this direction.

> The kids are like, "You know, I saw the farm, I went to the farm, and there were like carrots growing right next to onions and I didn't even know that you could use the same dirt." And kids say, "When I arrived, and they told me I was weeding, I thought, eeewww, I'm going to get dirty. But then when I realized that this is how food grows . . . I thought it always came from the supermarket in cellophane." Just those kind of breakthroughs in awareness I think are essential . . . We are getting further away from our connection to what sustains us. We've lost that link. And meantime, while that's been happening, the mega-corporations are working as hard as they can to patent the food so they can own it. So it is two converging trends that we are taking a small bit of pride in trying to interrupt.[37]

In some cases, educational activities in co-ops shaded into more explicitly political activities. For example, one respondent pointed out to me that her store not only distributed literature about the environmental risks of agricultural biotechnology, but also encouraged members to send letters to regulators at the Department of Agriculture during public comment periods for biotechnology regulation. A second respondent reported that her store had joined a statewide legislative action group called the Genetic Engineering Policy Alliance, which lobbied for stricter controls on the planting of engineered seeds. Co-op leaders also described their efforts to get members involved in campaigns that focused on the federal organic regulations (Allen and Kovach 2000). Recalling the public comment period for the first proposed regulations, one co-op manager explained, "We were definitely involved in getting our shoppers to write letters and sign petitions and say, wait a minute, sewage sludge does not equal organic fertilizer . . . If there are ways that we can get our membership interested in something that is going to affect everyone, when it comes to something as broad as the organic standards, then that is a way that we do get people involved in the food politics scene."[38]

However, co-op leaders carefully considered the scope of these activities and the sorts of issues that they engaged. Their tendency to defer to shoppers' sensibilities for commercial reasons—as one respondent put it, "We have a ton of Republicans and born-again Christians who come into the co-op, so it's important to be sensitive . . . [because] we don't want to alienate people"—often led them to back away from potentially controversial issues or from critiques of political leaders. One co-op manager articulated a sentiment shared by several of my respondents when she asserted, "We want Republicans who voted for [George W.] Bush to think that they can come in here and buy organic food just like anyone else, although in my heart I don't believe that they can be voting for Bush and believe in organics! [So] we stayed really clear from, say, putting 'Impeach Bush' . . . signs out on our lawn."[39] Others were quick to emphasize the *apolitical* nature of their stores. As one manager put it, "We want to be a place for expression, for our members and our communities to be tolerant and accept all viewpoints. And perhaps we're an area where folks can come and as part of their shopping and as part of their lives enter into dialogues with one another as part of the space. But in terms of the co-op taking a position, no, we don't do that. That's not our role here."[40]

At an individual level, co-op leaders often struggled with these limits on political activism. PFC's store manager noted, "I happen to be rabidly political, personally. I really work to separate my own sentiments . . . [and] I try not to use the [co-op's] resources to work my particular bias."[41] Their sense that the co-op's taking a position was neither appropriate nor in the best interests of the store often led them not to engage customers in systemic critiques, even though they might have been personally convinced of the importance of large-scale social and political change. For example, this manager noted that while she was deeply concerned about growing economic inequality in the United States, her store limited its anti-poverty activism to donating expired products to a local food bank. Similarly, it turned down a member's request to boycott a local newspaper whose owner supported restricting minors' access to abortions. This member had argued that just as the co-op avoided selling foods that harmed the health of farmworkers, consumers, and the environment, so should it also refuse to distribute a newspaper that had come out in favor of laws that would jeopardize the health of young women. While the manager and most of the co-op's board of directors were persuaded by this argument, they concluded that a boycott would antagonize the store's customers and amount to an imposition of their political beliefs. As one board member remarked, "We assume that people who eat organic foods have left politics, but all sorts of people shop at the co-op. We have a tendency to forget this."[42]

Conclusion

In this chapter, I have argued that co-op stores straddle the transformative and expansionary logics that exist in the organic sector. As organizations, co-ops offer examples of how compromises between these logics may be achieved through hybrid arrangements and practices. Co-op leaders have incorporated elements of mainstream business organization into their stores and abandoned some of their earlier collectivist practices, but they have also developed measures that protect store autonomy and that enable employees and customers to interact with stores as community institutions over which they have a degree of ownership and control. Co-ops have also contributed to (and benefited from) the growth of the organic market, even as they expose customers to some of the concerns about the increasing presence of mainstream food companies in the sector and provide support for alternative food networks.

These practices reflect the leaders' ambivalence about the organic sector's trajectory of market growth, and their negotiations about organizational identity and values play as much of a role in shaping hybrid arrangements as do efforts to satisfy external expectations. These negotiations and ambivalence lend dynamism to organizational compromise in co-ops: individual stores have crafted compromises in different ways and the character of these compromises continues to evolve in response to internal discussions and developments in larger markets.

The relationships that co-op leaders try to develop with their customers correspond in interesting ways with other understandings of consumers' roles and behaviors in the contemporary organic sector. Co-op leaders treat customers as sovereign, deferring to their prerogative to make shopping decisions without interference, but they also try to increase customers' knowledge of the implications of their choices in gentle, non-confrontational ways. This approach seems to fall into a middle ground between the new arrivals' assumptions that consumer behavior is usually individualistic and self-centered in its motivations and advocates' efforts to mobilize consumers to participate in boycott campaigns through the use of dramatic, conflict-oriented frames. As I argued previously, though, both the new arrivals and the advocates tend to focus on the aggregate effect of individual consumer choices and do less to advance consumers' capacity to participate in deliberations about the sector's governance. In contrast, co-ops' efforts to cultivate consumer reflexivity through educational activities have the potential to spur open-ended discussions about the values and priorities that should guide organic (and other) systems of food production (Haedicke 2014). Co-ops' relatively small size may also facilitate this sort of practical food democracy (Hassanein 2003). Small-scale organizations and locally oriented food systems have had an important place in transformative understandings of organic farming precisely because they are understood to allow farmers and consumers to form personal relationships and to become more knowledgeable about how people and environments are affected by the way that food is produced.

Reflexivity alone cannot change food systems, though (Johnston and Szabo 2011). Consumer knowledge needs to be coupled with opportunities for shared discussion and political influence. These opportunities exist in co-ops, as the ubiquity of food-related petitions attests. However, they are limited by the pressures of market competition, which along with assumptions about consumer sovereignty, make it difficult for co-op leaders to challenge customers to consider ways that food politics may be linked to or serve as a metaphor for other issues, such as those related to economic or gender inequality. An important feature of the countercultural movements from which co-ops emerged was the treatment of organic foods production and consumption as an "edible dynamic"—that is, as a means through which people could interact cooperatively, address important collective problems, and envision a new society (Belasco 1989, 22). However much early organic activism fell short of this ideal in practice, it is also true that the sector's shift in the direction of market expansion has limited the collective, exploratory aspects of organic foods systems. This is even the case in organizations that, like these co-ops, try to sustain their transformative roots.

CHAPTER 6

Institutional Logics and Social Processes Revisited

Insights from the Organic Sector

NEAR THE END OF MY RESEARCH for this book, I learned of a report titled *From the Margins to the Mainstream*, which had drawn the attention of many members of the organic sector. Produced by the National Organic Action Plan (or NOAP) Project, an initiative of a group of veteran organic sector participants, the report distilled the ideas and concerns that had emerged from a series of guided conversations with organic farmers, consumers, and other stakeholders. A key theme in these meetings was that "tensions exist between organic as a broad social movement and organic as a fast-growing industrial sector . . . Such tensions pivot around one central challenge: How can we facilitate the growth of organic food and agriculture while preserving organic integrity, maintaining diverse farms and agricultural systems, retaining farmer and consumer confidence, and furthering broader social and environmental values?" (Hoodes et al. 2010, 21). Phrased differently, the question might read: How can the organic sector pursue market growth without sacrificing the transformative ideas and organizational patterns that distinguish it from the mainstream food industry?

The tensions that the NOAP report identified are not new, and the question is one that organic advocates have confronted throughout the sector's history. This book has examined these tensions through the lens of social scientific work about institutional logics (Thornton, Ocasio, and Lounsbury 2012). The institutional logics perspective helps us see that different understandings of organic foods production exist at the level of shared symbols, as well as at the level of individual beliefs. It also highlights connections that exist between transformative and expansionary understandings in the organic sector and cultural ideas in other social arenas—from the 1960s counterculture to modern business education—that have impinged on the sector from outside its boundaries. Finally, the institutional logics perspective draws attention to reciprocity between symbolic understandings and the practical features of organizations and institutions. The book has also pushed the institutional logics approach further by examining how members of the sector engage with and elaborate these transformative and expansionary logics in daily life and how they mobilize these understandings in interactive processes of conflict and compromise. This chapter reviews the book's central arguments and explains how its analysis of the organic sector elucidates structure and action in other fields shaped by contradictory logics. It also discusses the study's implications for understanding the organic sector itself.

Transformative and Expansionary Logics in the Organic Sector

Transformative understandings and practices construe organic agriculture as a decentralized approach to food production rooted in small-scale farms and interpersonal relationships. Expansionary ones push the sector toward rapid market growth in order to maximize the social and environmental benefits of organic farming. In the sector's early years, advocates like J. I. Rodale blended elements of these understandings to create a vision for organic farming that emphasized market opportunities as well as food system changes. Critiques of mainstream agriculture and food processing shaped the agrarian tendencies in Rodale's writing, while his experiences as a successful entrepreneur and his desire to participate in the postwar economic boom influenced his descriptions of organic farming as a lucrative business opportunity. Later, countercultural critiques of hierarchy and technocracy added a radical flavor to some articles in *Organic Gardening and Farming*, while other writers looked to the business world for ideas about how to support and streamline the organic trade. While transformative and expansionary ideas shared space in *OGF*'s pages, the decentralized character of the sector as a whole allowed farmers and businesspeople in different regions of the country to practice organic farming in different ways. Different groups invested different amounts of energy in building markets or cultivating alternative ways of living, and conflicts between different visions of organic production took place mainly at a local level.

Today, expansionary ideas and practices occupy a central place in the organic sector, and transformative ones have retreated to the margins. How did this change occur? First, the passage of the Organic Foods Production Act and the implementation of the National Organic Program established market growth as the core principle of a national system of organic standards and certification. During the 1980s, private-sector certification programs had also tried to support the expanding organic trade, but their voluntary nature preserved some of the sector's decentralization and regional diversity. Mandatory federal regulations, which resulted both from these efforts to solve problems associated with expanding trade and from quickly organized responses to the Alar food contamination scare in 1989, eliminated this flexibility. Members of the sector worked to bring arrangements that reflected the sector's history of decentralized organization and grassroots participation into the law and the rulemaking process, but they found that legislative mandates and bureaucratic routines constrained their ability to affect the character of the final regulations. OFPA and the NOP show that while government regulation can be an effective way of achieving "field settlements," governments construct regulations at least partially according to their own logics of organization and the resulting settlements can increase tensions in multi-institutional fields (Fligstein and McAdam 2012, 88).

Second, the finalization and implementation of the NOP ushered in a period of convergence between the organic sector and the mainstream food industry. Organizationally, convergence has appeared in the erosion of the partitions that formerly separated organic and conventional food businesses (Carroll, Dobrev, and Swaminathan 2002; Sikavica and Pozner 2013). Conventional farms, manufacturers, and retailers have all entered the organic sector, and organic specialists find themselves pushed by competition and pulled by investors' expectations to operate in ways that resemble those of their mainstream counterparts. Culturally, convergence has resulted in the elaboration of expansionary understandings of organic production as new arrivals to the sector transpose cultural schemas and moral ideas from the mainstream business world to their work with organic foods (DiMaggio 1997; Sewell 1992). The place of many of the new arrivals on the National Organic Standards Board has helped to give political weight to these cultural understandings. In particular, these NOSB members have often supported the technical character of the organic standards, which makes it difficult to introduce broader questions about the organization of the sector itself (Guthman 2004a).

The contemporary experiences of organic farming advocacy groups and countercultural co-ops show the effects of expansionary ideas and practices. One of the consequences of the expansionary logic's dominance is a reduction of opportunities for advocates of alternative forms of organization to exert political and institutional influence (McAdam, McCarthy, and Zald 1996). Along these lines, advocacy groups often find their efforts to reassert transformative understandings in the federal regulations diverted by the need to focus on materials and blocked by NOSB members' and regulators' attention to the priority of market growth. Advocates have had somewhat more success with boycott and shaming campaigns against particular businesses, but these campaigns also reproduce expansionary understandings from the "inside out" (Swidler 2001) by providing few opportunities for consumer participants to deliberate about the organic sector's course of development. Similarly, co-ops have found themselves pushed by competition with larger retailers to incorporate mainstream organizational arrangements and practices, and co-op leaders bring assumptions about the benefits of market growth into their assessments of changes in the organic sector. These experiences show the power of the expansionary logic to shape the perceptions and activities of even those sector members who work in organizations modeled along transformative lines.

The changing relationship between expansionary and transformative logics creates a context for action in the organic sector. However, the organic sector is a place where "real people, in real contexts, with consequential past experiences of their own, play with [logics], question them, combine them with institutional logics from other domains, take what they can from them, and make them fit their needs" (Binder 2007, 568). How does this happen? First, members of the sector use expansionary and transformative understandings to make sense of their work with organic foods (Weick 1995). Guided by "consequential past experiences" in the worlds of business and activism, the new arrivals and contemporary critics of growth mobilize principles embedded in these understandings to interpret their activities in the organic sector and also elaborate these understandings by bringing in organizational principles from other settings. Leaders of co-ops, on the other hand, blend these understandings in a process of ambivalent sensemaking. Organizationally, co-ops and their leaders have one foot in the world of business and the other in the world of activism. The contradictory meanings that exist in these two social settings are evident in the ambivalent evaluations that they offer of the organic sector's recent growth.

Sensemaking feeds into the cultural frames that sector members develop to influence the behavior of other people. Research about framing has tended to focus on efforts to justify and sustain social conflict and oppositional activity (Benford and Snow 2000), but in this book, I have considered both conflict-oriented and compromise-oriented frames that appear in the organic sector. Conflict-oriented frames appear in the efforts of activist groups to define federal regulation and the convergence of the organic sector with the mainstream food industry as a takeover of organic farming by bureaucratic and corporate interests. The new arrivals' descriptions of activist groups as naive or destructive to the sector's mission of converting farmland to organic management are also examples of conflict-oriented framing. Compromise-oriented frames appeared in the work of early NOSB members, who defended the legitimacy of federal organic regulations by describing them as an effort to establish organic principles within the USDA, as well as in the writings of J. I. Rodale and other *OGF* authors, who argued that increases in consumer demand for organic foods would support small-scale organic farmers and create opportunities to develop alternative food distribution networks. Whether it is oriented toward conflict or compromise, framing involves interpretive work on the part of sector members who draw attention to particular elements of expansionary and transformative understandings and move others into the background.

Finally, sector members bring these understandings to bear in the collective work of creating organizations and regulatory institutions (Clemens 1996; Lawrence and Suddaby 2006). Like frames, organizational and institutional work may be oriented toward either conflict or compromise. The activist groups that regularly challenge the organic sector's convergence with the mainstream food industry and assert the value of small-scale, decentralized modes of food production provide examples of organized conflict, not least by orchestrating boycott campaigns against businesses that they perceive to be undermining organic integrity. On the other hand, the sector offers examples of attempts to build compromises between different understandings into the design of organizations and institutions. Sector members worked at both the legislative and the institutional levels to bring compromises into the federal rules through the creation and invigoration of the NOSB, although both OFPA and the NOP prioritized the expansion of the organic trade. Compromise also appears in hybrid organizations, like co-ops, which combine practices that stem from a countercultural history with organizational arrangements borrowed from the world of mainstream retailing. Focusing on the work of institutional design and organizational maintenance in these cases provides another way to see how expansionary and transformative understandings of organic production touch down in the collective life of sector members.

Embeddedness and Agency in Multi-institutional Fields

The institutional logics approach developed from an effort to understand how the divergent rationalities that exist in different spheres of modern societies shape the character of organizations within those spheres, as well as the understandings and practices of the people who participate in them (Friedland 2013; Friedland and Alford 1991). Contemporary studies of institutional logics continue to grapple with questions of the meaning and influence of diverse rationalities, although much of this work has shifted to focus on rationalities within, rather than across, organized fields of activity (Thornton and Ocasio 2008). Scholars have found no shortage of these divided organizational fields and settings. During their graduate training, aspiring doctors encounter models of medical professionalism based on the contrasting logics of care and science (Dunn and Jones 2010). Chefs in the high-stakes world of elite French restaurants find competing standards of judgment in the transgressive principles of the nouvelle cuisine movement and the tradition-inflected ones of classical cuisine (Rao, Monin, and Durand 2003). Public school teachers experience the pressure of new expectations of standardized accountability even as teacher education programs continue to encourage the cultivation of flexible and personalized techniques (Everitt 2013; Hallett 2010). Book publishers and booksellers struggle to hold on to an identity based on professionalism and literary knowledge even as their industry becomes more competitive and market-driven (Miller 2006; Thornton 2004). In each of these settings, institutional logics shape people's experiences from the "outside in" as well as from the "inside out" (Swidler 2001). In the former sense, logics influence the evaluative standards, organizational demands, and formal rules that constrain people's behavior and shape their position within the field (Clemens and Cook 1999). In the latter sense, they provide symbols and narratives that people use to account for the meaning and worth of their efforts. The fact that collective life revolves around the search for meaning and value as much as it does around jockeying for instrumental gain helps to explain the vigor with which people defend the legitimacy of institutional logics (Fligstein and McAdam 2012, 35–45).

Studies of multi-institutional fields offer purchase on perennial questions of creative agency and institutional change that, incidentally, also lie at the heart of my examination of the organic sector. In the more than two decades that have followed the rise of new institutionalism and the institutional logics approach, institutional theory has oscillated between a framework that emphasizes the constitutive power of logics to shape social action and organizational behavior in unnoticed and irresistible ways and a framework that posits that strategic and powerful individuals act as "institutional entrepreneurs" by crafting new logics and disseminating them through organizational fields (DiMaggio 1988; Hardy and Maguire 2008; Powell and DiMaggio 1991). Critiques have been leveled at both approaches: the first treats institutions, not people, as actors and obscures processes of institutional change, while the second offers few clues about how certain actors free themselves from institutional influences in order to become "entrepreneurs" (Powell and Colyvas 2008).

Recent scholarship has tried to synthesize these frameworks by arguing that institutional environments provide the symbolic and practical elements from which people construct identities, understandings, and strategies, while also asserting that people are creative actors who reinterpret and modify institutional logics through collaborative or conflictual interactions (Battliana and D'Aunno 2009; Garud, Hardy, and Maguire 2007; Hallett and Ventresca 2006). In general terms, this book affirms the notion that agency is simultaneously embedded in institutional logics and also functions to develop and modify these logics. The book also advances several specific ways to think about embeddedness of creative agency and, by extension, about the relationship between institutional logics and patterns of social action.

EMBEDDEDNESS HAS MORAL AND EMOTIONAL,
AS WELL AS COGNITIVE, DIMENSIONS

Organizational scholarship has historically placed greater emphasis on cognitive processes and rational action than on emotion or affective behavior (Domagalski 1999; Fineman 1999). The institutional logics approach, although it asserts the existence of multiple rationalities, tends to retain this cognitive focus (Powell and DiMaggio 1991, 11–15; Thornton, Ocasio, and Lounsbury 2012, ch. 4). In practice, it is extremely difficult to separate the cognitive and emotional components of action, since "feeling and thinking are parallel, interacting processes of evaluating and interacting with our worlds" (Jasper 2011, 286). A first lesson of this study is that it is important to expand the idea of the embeddedness of agency in institutional logics in order to show how those logics shape both cognition and emotion. Cognitive embeddedness certainly exists in the organic sector: the new arrivals draw on schemas from the business world to understand the sector's character and purpose, while contemporary activists use critical ideas developed in social movement settings to evaluate organic regulations. But the sector is also a place where moral outrage, as well as divergent cognitive understandings, fuels ongoing social conflict. When the new arrivals consider activists' efforts to restrict the businesses that are growing the organic market, they feel frustrated and angry; these feelings are reciprocated by activists when they observe that, as one person put it, the new arrivals are "dragging us down this road toward one system that looks pretty industrial."[1]

Scholars can understand responses like these by acknowledging that logics have moral dimensions that shape feelings and attributions of value, in addition to cognitive ones that shape attention and conceptual understanding. In the organic sector, transformative and expansionary understandings offer competing templates for understanding the sector's goals and for thinking about the sorts of organizations and practices that best suit those goals. They also offer rival ways of imagining the ethical value of organic farming, to which people become emotionally attached. The notions of shared moral understandings, emotional attachments, and resultant conflicts hark back to older versions of institutional theory that considered how people form affective connections with particular organizational arrangements and goals, and having done so, work to preserve these arrangements and goals against countervailing pressures (Selznick 1957, [1949] 1966). One of the advantages of this variety of institutional research was its attention to the complicated ways in which people experience and respond to practical problems in particular organizational settings, which avoided the tendency toward "infinite regression towards higher levels of abstraction" that characterized some of the more recent scholarship (Hirsch and Lounsbury 1997, 410). One of its disadvantages (which I will return to below) was its focus on culture within individual organizations, rather than on meanings that are shared and contested across social sectors and organizational fields. By paying attention to moral elements of logics and emotional (as well as cognitive) embeddedness, institutional logics scholars may be able to move past this myopia while generating richer understandings of action and problem solving in multi-institutional fields.

For example, thinking of multi-institutional fields as places where people encounter competing moral understandings, as well as divergent cognitive frameworks, highlights the complexities that these people face when combining rival logics in sensemaking and in organizational design. These complexities were clear in the case of co-op leaders. In interviews, leaders of co-ops offered ambivalent assessments of the organic market's growth and of their own place within it. They moved back and forth between evaluations based on expansionary understandings of the virtues of market growth and transformative understandings of the importance of localized, small-scale food systems, often failing to resolve the tensions between these competing principles. At the organizational level, co-op leaders tried to combine support for small-scale farms and independent organic foods businesses with deference to consumers' desires. Between stores, they developed arrangements that increased business efficiency while retaining a degree of local autonomy and democratic control. Ambivalent assessments and organizational hybridity reflect the economic struggles that co-op leaders face in increasingly competitive retailing markets, but they also reveal efforts to operate stores in virtuous ways in the context of competing moral accounts of organic foods production. Similarly, researchers studying the embeddedness of action in other multi-institutional fields should consider how moral dilemmas, as well as strategic considerations, shape organizational forms and individual accounts.

Additionally, paying attention to the way that logics shape emotional responses, as well as cognitive ones, clarifies the challenges that were involved in efforts to maintain the legitimacy of federal rulemaking during the 1990s.

Members of the sector who supported the federal regulations found themselves facing organic farmers, businesspeople, and consumers for whom the possibility of centralized government oversight evoked anxiety, if not outright hostility. In this context, compromise involved more than a search for ways to bring competing principles into the rules themselves. It also involved the manipulation of symbols and rituals to assuage doubt. The decision to hold open NOSB meetings at locations throughout the country displayed an openness and accountability of NOSB members to the organic sector's grassroots, which calmed some of the anger that erupted after the initial board appointments. Conversely, debates about the status of private certifiers and, later, about the "Big Three" in the USDA's initial draft of the organic rules were fueled by feelings of frustration and betrayal. The emotional symbolism of the issues at stake arguably exceeded their technical importance in the rules themselves, and the conflict-oriented frames that helped to rally the opposition played on this emotional symbolism to cast the agency as duplicitous and guilty of other moral transgressions.

MULTI-INSTITUTIONAL FIELDS ENCOURAGE REFLEXIVITY AND CREATIVE ACTION

Much action is routine and unthinking, but human agency also has projective and practical-evaluative dimensions: the former term "encompasses the imaginative generation by actors of possible future trajectories of action," while the latter refers to the work of making "practical and normative judgments among alternative possible trajectories" (Emirbayer and Mische 1998, 971). A good part of the action that I have discussed in this book leans in the direction of projectivity and practical evaluation. Members of the organic sector often engage imaginatively with different possible trajectories for themselves, their organizations, and the sector as a whole that are offered by the transformative and expansionary understandings as they carry out the activities of sensemaking, framing, and organization. Multi-institutional fields like the organic sector encourage this sort of imaginative and practical creativity: when people regularly encounter ideas, practices, and arrangements that differ from the ones that they are familiar with, they often begin to think more consciously and critically about those that they take for granted (if only to determine how to assert them more successfully), which can lead to innovations in ideas and actions (Hargrave and Ven de Ven 2009; Lounsbury and Crumley 2007). Scholars who are interested in how changes occur in multi-institutional fields should pay attention to this dynamic.

One promising approach to understanding this sort of reflexive creativity has developed within the research stream known as "inhabited institutions," which deploys ethnographic techniques to examine how people in organizational settings craft local variations of institutionalized meanings and practices (Haedicke and Hallett 2015; Nunn 2014). By rereading Gouldner's classic ethnography *Patterns of Industrial Bureaucracy* as an exemplar of inhabited institutions research, for example, Hallett and Ventresca show how the collision of local work routines and externally imposed production mandates resulted in distinctive varieties of bureaucratic management in a mid-twentieth-century gypsum mine. Supervisors and workers negotiated arrangements by which rules were sometimes respected and sometimes ignored, depending on the risks and demands of different work sites in the mine. By adopting a "skeptical, inquiring attitude towards the assumed operation" of institutions and their impact on organizational life, the inhabited institutions approach provides access to the imaginative and practical creativity that unfolds through situated interactions (Hallett and Ventresca 2006, 228). But (like older institutional scholarship) this approach is shortsighted when it comes to understanding how local innovations break free from the boundaries of organizations and become established in organizational fields. My description of the efforts of organic sector members to build compromise arrangements into sector-level governance institutions like the NOP offers one example of how to approach the study of innovation at the field level. In this case, individuals worked to establish and bring to life democratic arrangements in a context that was profoundly bureaucratic and market-oriented, and the unconventional strategies that they pursued to do this have had enduring consequences for the organic sector. As this work continues, scholars should consider how innovations that emerge at local organizational levels may affect larger fields—a point that I will return to in the final section of this chapter.

MECHANISMS CONNECT LOGICS WITH SOCIAL PROCESSES

As a number of organizations researchers have noted, the presence of contradictory institutional logics may contribute to social conflict in markets and other organizational fields (Marquis and Lounsbury 2007; Oakes, Townley, and Cooper 1998; Reay and Hinings 2005). However, it is not always clear how conflict results from rival logics, or under what conditions logics may coexist without the emergence of conflict.[2] In this book, I have tried to resolve this ambiguity by identifying two agentic mechanisms—framing and organization—that connect the organic sector's contradictory logics to social processes of conflict and compromise within organizations and within the sector as a whole. Mechanisms are the recurring and recognizable "nuts and bolts" of social organization that causally link events or states of being, and sociological explanation frequently involves the identification of mechanisms that contribute to observed relationships between events or patterns of interest (Elster 1989; Hedström and Swedberg 1998). In the organic sector, some frames have promoted conflict by emphasizing threats posed by one logic to another, while others have promoted compromise by emphasizing complementarity between logics. Similarly, some organizations have been designed to assert one logic at the expense of the other, while others have tried to accommodate both logics through hybrid arrangements. These mechanisms are agentic because they focus attention on the activities and strategies (i.e., the agency) of people doing the framing and designing the organizations, as well as on the ways in which frames and organizations influence the behavior of others (Campbell 2002). While mechanisms that affect processes of conflict and compromise may also operate at the level of social environments and relationships, agentic mechanisms highlight ways that people work to create, sustain, or dismantle institutional logics (Lawrence and Suddaby 2006).[3]

Scholars who study social movements have cultivated a number of concepts—including those of framing and the mobilization of resources through organizational work—that are oriented toward understanding mechanisms involved in contentious interactions and social change (McAdam, Tarrow, and Tilly 2001). Economic sociologists and organizational scholars are increasingly turning to this literature to understand the emergence and dynamics of markets and other fields, particularly those that contain multiple institutional logics (Weber and King 2014; Rao, Morrill, and Zald 2000). For example, McInerney's (2014) study of the nonprofit technology assistance industry identifies three mechanisms—the creation of accounts of worth (similar to frames), organizing, and the negotiation of conventions of coordination—that help to explain the interactions of activists and market builders in this emerging field of activity. Similarly, Bartley (2007) explains how firms' search for competitive advantage combined with activists' internal disagreements about the effectiveness of confrontational tactics and with a neoliberal political context to generate private environmental and social product certification programs. Although it lies beyond the scope of this study, it is also worth noting that some social movement researchers have argued that the institutional logics approach can expand studies of activism by providing a framework for understanding why protestors' grievances, goals, and strategies differ across different institutional settings (Armstrong and Bernstein 2008). My study of the organic sector contributes to this ongoing and fruitful collaboration between organizations and social movements researchers.

My attention to agentic mechanisms also incorporates the insights about the moral, emotional character of logics and about reflexive creativity that I have discussed. Frames often make use of the morally loaded ideas and symbols that constitute part of institutional logics to evoke the emotional responses that motivate people to action (Goodwin, Jasper, and Polletta 2000). This is true for conflict-oriented frames, as I have discussed, but it is also the case for compromise-oriented ones. For example, writers in *OGF* framed the growth of the organic market in a morally positive and emotionally satisfying fashion by explaining that sales of organic foods would support a growing number of hardworking, small-scale organic farmers. The work of crafting organizations and institutions, on the other hand, often leads people to grapple with competing logics, which in turn spurs innovation. The conflict-oriented boycott campaigns of advocacy groups, which stem from the challenge of finding ways to assert transformative organizational principles in a field dominated by the logic of market expansion, and the compromise-oriented arrangements in co-ops both illustrate this process.

CONSUMERS MAY PLAY A LIMITED ROLE IN GUIDING ETHICAL MARKETS

Finally, this study has implications for understanding a particular type of multi-institutional field: ethical markets where the exchange of goods is linked to efforts to produce positive social and environmental outcomes. Much of the research about the development of these markets has focused on consumers' political engagement and ability to push firms to factor social and environmental values, as well as economic ones, into decision making (Micheletti 2003; Stehr 2008). In contrast, I have argued that politically engaged consumers play a limited role in guiding the organic sector's development. This is not a coincidence. Both the sector's new arrivals and, more surprisingly, the advocates who assert transformative understandings tend to treat consumers as "purchasers" who support predetermined goals by "voting with their dollars," rather than as "citizens" who deliberate about the goals that the sector should pursue (Cohen 2003). In this sense, the organic sector resembles other product markets created by certifications related to sustainability and worker justice. These markets often result from negotiations between firms and professional social movement actors, rather than being produced by consumer initiatives (Bartley 2003; Jaffee 2007). Opportunities for greater deliberative participation by consumers exist in co-ops and in the alternative food networks created by efforts to move "beyond organic," but these opportunities are limited by the marginal position of these organizations and networks in the organic sector, by the pressures of market competition, and by the presence of assumptions about consumer sovereignty and individualism. With these findings in mind, scholars who study ethical markets should not take consumers' role in guiding firms' behavior for granted, but should rather investigate empirically how organizations in these markets channel consumer participation in more or less engaged and empowering directions.

Looking Forward: Democratic Organization in the Organic Sector and Beyond

The story of the organic sector is neither a triumph nor a tragedy. Both the transformative and the expansionary logics of development have the potential to deliver values that lie outside the market, despite the tensions between them. For the future, a key question is whether the sector will be able to develop institutions, organizations, and practices that advance the multiple values that derive from these different ways of understanding and carrying out the organic project. Looking forward, the dominance of the expansionary logic looms as an obstacle to this effort. Although organizing the sector around the goal of market growth has real benefits, it also limits the democratic and participatory principles that are at the core of the transformative vision.

New arrivals to the organic sector describe the conversion of farmland to organic management as one of the most rewarding parts of their efforts to increase organic sales. This is not a meaningless accomplishment. For a case in point, consider the description that the *New York Times* reporter Barry Estabrook provides of conventional tomato farming in Florida, a state that produces a third of the tomatoes sold in the United States. Tomato growers have employed "a witch's brew of toxic chemicals," including the acutely poisonous and environmentally destructive substances methyl bromide and methyl iodide, for much of the industry's history (Estabrook 2011, 34).[4] People who work on or live near farms face particular dangers. In one labor camp in the early 2000s, three women who regularly encountered synthetic pesticides gave birth to children with severe deformities, including one child who was born with neither arms nor legs. While it is difficult to make clear causal connections between pesticide exposure and birth defects in particular cases, finding ways to minimize or eliminate the use of synthetic pesticides certainly translates into reductions in the risks faced by farmworkers and near-farm communities (Harrison 2011).

Market growth also has the potential to expand consumers' access to organic products by making those products available at lower prices and in a wider range of locations. While there are real questions about whether organically raised fruits and vegetables are more nutritious than their conventional counterparts (Smith-Spangler et al. 2012), and while consuming large amounts of processed foods, whether or not those foods are organic, is often tied to health problems, this, again, is not a meaningless thing to do. One feature of American culture that curtails critical conversations about social inequality is its tendency to equate moral worth with consumption patterns, so that those individuals who are able to consume organic (or other sorts of "ethical") products are often able to advance claims to moral virtues that justify (or at least conceal) unearned social privileges (Guthman 2003; Johnston, Szabo, and Rodney 2011). Making the consumption of organic foods possible across social and geographic boundaries provides the potential for challenging some of these stereotypes. Additionally, market growth may translate into increased political influence for activists who are working to make food systems more sustainable and socially just, whether they are inside or outside the organic sector. When a shopper buys an organic product, she also encounters (however briefly and superficially) critiques of the conventional food system that help to motivate organic farming (Obach 2015). Shopping organic may provide a gateway to other interactions with advocacy groups, and may make consumers more aware of and more likely to support campaigns to strengthen laws and regulations that govern agriculture and food processing.

Yet there are also reasons to be skeptical of the equation of market growth only with social and environmental benefits. Despite their avoidance of synthetic inputs, organic operations may seek to drive down costs and meet consumer demand in ways that work against the goal of environmental sustainability. Reports about large organic farms in the northern Mexico desert that rely on artificial irrigation to raise tomatoes for U.S. consumers provide one example (Rosenthal 2011). Such operations are made possible by the emphasis within the federal organic regulations on technical—rather than holistic and substantive—criteria for organic farming. Additionally, the current organic regulations say nothing about the rights and treatment of workers, which has led to the replication of the exploitative labor relations that exist in the mainstream agricultural sector on many organic farms (Guthman 2004a).[5] Even if the regulations were to include more-robust labor and environmental requirements (which seems unlikely, given the structure imposed by OFPA and the priority of market growth), relying on sales of organic products to improve the overall social and environmental profile of agriculture is itself potentially problematic. Organic sales remain tiny in comparison to sales of conventional food products, and while the organic market continues to grow, this situation is not likely to change in the near future (Obach 2015). There is also a possibility that market growth may undermine, rather than strengthen, activist campaigns related to agricultural sustainability and food justice. The sense that social and environmental ends can be accomplished through shopping has the potential to reduce popular support for state regulation and activism in civil society, both of which may have more far-reaching and evenly distributed impacts (Szasz 2007).

Moreover, increased accessibility of organic products does not necessarily equate to the extension of democratic participation in food systems. Suggestions that food systems should move in the direction of decentralized, human-scaled arrangements are often dismissed as unrealistic with the argument that such arrangements cannot meet modern society's demand for food (Paarlberg

2013). This argument is something of a red herring, since few serious advocates for food system reform would argue for the overnight conversion of current systems to decentralized models. What experiments in decentralized, human-scaled organization can do, their supporters explain, is provide opportunities for ordinary people to understand, think critically about, and exercise some control over the economic and social arrangements that bring food from farm to plate. Practical food democracy, in this sense, is key to the creation of socially, environmentally, and ethically responsible food systems in a changing world (Hassanein 2003). In one way or another, this notion of civic involvement in food systems has been part of transformative visions of organic farming, from the Rodales' agricultural populism to the radical democracy of countercultural activists to the defense of the autonomy and authority of the NOSB in the 1990s. This book has joined other research in showing that the increasing dominance of expansionary understandings and the organic sector's convergence with the mainstream food industry have made it more difficult to sustain opportunities for civic involvement in the sector, though (DuPuis and Gillon 2009).

A key question for the organic sector, then, is whether organic advocates will be able to find creative ways to invigorate the democratic ideas and arrangements that are central to the vision of food system transformation, even as they take seriously the benefits of market growth. The NOAP Project, which I mentioned at the beginning of this chapter, is one example of an effort along these lines. In contrast to the boycott campaigns organized by activist groups and the public relations initiatives supported by new arrivals to the organic sector, the NOAP Project is fundamentally democratic in character. It is anchored in open-ended, grassroots meetings, in which participants work to identify the benefits and the problems associated with the organic sector's trajectory of development. In certain ways, the NOAP Project represents what the NOSB might have been had it not faced the constraints and duties imposed by OFPA, which channeled discussions down a few well-defined pathways. The challenge that this initiative faces, however, lies in spreading this model of organization and making these discussions matter to the sector at large. *From the Margins to the Mainstream* offered a number of specific policy proposals that were intended to encourage continued market growth while also supporting the existence of small farms and regional food systems in the organic sector, but the NOAP Project is dependent on policymakers and regulators to make these proposals a reality, and many of them have not come to pass. In addition, the energy and resources that organizers invested in NOAP are dwarfed by those expended to promote more-conventional patterns of market growth.

Finally, struggles to work out the relationships between competing logics in the organic sector are best understood as part of a broader effort to bring principles of democratic organization and governance into agriculture and food production. This is not a new goal—democratic themes existed in the alternative agriculture advocacy that preceded the popularization of organic farming—but it has arguably entered a new phase. Critical discussions of food systems are more part of popular culture today than they have been in years past, and the encounter of democratic visions with ideas of industrial efficiency generates individual and organizational creativity outside the organic sector as well as inside it. The spread of community-supported agriculture and collective neighborhood gardening, the organization of stakeholder food policy councils that advise city governments about food systems, and the development of city government offices charged with promoting food production in parks and other municipally owned areas are all examples of how this creativity occurs on a local level (Winne 2010). The questions of whether any or all of these initiatives will be able to cling to their democratic character in the face of commercial and bureaucratic pressures, as well as whether they will be able to "scale up" to impact food systems at a national level, have yet to be resolved. But despite the complexities involved in democratizing food systems, this is a challenge that is well worth the effort.

Research Methods and Data

Three sorts of data inform the analysis developed in this book: (1) semistructured interviews with sixty participants in the organic foods sector, (2) archival and other textual sources, and (3) observations at trade conferences and business meetings. I collected about half of the data during a two-year period between 2005 and 2007, and the remainder during the summer and fall of 2010 and the winter of 2011.

Interviews

I began this project without personal connections to people in the organic foods sector and set up my initial interviews on the basis of accessibility and convenience. Respondents in these interviews were mainly owners of small organic businesses and managers and directors of co-op stores. The experiences of co-op leaders struck me as particularly intriguing, and I focused on collecting additional interviews with people in this position at various stores around the country. Seeking a comparison group, I also pursued interviews with individuals who had arrived in the sector more recently and who worked for more-mainstream businesses—this is the group that I refer to in the book as the "new arrivals." I used several strategies to secure interviews, including approaching people at trade conferences, making connections through friends and relatives, snowball sampling (that is, asking respondents to recommend other individuals to contact for interviews), and cold calling.

During the second wave of data collection, I concentrated on making contact with environmental and consumer-interest advocates who were active in the organic sector. These interviews inform the analysis that appears in Chapter 4. I also interviewed several of the sector's acknowledged "leaders": these were people who had helped to develop farmers' groups and certification organizations in the 1970s and 1980s, who participated in the creation of the Organic Foods Production Act and the National Organic Program in the 1990s, and/or sat on the National Organic Standards Board during the 2000s. These interviews were particularly helpful when it came to understanding the history and structure of the organic regulations.

My interviews generally lasted between one and two hours, and were conducted in person, over the telephone, or using videoconferencing software. I recorded and transcribed all of the interviews, except in a few cases when respondents requested not to be recorded. Without exception, respondents were gracious and patient with the long list of questions that I asked about their experiences, their perceptions of current debates in the organic sector, and the operations of the businesses or other organizations in which they participated. The organic sector has attracted a good deal of public attention in recent years, and a number of my respondents were well versed in speaking with members of the media. The challenge in these interviews lay in moving the conversation beyond stock responses and sound bites. The length of the interviews, which far exceeded that of typical interactions with reporters, was helpful in this regard.

As is typical in social sciences research, I offered a guarantee of confidentiality to my respondents. Except in cases where respondents provided me with permission to identify them in publications, I have not included names of individuals or organizations, or other identifying information, in this book. This procedure was approved by institutional review boards at the University of California, San Diego and at Drake University.

Archival and Textual Sources

Archival and other textual sources played an essential role in helping me to understand the economic, cultural, and political contexts that shaped my interviewees' experiences. They also provided me with the ability to make broader claims about the organic sector. Because of the sector's size and diversity, I cannot claim that my interviews constitute anything like a representative sample; archival and textual sources enabled me to check the accuracy of information provided in the interviews and to assess the extent to which interviewees' statements spoke to collective experiences and shared cultural understandings.

Archival sources included: (1) the minutes of all NOSB meetings between 1992 and 1997; (2) documents related to OFPA and to the Harvey lawsuit, including the text of the law itself (including amendments) and various briefs and reports prepared by participants and *amici* in the lawsuit; (3) all issues of *Organic Gardening and Farming* between 1969 and 1978; (4) all issues of *Organic Farmer*, a policy-oriented magazine that reported on the development of the NOP, between 1990 and 1994; (5) all issues of *Cooperative Grocer*, a trade magazine for natural foods co-ops, published between 1987 and 2010, which are available through the magazine's website (www.cooperativegrocer.coop); and (6) transcripts of interviews from *Cultivating a Movement: An Oral History Series on Sustainable Agriculture and Organic Farming on California's Central Coast*, which are available through the website of the University of California, Santa Cruz Library (library.ucsc.edu).

I also followed contemporary business reporting about the organic foods sector during my research, and a number of articles from popular media sources made it into the book. Finally, I benefited from the generosity of Elizabeth Henderson, who shared with me an archive of papers that she had collected during her decades of leadership in the organic sector. These papers provided an insider's view of negotiations related to the development of federal regulations, which would otherwise have been inaccessible.

Observations

I attended several organic sector meetings and trade shows during this research, including the Natural Products Expo West in Anaheim, California, the New Mexico Organic Farming Conference in Albuquerque, and the Midwest Organic and Sustainable Education Service (MOSES) meeting in La Crosse, Wisconsin. These events provided opportunities to hear businesspeople, market researchers, and activists discuss the sector's development, as well as to meet with and interview several of my respondents. To the extent that conferences are places where members of an industry or profession celebrate collective identity, attendance also exposed me to symbols and narratives that make up the cultural side of the expansionary and transformative logics.

I also attended monthly meetings of the board of directors at the store that I refer to as Pacific Foods Co-op for a one-year period during this research. While I discuss these observations only briefly in the book, they provided insight into the everyday workings of food co-ops and the multiple negotiations between commercial and social change orientations that exist in these stores.

APPENDIX 2

List of Interviews

Interview Number	Interview Date	Respondent's Position
1	4/22/2005	Small business owner
2	6/6/2005	Small business owner
3	7/5/2005	Small business owner
4	10/10/2005	Co-op manager
5	10/26/2005	Co-op manager
6	11/21/2005	Small business owner
7	1/10/2006	Co-op manager
8	3/10/2006	Marketing researcher
9	3/30/2006	Co-op manager
10	3/31/2006	Co-op manager
11	5/2/2006	Organic farming advocate
12	5/16/2006	Co-op manager
13	5/26/2006	Co-op manager
14	5/29/2006	Co-op director
15	5/31/2006	Small business owner
16	6/20/2006	Co-op manager
17	6/20/2006	Co-op manager
18	6/21/2006	Co-op manager
19	6/21/2006	Co-op manager
20	6/22/2006	Organic farming advocate
21	6/23/2006	Co-op manager
22	8/16/2006	Co-op manager
23	8/26/2006	Grocery store manager
24	9/1/2006	Small business owner
25	9/11/2006	Marketing researcher
26	9/22/2006	Logistics manager (distribution)

Interview Number	Interview Date	Respondent's Position
27	11/18/2006	Small business owner
28	11/20/2006	Marketing manager (consumer products)
29	12/5/2006	Executive vice president (distribution)
30	12/7/2006	Trade association representative
31	12/13/2006	Logistics manager (distribution)
32	2/20/2007	Co-op manager
33	2/25/2007	Co-op manager
34	3/28/2007	Public relations consultant
35	4/05/2007	Sales manager (retail)
36	4/10/2007	Marketing manager (consumer products)/ NOSB member
37	5/1/2007	Co-op manager
38	10/12/2007	Co-op manager
39	11/12/2007	Farming consultant/NOSB member
40	7/19/2010	Co-op director
41	7/19/2010	Co-op manager
42	7/20/2010	Small business owner
43	7/20/2010	Consumer/environmental advocate
44	8/19/2010	Organic farming advocate
45	8/20/2010	Logistics manager (consumer products)
46	8/20/2010	Chief executive officer (consumer products)
47	9/17/2010	Trade association representative
48	10/27/2010	Certifier
49	11/5/2010	Organic farming advocate
50	11/12/2010	Certifier/NOSB member
51	12/3/2010	Certifier
52	12/8/2010	Marketing manager (consumer products)/ NOSB member
53	12/13/2010	Certifier
54	2/11/2011	Certifier
55	2/25/2011	Organic farming advocate/NOSB member
56	3/3/2011	Organic farming advocate
57	4/14/2011	Consumer interest advocate
58	4/15/2011	Organic farming advocate
59	4/22/2011	Environmental advocate
60	4/30/2011	Marketing manager (consumer products)

Notes

Introduction

1. The full text of Henderson's speech is available at http://www.gvocsa.org/web/archive/keynote_UMOFC_2004.html. Fromartz (2006) also describes the talk.

2. Smillie spoke on a panel titled "Organic Standards: Where We Are and Where We're Going" at the 2006 Natural Products Expo West in Anaheim, California. This excerpt is transcribed from an audio recording of the panel that was made available to the expo's attendees.

3. Details about data collection and analysis are included in the methodological appendices at the end of this book.

4. In contrast, Fromartz (2006) offers a detailed and thoughtful history of the organic sector without staking out a partisan position.

5. Scholarship about the organic sector and other alternative farming initiatives has remarked on the existence of these shared—but mutually contradictory—cultural understandings for a number of years (Beus and Dunlap 1990; DuPuis and Gillon 2009; Obach 2015; Vos 2000).

6. More recently, institutional logics have been defined as "socially constructed, historical patterns of cultural symbols and material practices, including assumptions, values, and beliefs, by which individuals and organizations provide meaning to their daily activity, organize time and space, and reproduce their lives and experiences" (Thornton, Ocasio, and Lounsbury 2012, 2).

7. Like other scholars who have studied institutional logics, I used a Weberian "ideal-typical" approach to construct this table (Weber 1978, 1949). Ideal types are a useful analytic device for highlighting contrasts between "publicly available understandings" (Blair-Loy 2003, 5) about appropriate forms of organization and behavior and for suggesting that different sets of ideas have a logical affinity with one another, whether or not they appear together in the things that people actually say and do.

Chapter 1

1. Peters (1979) and Belasco (1989) offer comprehensive histories of early organic farming advocacy.

2. As Levenstein (2003a) points out, the irony was that much of the demand for convenience food stemmed from women's increasing participation in paid employment. Women's contribution to household salaries also brought value-added processed foods within the financial means of more American families during this time.

3. Upton Sinclair ([1906] 2004) sought to make a similar point in his turn-of-the-century portrayal of the meat industry.

4. The magazine began publication under the title *Organic Farmer*, but Rodale changed its name to *Organic Gardening and Farming* after realizing that home gardeners accounted for a more significant portion of organic practitioners than commercial farmers did.

5. In this respect, Rodale also conforms to organizational theorists' ideas. Scholars argue that entrepreneurial accounts are rarely wholly new—indeed, truly innovative accounts often experience "liabilities of newness" (Stinchcombe 1965) that limit their impact—but instead consist of familiar cultural elements assembled in different ways through a process known as "bricolage" (Binder 2007; Campbell 2002).

6. This discussion extends Haydu's (2011) analysis of the transposition of cultural scripts from the environmental and New Left movements to organic foods advocacy in the 1970s.

7. Rao, Monin, and Durand (2003) documented a similar phenomenon in their study of the nouvelle cuisine movement among elite chefs in France, where assertions of personal autonomy and critiques of institutional authorities during the country's May 1968 protests gave revolutionary meaning to culinary techniques that challenged classical traditions. Both nouvelle cuisine and the organic sector illustrate the ability of society-wide social movements to influence discourse and understandings within more circumscribed fields of activity.

8. I am grateful to Jeffrey Haydu for this observation.

9. Interview (Int.) 49. See Appendix 2 for additional details about the research interviews.

10. Int. 50.

11. Int. 56.

12. Excerpted from "Janet Brians and Grant Brians: Brians Ranch, Hollister, CA," a transcribed interview conducted by Ellen Farmer and included in *Cultivating a Movement: An Oral History Series on Organic Farming and Sustainable Agriculture*, published by the University of California, Santa Cruz Library Regional Oral History Project, 2010. http://library.ucsc.edu/reg-hist/cultiv/home.

13. Excerpted from "Russel and Karen Wolter: Down to Earth Farm," a transcribed interview conducted by Ellen Farmer and included in *Cultivating a Movement*.

14. Int. 49.

15. Excerpted from "Melody Meyer: Organic Foods Distributor," a transcribed interview conducted by Ellen Farmer and included in *Cultivating a Movement*.

Chapter 2

1. This information is from "Whole Foods Market History," an online account

published on the company's website at http://www.wholefoodsmarket.com/company
-info/whole-foods-market-history.

2. The first states to create certification programs were Washington in 1985 and
Texas in 1988. Oregon, Massachusetts, Connecticut, Maine, and California created
organic foods labeling statutes, but not certification programs, during the 1970s.

3. Guthman (2004a) explains that procedural variations between certifiers exceeded differences in these groups' standards.

4. This episode is described in "Mark Lipson: Senior Analyst and Policy Program
Director, Organic Farming Research Foundation," a transcribed interview conducted
by Ellen Farmer and included in *Cultivating a Movement*.

5. Int. 49.

6. Int. 50.

7. More specifically, the problems heightened transaction costs in the national
organic market. These costs are high in situations in which information and trust between parties in a transaction are limited, and they may impede the flow of goods and
services in a market (Williamson 1981).

8. Int. 50.

9. NOSB Minutes, July 1993. Incidentally, this effort illustrates Fligstein's assertion that "the source of rules for new fields is often understandings brought in from
other fields" (Fligstein 2001a, 27). This process is referred to as "institutional isomorphism" (DiMaggio and Powell 1983).

10. Int. 53. The story of the destruction of remaining copies of the report may
be apocryphal, but the fact that this respondent found it to be credible illustrates the
depth of resistance that organic farmers faced from the federal government.

11. It is worth noting that one of my respondents asserted that federal intervention would have occurred eventually, with or without the Alar report, as a result of the
federal government's responsibility to regulate interstate trade. While this may be true,
it is also clear that the Alar report and the resulting public concern about food safety
affected the timing of regulation and the character of the coalition that advocated an
organic labeling law.

12. Int. 47. Several other food scares that increased demand for organic products
took place during the 1980s. One of the most notable involved the contamination of
watermelons in several states with aldicarb, a highly toxic insecticide, in the summer
of 1985. A number of people fell ill after eating contaminated watermelons at Independence Day parties. However, the Alar scare was the most significant in terms of size
and impact on the sector.

13. Int. 55.

14. Int. 53.

15. In early 1990, for example, the consumer activist Roger Blobaum delivered to
the U.S. Senate Committee on Agriculture, Nutrition, and Forestry a petition signed
by 136,000 members of the Center for Science in the Public Interest.

16. Int. 47.

17. Int. 53.

18. This account is taken from "Mark Lipson: Senior Analyst and Policy Program Director, Organic Farming Research Foundation," a transcribed interview conducted by Ellen Farmer and included in *Cultivating a Movement*. Obach (2015), drawing from an interview with Kathleen Merrigan, offers a similar account of OFPA's origin.

19. Int. 56.

20. Senator Leahy's remarks were reproduced in the 1990 Congressional Record Index Online. Whatever Leahy's personal feelings, justifying organic regulations in market-based terms was probably necessary to win support for the legislation from his farm-state colleagues, who were likely to resist any implication that organic methods were more sustainable or otherwise superior to those used in conventional agriculture.

21. Int. 49.

22. The initial NOSB consisted of fourteen members. The fifteenth seat, designated for a representative from a certification organization, was filled later.

23. Int. 52.

24. Int. 55.

25. Int. 55.

26. Grace Gershuny, n.d., "The National Organic Program Process: Points of Clarification for the Grassroots Organic Community" (personal collection of Elizabeth Henderson).

27. NOSB Minutes, May 1992.

28. NOSB Minutes, May–June 1994.

29. Letter from Elizabeth Henderson to Michael Hankin, December 2, 1993 (personal collection of Elizabeth Henderson).

30. NOSB Minutes, July 1993.

31. NOSB Minutes, October 1994.

32. NOSB Minutes, April 1995. USDA confusion over the extent of the NOSB's authority was understandable. The Federal Advisory Committee Act (FACA) of 1972, the law that governs the operation of stakeholder advisory groups like the NOSB, limits their role to conducting research and developing policy recommendations. FACA states that these groups do not have the authority to set policy. OFPA, on the other hand, granted the NOSB limited policymaking ability by stating that the secretary of agriculture could not allow synthetic materials in organic production without NOSB review and approval.

33. Grace Gershuny, a member of the organic sector who worked with the USDA to draft the proposed rule, has explained that most of the deviations from the NOSB's recommendations occurred during the interagency review process. In particular, substantial changes were made at the behest of the Office of Management and Budget. This account appears in Obach (2015, 117–119) and in a series of articles written by Gershuny in the European periodical *The Organic Standard* (author's personal collection).

34. "Joint Press Release of the Organic Farmers Marketing Association and the National Coalition against the Misuse of Pesticides," December 29, 1997 (personal collection of Elizabeth Henderson).

35. "The Sixty-Six Points of Darkness," January 16, 1998 (personal collection of Elizabeth Henderson).

36. "Natural Organic Farmers Association Press Release," February 3, 1998 (personal collection of Elizabeth Henderson).

37. Frederick Kirschenmann, n.d., "The Proposed Organic Rules: It's Not Just about Sewage Sludge, GEO's, and Irradiation" (personal collection of Elizabeth Henderson).

38. Int. 55.

39. Int. 50.

40. The quote is from Joan Gussow, n.d., "Where Is Organic Going?" (personal collection of Elizabeth Henderson).

41. Jasper's concept of "moral shocks" is helpful for understanding this reaction. Moral shocks occur when unexpected, highly public events "raise such a sense of outrage in people that they become inclined toward political action" (Jasper and Poulsen 1995, 498). Social movement organizers often try to evoke moral shocks through the use of frames and "condensing symbols" in order to mobilize people with no previous connection to the social movement. The emphasis that organic advocates placed on the "Big Three" is an example of this strategy.

Chapter 3

1. Scholars have also pointed out that conventionalization is not a uniform process, but one that varies across geographic regions and commodity sectors. It is extensive in California as a result of the state's agro-industrial history, but other areas of organic production display slower rates of conventionalization and more variety in the structures and practices of organic farms (Guptill 2009; Guthman 2004c; Lockie and Halpin 2005).

2. Int. 26.

3. Int. 6.

4. Int. 23.

5. Mackey posted the tips anonymously on a Yahoo! Finance bulletin board, using a pseudonym based on his wife's name. Several of the postings denigrated the Wild Oats operation and suggested that the company's stock price was overvalued. After FTC attorneys discovered his identity, Mackey explained his decision to post anonymously by saying that he simply had fun doing it (Martin 2007).

6. Int. 22.

7. I thank Paul-Brian McInerney for this observation.

8. In interviews, respondents described how they evaluated merchandise category performance, negotiated slotting fees, analyzed supply chains, and organized launch campaigns for new products. These procedures would occur in much the same form in any sector that involves the distribution and retail sale of merchandise.

9. In another validation of the ability of mainstream business thinking to accomplish ethical goals, Mackey and Sisodia offer four abstract tenets that might be implemented across businesses and industries to increase social and environmental value: defining a higher purpose, integrating stakeholders, conscious leadership, and

conscious culture and management. The authors profile the efforts of entrepreneurs who have adopted these tenets—"the true heroes in a free-enterprise economy, driving progress in business, society, and the world"—and suggest that business leaders follow in their footsteps by hiring expert consultants to conduct a "conscious business audit" (Mackey and Sisodia 2013, 14).

10. For example, I participated in a chapter of the business student organization Net Impact while in graduate school. This organization had active chapters in most major American business schools, and served as an organizational center for students who wanted to learn more about combining business activities with social and environmental values. I also attended meetings of the Natural Products Expo West, an organic industry trade show, during this research. At one of these meetings, Jeffrey Hollender, who founded the mission-driven company Seventh Generation, was featured as a keynote speaker.

11. Int. 36.

12. According to Weick (1995), much of organizational life consists of efforts to make sense of events in a retrospective fashion. Studying the "vocabularies of motive" that people use to construct these explanations provides insight into prominent cultural themes in a particular institutional or social settings (Mills 1940).

13. Int. 35.

14. Int. 39.

15. Int. 31.

16. Int. 29.

17. Int. 47.

18. Int. 30.

19. Int. 36.

20. Int. 47.

21. Int. 36.

22. Int. 34.

23. Int. 34.

24. Int. 34.

25. Int. 28.

26. Int. 46.

27. Though these authors emphasize the newness of moral markets, there is also evidence to suggest that consumers have examined and critically assessed business practices in similar ways for some time (Haydu and Kadanoff 2010).

28. Here, my respondents echoed the ideology of consumerism, pervasive in both business communities and popular culture, which presents consumer individualism as a reflection of human nature and elevates consumer satisfaction to the status of an important institutional goal (Johnston 2008; Kellner 1983).

29. Int. 25.

30. Int. 8.

31. Int. 30.

32. Int. 35.

33. Int. 39.

34. Int. 36.

35. Int. 45.

36. The website for the Organic Center is located at http://organic-center.org. The organization lists as one of its goals "to empower consumers to make choices that will improve their health, the health of the environment, and the health of their communities through education and outreach." The implication is clear: consumers are to be empowered as knowledgeable purchasers but not as participants in governance.

37. To be clear, this has resulted from both economic competition and "mimetic isomorphism," a process whereby organizations emulate the practices of peers that they perceive to be successful (DiMaggio and Powell 1983). I discuss isomorphic processes at greater length in Chapter 5.

Chapter 4

1. According to the original version of OFPA, processors were not allowed to "add any synthetic ingredient during the processing or postharvest handling of the product." These terms applied only to processed foods marketed as "organic." OFPA allowed processed foods that combined organic and non-organic (including synthetic) ingredients to be labeled "Made with Organic [Ingredient]." Thus, a cookie that included organic raisins, non-organic flour, and synthetic baking soda could be labeled "Made with Organic Raisins" but not "Organic."

2. Int. 53.

3. NOSB Minutes, April 1995.

4. NOSB Minutes, September 1993. Apparently, NOSB member Merrill Clark was the most vigorous opponent of this decision, but the minutes show little evidence of other dissent. USDA staff also supported the creation of a list of approved synthetic ingredients and argued that apparent contradictions in OFPA rendered the intent of its authors regarding synthetic ingredients unclear.

5. As Fromartz (2006) points out, Gussow later voted in favor of a list of permitted synthetic ingredients as a member of the National Organic Standards Board.

6. Kate Clancy and Frederick Kirschenmann, n.d., "Keeping it 'Organic': Making Sense Out of the Processing of Organic Food" (personal collection of Elizabeth Henderson).

7. Joan Gussow, n.d., "Gussow Draft—Processing" (personal collection of Elizabeth Henderson; emphasis in original).

8. Gene Kahn, Craig Weakley, and Steven Harper, n.d., "A Response from Small Planet Foods to 'Keeping It "Organic"': Making Sense Out of the Processing of Organic Food" (personal collection of Elizabeth Henderson).

9. These arguments appear in a document titled "Harvey v. Veneman and Its Impact on the Organic Supply Chain" (author's personal collection).

10. Int. 7.

11. Int. 43.

12. Int. 57.

13. Int. 57.

14. Int. 36.

15. Int. 59.

16. Synthetic methionine is currently included on the National List and therefore permitted in organic egg production, although only in limited quantities. As I describe below, the politics of the National List are complex. Although synthetic methionine was slated for "sunset" (to be removed from the list and prohibited in organic production), in 2017, recent changes in the sunset review procedures make it uncertain that this will take place.

17. This phrase comes from Interview 53.

18. These arguments appear in the document "Corn Steep Liquor," published online by Beyond Pesticides. The document is available at www.beyondpesticides.org/organicfood/action/spring2011/CSL.pdf.

19. Letter from Gwendolyn Wyard, associate director of organic standards and industry outreach, Organic Trade Association, to Patricia Atkins, National Organic Standards Board, April 10, 2011 (author's personal collection).

20. Int. 58.

21. Discussions of these events appeared on the websites of several organizations and Internet news sources, including the Organic Consumers Association (www.organicconsumers.org), the National Organic Coalition (www.nationalorganiccoalition.org), and *Health Impact News Daily* (www.healthimpactnews.com). The significance of this procedural change becomes clear if one considers the case of tetracycline, one of the antibiotics used to prevent fire blight in organic apple and pear orchards. Tetracycline underwent a "sunset" review under the old rules at an NOSB meeting in early 2013. During the review, nine board members voted to renew the material's listing, while six members voted to remove it from the National List. Since the votes in favor of renewal did not meet the supermajority requirement, tetracycline use has not been allowed in organic production since October 2014. Under the new rules, the same voting pattern would have resulted in a renewal of tetracycline's National List entry.

22. Int. 59.

23. For a more extensive discussion of the pasturing debate, see Fromartz (2006).

24. Int. 44.

25. Space limitations preclude detailed discussion of these campaigns. The Cornucopia Institute alone has mobilized consumer pressure to challenge the presence of mainstream food companies and agricultural practices in markets for organic yogurt, infant formula, eggs, and soy, and has also challenged the organic foods retailing strategies of Wal-Mart and other major retailers. The Organic Consumers Association and its partner organization, the Center for Food Safety, have launched campaigns related to organic eggs, chickens, and fish (which, at the time of this writing, could not be certified as organic).

26. Int. 1.

27. The OCA provides historical summaries and documents related to this campaign on its website at https://www.organicconsumers.org/campaigns/coming-clean.

Dr. Bronner's Magic Soaps, a body care company that helped to lead the campaign, also provides information at https://www.drbronner.com/impact/activism/organic -integrity/coming-clean-campaign/.

28. As Schurman and Munro (2010) explain, anti-biotechnology activists used a similar strategy in Western Europe. When activists mobilized consumers against genetically modified foods, retailers removed these products from their shelves, and companies like Monsanto were left without access to markets.

29. For example, one activist that I interviewed described being asked not to speak at the MOSES organic farming conference, which attracts mainly small-scale farmers and independent producers.

30. Int. 43.

31. The sociologist E. Melanie Dupuis describes one example of how this simplification occurred in the Cornucopia Institute's dairy campaign in a blog post titled "The Organic Movement Is a Civic Process, Not a Set of Standards" at Grist.org. The post is available at http://grist.org/article/2010–02–08–organic-dairy-dispute-strauss -cornucopia/.

32. Schudson (2007, 238) offers a more skeptical analysis of the relationship between consumerism and political activity, noting that deliberative "politics is time-consuming, alternately boring and scary, often contentious, often remote from the present and concrete, and often makes people feel ineffectual, not empowered" and that it is unnecessary to posit consumerism "to distract people from something that they were not attracted to in the first place." Although I also doubt that people would race toward public-spirited deliberation if only they were not distracted by the lure of shopping, I find Schudson's description of politics in this passage to be unnecessarily cynical.

33. Int. 12.

34. Int. 13.

35. Int. 13.

36. Int. 13.

37. Int. 13.

38. Problematically, workers on small-scale farms are often left out of the development of these relationships and visions (Gray 2014).

39. This passage is taken from the document titled "Frequently Asked Questions," available on the website of Certified Naturally Grown at www.naturallygrown.org.

40. Int. 23.

41. This passage is taken from "Only Organic?" a blog post by Alice Varon, the executive director of Certified Naturally Grown, The post is available at www.community .naturallygrown.org/reclaim_natural.

42. Other alternative certification advocates go further. The farmer Eliot Coleman, who advocates using the term "authentic" for food grown on chemical-free, small-scale farms, has described "organic" as a category that has been compromised by the entrance of the federal government and commercially-oriented farmers (Coleman 2002). For their part, larger organic businesses have also challenged repartitioning

efforts by launching products that are designed to appeal to consumers who want to support small-scale farms. In 2012, CROPP/Organic Valley (unique among large organic businesses in that it is an independently-owned producers cooperative) introduced Grassmilk™, which according to the company's press release is only "sourced from pasture-raised cows grazing in the lush pastures of California's north coast" (Organic Valley 2012).

Chapter 5

1. Pacific Food Co-op is a pseudonym for the store.

2. National Co+op Grocers (NCG), an association for natural foods co-ops, currently lists 143 member co-ops, which collectively operate 195 stores. The NCG listing provides a rough estimate of the number of these co-ops in the United States. However, not all natural foods co-ops are members of this association.

3. Int. 7.

4. Int. 38.

5. Int. 22.

6. Int. 4.

7. Int. 9.

8. Int. 14.

9. Int. 22.

10. Int. 40.

11. In 2015, the organization changed its name to National Co+op Grocers (NCG).

12. Int. 4.

13. Elsewhere, I have argued that the NCGA's creation shows how organizational forms are translated to suit local conditions as they become diffused through organizational fields (Haedicke 2012). The notion of translation challenges the emphasis that new institutional research has traditionally placed on organizational isomorphism (Sahlin and Wedlin 2008).

14. Int. 22.

15. Int. 10.

16. Int. 5.

17. Int. 41.

18. Int. 12.

19. Int. 19.

20. Int. 21.

21. Int. 4.

22. Int. 22.

23. Int. 10.

24. Int. 32.

25. Int. 21.

26. Int. 19.

27. Int. 10.

28. Int. 10.
29. Int. 4.
30. Int. 10.
31. Int. 33.
32. Int. 12.
33. Int. 41.
34. Int. 32.
35. Int. 32.
36. Int. 32.
37. Int. 4.
38. Int. 10.
39. Int. 22.
40. Int. 32.
41. Int. 4.
42. Fieldnotes, November 20, 2006.

Chapter 6

1. Int. 59

2. The failure of researchers working in the institutional logics approach to examine the dynamics of conflict has led Fligstein and McAdam to charge that the approach assumes "way too much consensus in a field about what is going on and why and way too little concern over actors' positions, the creation of rules in the field that favor the more powerful over the less powerful, and the general use of power in strategic action fields" (Fligstein and McAdam 2012, 11). I think that rather than discarding the institutional logics approach entirely, it is more productive to bring the approach into dialogue with scholarship that has more closely examined issues of power and politics.

3. The growth in the national trade in organic foods and the exogenous shock produced by the Alar report might be seen as examples of environmental mechanisms that contributed to conflict in the sector.

4. Methyl bromide is near the end of a phase-out process mandated by the Montreal Protocol on Substances that Deplete the Ozone Layer, although it will be possible to apply for a "critical use exemption" until 2017. Methyl iodide was originally advertised as a replacement for methyl bromide, but its manufacturer withdrew the product from the market in response to a campaign organized by the Pesticide Action Network. Although these substances are unlikely to be used in coming years, their replacements are also quite dangerous.

5. In a recent book, Gray (2014) demonstrates that large-scale organic farms do not have a monopoly on abusive labor practices. She shows that despite the ethical reputation of small farms, those that participate in alternative food networks in New York's Hudson Valley demand long hours at low pay and provide substandard housing and little job security to a vulnerable, migratory workforce.

References

Abolafia, Mitchel. 1996. *Making Markets: Opportunism and Restraint on Wall Street.* Cambridge, MA: Harvard University Press.

Albert, Stuart, and David A. Whetten. 1985. "Organizational Identity." *Research in Organizational Behavior* 7: 263–295.

Alkon, Alison Hope. 2012. *Black, White, and Green: Farmers Markets, Race, and the Green Economy.* Athens: University of Georgia Press.

Allen, Floyd. 1971. "The Program to Certify Organic Farmers." *Organic Gardening and Farming*, September, 80–83.

Allen, Patricia, and Michael Kovach. 2000. "The Capitalist Composition of Organic: The Potential of Markets in Fulfilling the Promise of Alternative Agriculture." *Agriculture and Human Values* 17 (3): 221–232.

Armstrong, Elizabeth A., and Mary Bernstein. 2008. "Culture, Power, and Institutions: A Multi-Institutional Politics Approach to Social Movements." *Sociological Theory* 26 (1): 74–99.

Ashcraft, Karen Lee. 2001. "Organized Dissonance: Feminist Bureaucracy as Hybrid Form." *Academy of Management Journal* 44 (6): 1301–1322.

Aurini, Janice Danielle. 2012. "Patterns of Tight and Loose Coupling in a Competitive Marketplace: The Case of Learning Center Franchises." *Sociology of Education* 85 (4): 373–387.

Barley, Stephen R. 2008. "Coalface Institutionalism." In *The SAGE Handbook of Organizational Institutionalism*, edited by Royston Greenwood, Christine Oliver, Kerstin Sahlin-Anderson, and Roy Suddaby, 491–518. Los Angeles: Sage.

Bartley, Tim. 2003. "Certifying Forests and Factories: States, Social Movements, and the Rise of Private Regulation in the Apparel and Forest Products Fields." *Politics and Society* 31 (3): 433–464.

———. 2007. "Institutional Emergence in an Era of Globalization: The Rise of Transnational Private Regulation of Labor and Environmental Conditions." *American Journal of Sociology* 113 (2): 297–351.

Battilana, Julie. 2006. "Agency and Institution: The Enabling Role of Individuals' Social Position." *Organization* 13 (5): 653–676.

Battilana, Julie, and Thomas D'Aunno. 2009. "Institutional Work and the Paradox of Embedded Agency." In *Institutional Work: Actors and Agency in Institutional Studies of Organizations*, edited by Thomas B. Lawrence, Roy Suddaby, and Bernard Leca, 31–58. New York: Cambridge University Press.

Battilana, Julie, and Sylvia Dorado. 2010. "Building Sustainable Hybrid Organizations: The Case of Commercial Microfinance Organizations." *Academy of Management Journal* 53 (6): 1419–1440.

Bechky, Beth A. 2011. "Making Organizational Theory Work: Institutions, Occupations, and Negotiated Orders." *Organization Science* 22 (5): 1157–1167.

Beckert, Jens. 1998. "What Is Sociological about Economic Sociology? Uncertainty and the Embeddedness of Economic Action." *Theory and Society* 25 (6): 803–840.

Beeman, Randal S., and James A. Pritchard. 2001. *A Green and Permanent Land: Ecology and Agriculture in the Twentieth Century*. Lawrence: University of Kansas Press.

Belasco, Warren J. 1989. *Appetite for Change: How the Counterculture Took on the Food Industry, 1966–1988*. New York: Pantheon Books.

Benford, Robert D., and David A. Snow. 2000. "Framing Processes and Social Movements: An Overview and Assessment." *Annual Review of Sociology* 26: 611–639.

Benner, Patricia. 1994. "The Role of Articulation in Understanding Practices and Experience as Sources of Knowledge in Clinical Nursing." In *Philosophy in an Age of Pluralism: The Philosophy of Charles Taylor in Question*, edited by James Tully, 136–155. New York: Cambridge University Press.

Benson, Mitchel. 1988. "Carrot Crisis Organic Veggie Scam Alleged." *San Jose Mercury News*, May 11.

Berger, Bennett M. 2004. *The Survival of a Counterculture: Ideological Work and Everyday Life among Rural Communards*. New Brunswick, NJ: Transaction Publishers.

Beus, C. E., and Riley E. Dunlap. 1990. "Conventional Versus Alternative Agriculture: The Paradigmatic Roots of the Debate." *Rural Sociology* 55 (4): 590–616.

Binder, Amy J. 2007. "For Love and Money: Organizations' Creative Responses to Multiple Environmental Logics." *Theory and Society* 36 (6): 547–571.

Blair-Loy, Mary. 2003. *Competing Devotions: Career and Family Among Women Executives*. Cambridge, MA: Harvard University Press.

Bones, Gordon G. 1992. "State and Federal Organic Food Certification Laws: Coming of Age." *North Dakota Law Review* 68: 405–444.

Borys, Bryan, and David B. Jemison. 1989. "Hybrid Arrangements as Strategic Alliances: Theoretical Issues in Organizational Combinations." *Academy of Management Review* 14 (2): 234–249.

Breines, Wini. 1989. *Community and Organization in the New Left, 1962–1968*. New Brunswick, NJ: Rutgers University Press.

Buck, Daniel, Christina Getz, and Julie Guthman. 1997. "From Farm to Table: The Organic Vegetable Commodity Chain of Northern California." *Sociologia Ruralis* 37 (1): 3–20.

Campbell, John L. 2002. "Where Do We Stand? Common Mechanisms in Organizations and Social Movements Research." In *Social Movements and Organization*

Theory, edited by Gerald F. Davis, Doug McAdam, W. Richard Scott, and Mayer Zald, 41–68. New York: Cambridge University Press.

Cantisano, Amigo, Gene Kahn, and Margaret Clark. 1992. "Letter Blasting NOSB Draws Response." *Organic Farmer*, Summer, 16–18.

Capek, Stella M. 1993. "The 'Environmental Justice' Frame: A Conceptual Discussion and an Application." *Social Problems* 40 (1): 5–24.

Carroll, Glenn R. 1985. "Concentration and Specialization: Dynamics of Niche Width in Populations of Organizations." *American Journal of Sociology* 90 (6): 1262–1283.

Carroll, Glenn R., Stanislav D. Dobrev, and Anand Swaminathan. 2002. "Organizational Processes of Resource Partitioning." *Research in Organizational Behavior* 24 (1): 1–40.

Carroll, Glenn R., and Anand Swaminathan. 2000. "Why the Microbrewery Movement? Organizational Dynamics of Resource Partitioning in the U.S. Brewing Industry." *American Journal of Sociology* 106 (3): 715–762.

Carson, Rachel. (1962) 2002. *Silent Spring*. New York: Mariner Books.

Clemens, Elizabeth S. 1996. "Organizational Form as Frame: Collective Identity and Political Strategy in the American Labor Movement." In *Comparative Perspectives on Social Movements*, edited by Doug McAdam, John D. McCarthy, and Mayer Zald, 205–226. Cambridge: Cambridge University Press.

Clemens, Elizabeth S., and James M. Cook. 1999. "Politics and Institutionalism: Explaining Durability and Change." *Annual Review of Sociology* 25: 441–466.

Cohen, Lizabeth. 2003. *A Consumers' Republic: The Politics of Mass Consumption in Postwar America*. New York: Vintage.

Coleman, Eliot. 2002. "Beyond Organic." *Mother Earth News*, December–January. http://www.fourseasonfarm.com/pdfs/beyondorganic.pdf.

Collins, Randall. 1975. *Conflict Sociology: Toward an Explanatory Science*. New York: Academic Press.

Conford, Philip. 2001. *The Origins of the Organic Movement*. Edinburgh: Floris Books.

Conkin, Paul Keith. 2008. *A Revolution Down on the Farm: The Transformation of American Agriculture since 1929*. Lexington: University Press of Kentucky.

Cox, Craig. 1994. *Storefront Revolution: Food Co-ops and the Counterculture*. New Brunswick, NJ: Rutgers University Press.

Cronon, William. 1992. *Nature's Metropolis: Chicago and the Great West*. New York: W. W. Norton.

D'Aunno, Thomas, Robert I. Sutton, and Richard H. Price. 1991. "Isomorphism and External Support in Conflicting Institutional Environments: A Study of Drug Abuse Treatment Units." *Academy of Management Journal* 34 (3): 636–661.

Dezember, Ryan. 2012. "The Buyout Brain behind Annie's IPO." *Wall Street Journal*, April 13. http://www.wsj.com/articles/SB10001424052702303624004577339743538261650.

DiMaggio, Paul. 1988. "Interest and Agency in Institutional Theory." In *Institutional Patterns and Organizations: Culture and Environment*, edited by Lynne G. Zucker, 3–22. Cambridge, MA: Ballinger.

———. 1994. "Culture and Economy." In *The Handbook of Economic Sociology*, edited by Neil J. Smelser and Richard Swedberg, 27–57. Princeton, NJ: Princeton University Press.

———. 1997. "Culture and Cognition." *Annual Review of Sociology* 23:263–287.

DiMaggio, Paul, and Walter W. Powell. 1983. "The Iron Cage Revisited: Institutional Isomorphism and Collective Rationality in Organizational Fields." *American Sociological Review* 48 (2): 147–160.

Dimitri, Carolyn, and Lydia Oberholtzer. 2009. *Marketing U.S. Organic Foods: Recent Trends from Farms to Consumers*. Washington, DC: U.S. Department of Agriculture Economic Research Service.

Dimitri, Carolyn, and Nessa J. Richman. 2000. *Organic Food Markets in Transition*. Greenbelt, MD: Henry A. Wallace Center for Agricultural and Environmental Policy.

Domagalski, Theresa A. 1999. "Emotions in Organizations: Main Currents." *Human Relations* 52 (6): 833–852.

Dunn, Mary B., and Candace Jones. 2010. "Institutional Logics and Institutional Pluralism: The Contestation of Care and Science Logics in Medical Education, 1967–2005." *Administrative Science Quarterly* 55 (1): 114–149.

DuPuis, E. Melanie. 2000. "Not in My Body: rBGH and the Rise of Organic Milk." *Agriculture and Human Values* 17 (3): 285–295.

DuPuis, E. Melanie, and Sean Gillon. 2009. "Alternative Modes of Governance: Organic as Civic Engagement." *Agriculture and Human Values* 26 (1–2): 43–56.

Dutton, Jane, and Janet Dukerich. 1991. "Keeping an Eye on the Mirror: Image and Identity in Organizational Adaptation." *Academy of Management Journal* 34 (3): 517–554.

Elster, Jon. 1989. *Nuts and Bolts for the Social Sciences*. Cambridge: Cambridge University Press.

Emirbayer, Mustafa, and Ann Mische. 1998. "What Is Agency?" *American Journal of Sociology* 103 (4): 962–1023.

Espeland, Wendy Nelson, and Mitchell L. Stevens. 1998. "Commensuration as a Social Process." *Annual Review of Sociology* 24: 313–343.

Estabrook, Barry. 2011. *Tomatoland: How Modern Industrial Agriculture Destroyed Our Most Alluring Fruit*. Kansas City, MO: Andrews McMeel.

Everitt, Judson G. 2013. "Inhabitants Moving In: Prospective Sensemaking and the Reproduction of Inhabited Institutions in Teacher Education." *Symbolic Interaction* 36 (2): 177–196.

Ferree, Myra Marx, and Patricia Yancey Martin. 1995. "Doing the Work of the Movement: Feminist Organizations." In *Feminist Organizations: Harvest of the New Women's Movement*, edited by Myra Marx Ferree and Patricia Yancey Martin, 3–25. Philadelphia: Temple University Press.

Fetter, Robert T., and Julie A. Caswell. 2002. *Variation in Organic Standards Prior to the National Organic Program*. Storrs-Mansfield, CT: University of Connecticut Department of Agricultural and Resource Economics.

Fields, Gary. 2003. *Territories of Profit: Communications, Capitalist Development and the Innovative Enterprises of G. F. Swift and Dell Computer*. Stanford, CA: Stanford Business Books.

Fine, Gary Alan. 1984. "Negotiated Orders and Organizational Cultures." *Annual Review of Sociology* 10: 239–262.

Fineman, Stephen. 1999. "Emotions and Organizing." In *Studying Organization: Theory and Method*, edited by Stewart R. Clegg and Cynthia Hardy, 289–310. London: Sage.

Fligstein, Neil. 1996. "Markets as Politics: A Political-Cultural Approach to Market Institutions." *American Sociological Review* 61 (4): 656–673.

———. 2001a. *The Architecture of Markets: An Economic Sociology of Twenty-First-Century Capitalist Societies*. Princeton, NJ: Princeton University Press.

———. 2001b. "Social Skill and the Theory of Fields." *Sociological Theory* 19 (2): 105–125.

Fligstein, Neil, and Doug McAdam. 2012. *A Theory of Fields*. New York: Oxford University Press.

Foote, James, and Jerome Goldstein. 1973. "1973 OGF Certification Program." *Organic Gardening and Farming*, April, 89–92.

Forster, Thomas. 1990. "The Crafting of a Legislative Miracle." *Organic Farmer*, Summer, 25–27.

Fourcade, Marion, and Kieran Healy. 2007. "Moral Views of Market Society." *Annual Review of Sociology* 33: 285–311.

Franz, Maurice. 1970. "To Market, To Market . . . for Organic Foods." *Organic Gardening and Farming*, January, 62–64.

Friedland, Roger. 2013. "God, Love, and Other Good Reasons for Practice: Thinking through Institutional Logics." In *Institutional Logics in Action*, Part A, edited by Eva Boxenbaum and Michael Lounsbury, 25–50. London: Emerald Group Publishing.

Friedland, Roger, and Robert R. Alford. 1991. "Bringing Society Back In: Symbols, Practices, and Institutional Contradictions." In *The New Institutionalism in Organizational Analysis*, edited by Paul J. DiMaggio and Walter W. Powell, 232–263. Chicago: University of Chicago Press.

Fromartz, Samuel. 2006. *Organic, Inc.: Natural Foods and How They Grew*. Orlando: Harcourt.

Gamson, William A. 1992. *Talking Politics*. New York: Cambridge University Press.

Garud, Raghu, Cynthia Hardy, and Steve Maguire. 2007. "Institutional Entrepreneurship as Embedded Agency." *Organization Studies* 28 (7): 957–969.

Gershuny, Grace. 1991. "NOSB Slate Submitted by Organic Industry." *Organic Farmer*, Summer, 25.

———. 1993. "Do We Continue to Support the Organic Foods Production Act?" *Organic Farmer*, Fall, 31–32.

Gershuny, Grace, and Thomas Forster. 1992. "Does Organic Mean Socially Responsible?" *Organic Farmer*, Winter, 7–11.

Gieryn, Thomas F. 1983. "Boundary-Work and the Demarcation of Science from Non-

Science: Strains and Interests in Professional Ideologies of Scientists." *American Sociological Review* 48 (6): 781–795.

Gilman, Steve. 2006. "Holding On to Organic!! A Grassroots Perspective Concerning Big Food's Threat to Organic Standards." *Natural Farmer*, Spring, 25–28.

Goldman, M. G. 1969. "Getting Organic Beef to the Public." *Organic Gardening and Farming*, February, 34–37.

———. 1970. "More Organic Foods for Wise Shoppers." *Organic Gardening and Farming*, March, 78–82.

Goldstein, Jerome. 1976. "Organic Force." In *Radical Agriculture*, edited by Richard Merrill, 212–214. New York: NYU Press.

Goodman, David, E. Melanie DuPuis, and Michael K. Goodman. 2011. *Alternative Food Networks: Knowledge, Practice, and Politics*. Hoboken, NJ: Taylor and Francis.

Goodman, David, and Michael Redclift. 1991. *Refashioning Nature: Food, Ecology, and Culture*. London: Routledge.

Goodwin, Jeff, James M. Jasper, and Francesca Polletta. 2000. "The Return of the Repressed: The Fall and Rise of Emotions in Social Movement Theory." *Mobilization* 5 (1): 65–84.

Gray, Margaret. 2014. *Labor and the Locavore: The Making of a Comprehensive Food Ethic*. Berkeley: University of California Press.

Greenwood, Royston, Roy Suddaby, and C. R. Hinings. 2002. "Theorizing Change: The Role of Professional Associations in the Transformation of Institutionalized Fields." *Academy of Management Journal* 45 (1): 58–80.

Guptill, Amy. 2009. "Exploring the Conventionalization of Organic Dairy: Trends and Countertrends in Upstate New York." *Agriculture and Human Values* 26 (1–2): 29–42.

Guptill, Amy, and Jennifer L. Wilkins. 2002. "Buying into the Food System: Trends in Food Retailing in the U.S. and Implications for Local Foods." *Agriculture and Human Values* 19 (1): 39–51.

Gusfield, Joseph R. 1992. "Nature's Body and the Metaphors of Food." In *Cultivating Differences: Symbolic Boundaries and the Making of Inequality*, edited by Michèle Lamont and Michel Fournier, 75–103. Chicago: University of Chicago Press.

Gussow, Joan Dye. 1997. "Can an Organic Twinkie Be Certified?" In *For All Generations: Making World Agriculture More Sustainable*, edited by J. Patrick Madden and Scott G. Chaplowe, 143–153. Glendale, CA: WSAA Publications.

Guthman, Julie. 1998. "Regulating Meaning, Appropriating Nature: The Codification of California Organic Agriculture." *Antipode* 30 (2): 135–154.

———. 2003. "Fast Food/Organic Food: Reflexive Tastes and the Making of 'Yuppie Chow.'" *Social and Cultural Geography* 4 (1): 45–58.

———. 2004a. *Agrarian Dreams: The Paradox of Organic Farming in California*. Berkeley: University of California Press.

———. 2004b. "Back to the Land: The Paradox of Organic Food Standards." *Environment and Planning A* 36 (3): 511–528.

———. 2004c. "The Trouble with 'Organic Lite' in California: A Rejoinder to the 'Conventionalization' Debate." *Sociologia Ruralis* 44 (3): 301–316.

Gutknecht, Dave. 2003. "Co-op Devolution Part 2: Northeast Cooperatives to Fold, United Natural Foods, Inc. Assuming Services after Merger Vote." *Cooperative Grocer*, January–February.

Gutknecht, Dave, and Michael Funk. 2003. "Food Co-ops Rock!" *Cooperative Grocer*, July–August.

Haedicke, Michael A. 2012. "'Keeping Our Mission, Changing Our System': Translation and Organizational Change in Natural Foods Co-ops." *Sociological Quarterly* 53 (1): 44–67.

———. 2014. "Small Food Co-ops in a Whole Foods World." *Contexts* 13:32–37.

Haedicke, Michael A., and Tim Hallett. 2015. "How to Look Two Ways at Once: Research Strategies for an Inhabited Institutionalism." In *The Handbook of Qualitative Organizational Research: Innovative Pathways and Methods*, edited by Kimberly D. Elsbach and Roderick M. Kramer, 99–111. New York: Routledge.

Hallett, Tim. 2010. "The Myth Incarnate: Recoupling Processes, Turmoil, and Inhabited Institutions in an Urban Elementary School." *American Sociological Review* 75 (1): 52–74.

Hallett, Tim, David Shulman, and Gary Alan Fine. 2009. "Peopling Organizations: The Promise of Classic Symbolic Interactionism for an Inhabited Institutionalism." In *The Oxford Handbook of Sociology and Organization Studies*, edited by Paul S. Adler, 486–509. Oxford: Oxford University Press.

Hallett, Tim, and Marc Ventresca. 2006. "Inhabited Institutions: Social Interactions and Organizational Forms in Gouldner's *Patterns of Industrial Bureaucracy*." *Theory and Society* 35 (2): 213–236.

Hardy, Cynthia, and Steve Maguire. 2008. "Institutional Entrepreneurship." In *The Sage Handbook of Organizational Institutionalism*, edited by Royston Greenwood, Christine Oliver, Kerstin Sahlin, and Roy Suddaby, 198–217. Thousand Oaks, CA: Sage.

Hargrave, Timothy J., and Andrew H. Ven de Ven. 2009. "Institutional Work as the Creative Embrace of Contradiction." In *Institutional Work: Actors and Agency in Institutional Studies of Organizations*, edited by Thomas B. Lawrence, Roy Suddaby, and Bernard Leca, 120–140. New York: Cambridge University Press.

Harrison, Jill Lindsey. 2011. *Pesticide Drift and the Pursuit of Environmental Justice*. Cambridge, MA: MIT Press.

Hassanein, Neva. 2003. "Practising Food Democracy: A Pragmatic Politics of Transformation." *Journal of Rural Studies* 19 (1): 77–86.

Hawken, Paul, Amory B. Lovins, and L. Hunter Lovins. 1999. *Natural Capitalism: Creating the Next Industrial Revolution*. New York: Little, Brown.

Haydu, Jeffrey. 1999. "Counter Action Frames: Employer Repertoires and the Union Menace in the Late Nineteenth Century." *Social Problems* 46 (3): 313–331.

———. 2011. "Cultural Modeling in Two Eras of U.S. Food Protest: Grahamites (1830s) and Organic Advocates (1960s–70s)." *Social Problems* 58 (3): 461–487.

Haydu, Jeffrey, and David Kadanoff. 2010. "Casing Political Consumerism." *Mobilization* 15 (2): 159–177.

Hedström, Peter, and Richard Swedberg. 1998. *Social Mechanisms: An Analytical Approach to Social Theory*. Cambridge: Cambridge University Press.

Henderson, Elizabeth. 1991. "Organic Legislation: The Next Steps." *Organic Farmer*, Winter, 20.

Henderson, Elizabeth, and Peter LeCompte. 1992. "USDA Names National Organic Standards Board." *Organic Farmer*, Spring, 22–23.

Henderson, Gary. 1989. "Member Labor: Models and Measures." *Cooperative Grocer*, February–March.

Henke, Christopher R. 2008. *Cultivating Science, Harvesting Power: Science and Industrial Agriculture in California*. Cambridge, MA: MIT Press.

Hewitt, Jean. 1970. "Organic Food Fanciers Go to Great Lengths for the Real Thing." *New York Times*, September 7. http://query.nytimes.com/gst/abstract.html?res=9F 05E1DA1731EE34BC4F53DFBF66838B669EDE.

Hibbard, Justin. 2006. "Put Your Money Where Your Mouth Is." *BusinessWeek*, September 18. http://www.bloomberg.com/bw/stories/2006–09–17/put-your-money -where-your-mouth-is.

Hirsch, Paul M. 1986. "From Ambushes to Golden Parachutes: Corporate Takeovers as an Instance of Cultural Framing and Institutional Integration." *American Journal of Sociology* 91 (4): 800–837.

Hirsch, Paul M., and Michael Lounsbury. 1997. "Ending the Family Quarrel: Toward a Reconciliation of 'Old' and 'New' Institutionalisms." *American Behavioral Scientist* 40 (4): 406–418.

Hirschman, Albert O. 1970. *Exit, Voice, and Loyalty: Responses to Decline in Firms, Organizations, and States*. Cambridge, MA: Harvard University Press.

Hoodes, Liana, Michael Sligh, Harriet Behar, Roger Blobaum, Lisa J. Bunin, Lynn Coody, Elizabeth Henderson, Faye Jones, Mark Lipson, and Jim Riddle. 2010. *National Organic Action Plan: From the Margins to the Mainstream—Advancing Organic Agriculture in the U.S.* Pittsboro, NC: Rural Advancement Foundation International—USA.

Howard, Philip H. 2009. "Consolidation in the North American Organic Food Processing Sector, 1997 to 2007." *International Journal of Sociology of Agriculture and Food* 16 (1): 13–30.

Ingram, Mrill, and Helen Ingram. 2005. "Creating Credible Edibles: The Organic Agriculture Movement and the Emergence of U.S. Federal Organic Standards." In *Routing the Opposition: Social Movements, Public Policy and Democracy*, edited by David S. Meyer, Valerie Jenness, and Helen Ingram, 121–149. Minneapolis: University of Minnesota Press.

Jaffee, Daniel. 2007. *Brewing Justice: Fair Trade Coffee, Sustainability, and Survival*. Berkeley: University of California Press.

Jaffee, Daniel, and Philip Howard. 2010. "Corporate Cooptation of Organic and Fair Trade Standards." *Agriculture and Human Values* 27 (4): 387–399.

Jagiello, Joseph. 1999. "CoCoFiSt Data Sharing Strengthens Co-ops." *Cooperative Grocer*, November–December.

Jansen, Erik, and Mary Ann Von Glinow. 1985. "Ethical Ambivalence and Organizational Reward Systems." *Academy of Management Review* 10 (4): 814–822.

Jasper, James M. 2011. "Emotions and Social Movements: Twenty Years of Theory and Research." *Annual Review of Sociology* 37:285–303.

Jasper, James M., and Jane Poulsen. 1995. "Recruiting Strangers and Friends: Moral Shocks and Social Networks in Animal Rights and Anti-Nuclear Protests." *Social Problems* 42 (4): 493–512.

Jepperson, Ronald. 1991. "Institutions, Institutional Effects, and Institutionalism." In *The New Institutionalism in Organizational Analysis*, edited by Walter W. Powell and Paul DiMaggio, 143–163. Chicago: University of Chicago Press.

Johnston, Josée. 2008. "The Citizen-Consumer Hybrid: Ideological Tensions and the Case of Whole Foods Market." *Theory and Society* 37 (3): 229–270.

Johnston, Josée, and Michelle Szabo. 2011. "Reflexivity and the Whole Foods Market Consumer: The Lived Experience of Shopping for Change." *Agriculture and Human Values* 28: 303–319.

Johnston, Josée, Michelle Szabo, and Alexandra Rodney. 2011. "Good Food, Good People: Understanding the Cultural Repertoire of Ethical Eating." *Journal of Consumer Culture* 11 (3): 293–318.

Kallett, Arthur, and F. J. Schlink. 1932. *100,000,000 Guinea Pigs: Danger in Everyday Foods, Drugs, and Cosmetics*. New York: Vanguard Press.

Kastel, Mark Alan. 2006. *Maintaining the Integrity of Organic Milk: Showcasing Ethical Family Farm Producers, Exposing the Corporate Takeover—Factory Farm Production*. Cornucopia, WI: Cornucopia Institute.

Kellner, Douglas. 1983. "Critical Theory, Commodities, and the Consumer Society." *Theory, Culture, and Society* 1 (3): 64–84.

Khurana, Rakesh. 2007. *From Higher Aims to Hired Hands: The Social Transformation of American Business Schools and the Unfulfilled Promise of Management as a Profession*. Princeton, NJ: Princeton University Press.

King, Brayden G. 2008. "A Political Mediation Model of Corporate Response to Social Movement Activism." *Administrative Science Quarterly* 53 (3): 395–421.

King, Brayden G., and Nicholas A. Pearce. 2010. "The Contentiousness of Markets: Politics, Social Movements, and Institutional Change in Markets." *Annual Review of Sociology* 36: 249–267.

King, Franklin H. 1927. *Farmers of Forty Centuries: Permanent Agriculture in China, Korea, and Japan*. New York: Harcourt and Brace.

Kingsolver, Barbara. 2007. *Animal, Vegetable, Miracle*. New York: HarperCollins.

Kirschenmann, Frederick, G. W. Stevenson, Frederick Buttel, Thomas A. Lyson, and Mike Duffy. 2008. "Why Worry about the Agriculture of the Middle?" In *Food and the Mid-Level Farm: Renewing an Agriculture of the Middle*, edited by Thomas A. Lyson, G. W. Stevenson, and Rick Welsh, 3–22. Cambridge: MIT Press.

Kirschenmann, Frederick, Gene Kahn, and Andrew Ferguson. 1993. "Towards a Sustainable, Organic Food Marketing System." *Organic Farmer*, Spring, 19–20.

Klonsky, Karen. 2000. "Forces Impacting the Production of Organic Foods." *Agriculture and Human Values* 17 (3): 233–243.

Knox, Reggie, and Elizabeth Henderson. 1992. "OFAC Update." *Organic Farmer*, Fall, 34–35.

Knupfer, Anne Meis. 2013. *Food Co-ops in America: Communities, Consumption, and Economic Democracy*. Ithaca, NY: Cornell University Press.

Kowitt, Beth. 2015. "Special Report: The War on Big Food." *Fortune*, June 1.

Kraatz, Matthew S., and Emily S. Block. 2008. "Organizational Implications of Institutional Pluralism." In *The SAGE Handbook of Organizational Institutionalism*, edited by S. R. Clegg, C. Hardy, Thomas B. Lawrence, and W. R. Nord, 243–275. London: Sage.

Lamont, Michèle. 1992. *Money, Morals, and Manners: The Culture of the French and American Upper-Middle Class*. Chicago: University of Chicago Press.

Lamont, Michèle, and Virág Molnár. 2002. "The Study of Boundaries in the Social Sciences." *Annual Review of Sociology* 28 (1): 167–196.

Lawrence, Thomas B., and Roy Suddaby. 2006. "Institutions and Institutional Work." In *The SAGE Handbook of Organizational Studies*, edited by S. R. Clegg, C. Hardy, Thomas B. Lawrence, and W. R. Nord, 215–254. London: Sage.

Lawrence, Thomas B., Roy Suddaby, and Bernard Leca. 2009. "Introduction: Theorizing and Studying Institutional Work." In *Institutional Work: Actors and Agency in Institutional Studies of Organizations*, edited by Thomas B. Lawrence, Roy Suddaby, and Bernard Leca, 1–28. New York: Cambridge University Press.

Lee, Brandon H. 2009. "The Infrastructure of Collective Action and Policy Content Diffusion in the Organic Food Industry." *Academy of Management Journal* 52 (6): 1247–1269.

Lee, Caroline. 2015. *Do-It-Yourself Democracy: The Rise of the Public Engagement Industry*. New York: Oxford University Press.

Levenstein, Harvey. 2003a. *Paradox of Plenty: A Social History of Eating in Modern America*. Rev. ed. Berkeley: University of California Press.

———. 2003b. *Revolution at the Table: The Transformation of the American Diet*. Rev. ed. Berkeley: University of California Press.

Lockie, Stewart, and Darren Halpin. 2005. "The 'Conventionalisation' Thesis Reconsidered: Structural and Ideological Transformation of Australian Organic Agriculture." *Sociologia Ruralis* 45 (4): 284–307.

Lounsbury, Michael, and Ellen T. Crumley. 2007. "New Practice Creation: An Institutional Perspective on Innovation." *Organization Studies* 28 (7): 993–1012.

Lounsbury, Michael, and Mary Ann Glynn. 2001. "Cultural Entrepreneurship: Stories, Legitimacy, and the Acquisition of Resources." *Strategic Management Journal* 22 (6–7): 545–564.

Lyson, Thomas A. 2004. *Civic Agriculture: Reconnecting Farm, Food, and Community*. Medford, MA: Tufts University Press.

Mackey, John, and Raj Sisodia. 2013. *Conscious Capitalism: Liberating the Heroic Spirit of Business*. Boston: Harvard Business Review Press.

Maguire, Steve, Cynthia Hardy, and Thomas B. Lawrence. 2004. "Institutional Entrepreneurship in Emerging Fields: HIV/AIDS Treatment Advocacy in Canada." *Academy of Management Journal* 47 (5): 657–679.

Marquis, Christopher, and Michael Lounsbury. 2007. "Vive La Résistance: Competing Logics and the Consolidation of U.S. Community Banking." *Academy of Management Journal* 50 (4): 799–820.

Martin, Andrew. 2007. "Whole Foods Executive Used Alias." *New York Times*, July 12. http://www.nytimes.com/2007/07/12/business/12foods.html?_r=0.

———. 2008. "Wait. Why Is the F.T.C. after Whole Foods?" *New York Times*, December 14. http://www.nytimes.com/2008/12/14/business/14feed.html?_r=0.

Maxwell, Joseph A. 2005. *Qualitative Research Design: An Interactive Approach*. 2nd ed. Thousand Oaks, CA: Sage Publications.

Mayo, James M. 1993. *The American Grocery Store: The Business Evolution of an Architectural Space*. Westport, CT: Greenwood Press.

McAdam, Doug, and Neil Fligstein. 2011. "Towards a General Theory of Strategic Action Fields." *Sociological Theory* 29 (1): 1–26.

McAdam, Doug, John D. McCarthy, and Mayer Zald. 1996. "Introduction: Opportunities, Mobilizing Structures, and Framing Processes—Toward a Synthetic, Comparative Perspective on Social Movements." In *Comparative Perspectives on Social Movements*, edited by Doug McAdam, John D. McCarthy, and Mayer Zald, 1–20. Cambridge: Cambridge University Press.

McAdam, Doug, Sidney G. Tarrow, and Charles Tilly. 2001. *Dynamics of Contention*. New York: Cambridge University Press.

McGrath, Maria. 2004. "'That's Capitalism, Not a Co-op': Countercultural Idealism and Business Realism in 1970s U.S. Food Co-ops." *Business and Economic History On-Line* 2: 1–14.

McInerney, Paul-Brian. 2014. *From Social Movement to Moral Market: How the Circuit Riders Sparked an IT Revolution and Created a Technology Market*. Stanford: Stanford University Press.

McPherson, Chad Michael, and Michael Sauder. 2013. "Logics in Action: Institutional Complexity in a Drug Court." *Administrative Science Quarterly* 58 (2): 165–196.

McVeigh, Rory, Daniel J. Myers, and David Sikkink. 2004. "Corn, Klansmen, and Coolidge: Structure and Framing in Social Movements." *Social Forces* 83 (2): 653–690.

Merrigan, Kathleen. 1991. "And Now for the Real Work . . ." *Organic Farmer*, Spring, 4.

Merton, Robert. 1976. *Sociological Ambivalence and Other Essays*. New York: Free Press.

Meyer, David S., and Nancy Whittier. 1994. "Social Movement Spillover." *Social Problems* 41 (2): 277–298.

Meyer, Harlyn. 1990. "Position Papers." *Organic Farmer*, Winter, 18–20.

Micheletti, Michele. 2003. *Political Virtue and Shopping: Individuals, Consumerism, and Collective Action*. New York: Palgrave Macmillan.

Micheletti, Michele, Andreas Føllesdal, and Dietlind Stolle, eds. 2004. *Politics, Products, and Markets: Exploring Political Consumerism Past and Present.* New Brunswick, NJ: Transaction.

Miller, Laura J. 2006. *Reluctant Capitalists: Bookselling and the Culture of Consumption.* Chicago: University of Chicago Press.

Mills, C. Wright. 1940. "Situated Actions and Vocabularies of Motive." *American Sociological Review* 5 (6): 904–913.

Mullen, Shannon. 2013. "Target Wants to Take a Bite Out of the Organic Market." *Marketplace*, June 10. http://www.marketplace.org/topics/sustainability/numbers/target-wants-take-bite-out-organic-market.

Nauman, Ben. 2007. "Support Our Success: A Systematic Store Improvement Program." *Cooperative Grocer*, July–August.

Nunn, Lisa M. 2014. *Defining Student Success: The Role of School and Culture.* New Brunswick, NJ: Rutgers University Press.

Oakes, Leslie S., Barbara Townley, and David J. Cooper. 1998. "Business Planning as Pedagogy: Language and Control in a Changing Institutional Field." *Administrative Science Quarterly* 43 (2): 257–292.

Obach, Brian K. 2015. *Organic Struggle: The Movement for Sustainable Agriculture in the United States.* Cambridge, MA: MIT Press.

Oberschall, Anthony. 1978. "Theories of Social Conflict." *Annual Review of Sociology* 4: 291–314.

Olds, Jerome. 1969a. "Announcing: The Organic Foods Shopper." *Organic Gardening and Farming*, February, 39–40.

———. 1969b. "Presenting the Organic Market Center." *Organic Gardening and Farming*, April, 56–58.

———. 1969c. "The Teen Age of Organic Food Marketing." *Organic Gardening and Farming*, March, 66–67.

———. 1970a. "Help Farmers Become Organic." *Organic Gardening and Farming*, June, 88–89.

———. 1970b. "The Social Significance of Organic Foods." *Organic Gardening and Farming*, August, 48–51.

Oliver, Christine. 1991. "Strategic Responses to Institutional Processes." *Academy of Management Review* 16 (1): 145–179.

Organic Valley. 2012. "Organic Valley Launches Grassmilk™." http://www.prweb.com/releases/prweb2012/3/prweb9262440.htm.

Paarlberg, Robert. 2013. *Food Politics: What Everyone Needs to Know.* 2nd ed. New York: Oxford University Press.

Pache, Anne-Claire, and Filipe M. Santos. 2012. "Inside the Hybrid Organization: Selective Coupling as a Response to Competing Institutional Logics." *Academy of Management Journal* 56 (4): 972–1001.

Padgett, John F., and Christopher K. Ansell. 1993. "Robust Action and the Rise of the Medici, 1400–1434." *American Journal of Sociology* 98 (6): 1259–1319.

Papendick, Robert I., Larry L. Boersma, Daniel Colacicco, Joanne Kla, Charles A. Kraenzle, Paul B. Marsh, Arthur S. Newman, James F. Parr, James B. Swan, and

I. Garth Youngberg. 1980. *Report and Recommendations on Organic Farming.* Washington, DC: United States Department of Agriculture.

Peters, Suzanne. 1979. "The Land in Trust: A Social History of the Organic Farming Movement." Ph.D. diss., McGill University.

Phillips, Nelson, Thomas B. Lawrence, and Cynthia Hardy. 2004. "Discourse and Institutions." *Academy of Management Review* 29 (4): 635–652.

Pollan, Michael. 2006a. "Mass Natural." *New York Times Magazine,* June 4. http://www.nytimes.com/2006/06/04/magazine/04wwln_lede.html.

———. 2006b. "My Second Letter to Whole Foods." http://michaelpollan.com/articles-archive/my-second-letter-to-whole-foods/.

———. 2006c. *The Omnivore's Dilemma: A Natural History of Four Meals.* New York: Penguin Press.

Polletta, Francesca. 1999. "'Free Spaces' in Collective Action." *Theory and Society* 28 (1): 1–38.

Polletta, Francesca, and James M. Jasper. 2001. "Collective Identity and Social Movements." *Annual Review of Sociology* 27: 283–305.

Powell, Walter W. 1987. "Hybrid Organizational Arrangements: New Form or Transitional Development." *California Management Review* 30 (1): 67–87.

Powell, Walter W., and Jeanette A. Colyvas. 2008. "Microfoundations of Institutional Theory." In *The SAGE Handbook of Organizational Institutionalism,* edited by S. R. Clegg, C. Hardy, Thomas B. Lawrence, and W. R. Nord, 276–298. London: Sage.

Powell, Walter W., and Paul J. DiMaggio. 1991. Introduction to *The New Institutionalism in Organizational Analysis,* edited by Walter W. Powell and Paul J. DiMaggio, 1–40. Chicago: University of Chicago Press.

Quinn, Sarah. 2008. "The Transformation of Morals in Markets: Death, Benefits, and the Exchange of Life Insurance Policies." *American Journal of Sociology* 114 (3): 738–780.

Rao, Hayagreeva. 1998. "Caveat Emptor: The Construction of Nonprofit Consumer Watchdog Organizations." *American Journal of Sociology* 103 (4): 912–961.

———. 2009. *Market Rebels: How Activists Make or Break Radical Innovations.* Princeton, NJ: Princeton University Press.

Rao, Hayagreeva, Philippe Monin, and Rodolphe Durand. 2003. "Institutional Change in Toque Ville: Nouvelle Cuisine as an Identity Movement in French Gastronomy." *American Journal of Sociology* 108 (4): 795–843.

Rao, Hayagreeva, Calvin Morrill, and Mayer Zald. 2000. "Power Plays: How Social Movements and Collective Action Create New Organizational Forms." *Research in Organizational Behavior* 22: 237–281.

Ravasi, Davide, and Majken Schultz. 2006. "Responding to Organizational Identity Threats: Exploring the Role of Organizational Culture." *Academy of Management Journal* 49 (3): 433–458.

Reay, Trish, and C. R. (Bob) Hinings. 2005. "The Recomposition of an Organizational Field: Health Care in Alberta." *Organization Studies* 26 (3): 351–384.

Riddle, Jim. 2005. "The Fractured State of the Organic Community." http://www.cornucopia.org/2005/09/the-fractured-state-of-the-organic-community/.

Rodale, Jerome Irving. (1945) 1959. *Pay Dirt: Farming and Gardening with Composts.* Emmaus, PA: Rodale Press.

Rodale, Maria. 2010. *Organic Manifesto: How Organic Farming Can Heal Our Planet, Feed the World, and Keep Us Safe.* New York: Rodale.

Rodale, Robert. 1969. "The New 'Back to the Land' Movement." *Organic Gardening and Farming*, September, 21–24.

———. 1970a. "Coming—A New Kind of Organic Gardening Club." *Organic Gardening and Farming*, April, 28–31.

———. 1970b. "Ordinary Housewives Flocking to Health Food Stores? There Must Be a Reason—Maybe It's DDT!" *Organic Gardening and Farming*, March, 47.

———. 1970c. "What Can I Do?" *Organic Gardening and Farming*, February, 31–34.

———. 1971. "Join the Fight against Organic Phonies." *Organic Gardening and Farming*, June, 73–74.

Rojas, Fabio. 2010. "Power through Institutional Work: Acquiring Academic Authority in the 1968 Third World Strike." *Academy of Management Journal* 53 (6): 1263–1280.

Rosenthal, Elizabeth. 2011. "Organic Agriculture May Be Outgrowing Its Ideals." *New York Times*, December 30. http://www.nytimes.com/2011/12/31/science/earth/questions-about-organic-produce-and-sustainability.html.

Roszak, Theodore. 1969. *The Making of a Counter Culture: Reflections on the Technocratic Society and Its Youthful Critics.* Garden City, NY: Anchor Books.

Rothschild, Joyce, and Raymond Russell. 1986. "Alternatives to Bureaucracy: Democratic Participation in the Economy." *Annual Review of Sociology* 12: 307–328.

Rothschild-Whitt, Joyce. 1979. "The Collectivist Organization: An Alternative to Rational-Bureaucratic Models." *American Sociological Review* 44 (4): 509–527.

Russo, Michael V. 2010. *Companies on a Mission.* Stanford, CA: Stanford Business Books.

Sahlin, Kerstin, and Linda Wedlin. 2008. "Circulating Ideas: Imitation, Translation, and Editing." In *The Sage Handbook of Organizational Institutionalism*, edited by Royston Greenwood, Christine Oliver, Kerstin Sahlin, and Roy Suddaby, 218–242. Thousand Oaks, CA: Sage.

Schleifer, David, and Michaela DeSoucey. 2015. "What Your Consumer Wants: Business-to-Business Advertising as a Mechanism of Market Change." *Journal of Cultural Economy* 8 (2): 218–234.

Schrader, Robynn. 2000. "Momentum Is a Powerful Thing: NCGA and Creating a Virtual Chain of Co-ops." *Cooperative Grocer*, May–June.

Schudson, Michael. 2007. "Citizens, Consumers, and the Good Society." *Annals of the American Academy of Political and Social Science* 611: 236–249.

Schurman, Rachel, and William A. Munro. 2010. *Fighting for the Future of Food: Activists versus Agribusiness in the Struggle over Biotechnology.* Minneapolis: University of Minnesota Press.

Schwartz, Anne. 1991. "Issues to Be Addressed by the Organic Foods Trade." *Organic Farmer*, Summer, 23–24.

————. 1992. "First Impressions of the NOSB." *Organic Farmer*, Summer, 18.

Schwartz, Rachel A., and Thomas A. Lyson. 2007. "Retail Relations: An Interlocking Directorate Analysis of Food Retailing Corporations in the United States." *Agriculture and Human Values* 24 (4): 489–498.

Scott, Marvin B., and Stanford M. Lyman. 1968. "Accounts." *American Sociological Review* 33 (1): 806–828.

Scott, W. Richard. 2007. *Institutions and Organizations: Ideas and Interests.* Thousand Oaks, CA: Sage.

Selznick, Philip. (1949) 1966. *TVA and the Grass Roots: A Study in the Sociology of Formal Organization.* New York: Harper and Row.

————. 1957. *Leadership in Administration: A Sociological Interpretation.* Berkeley: University of California Press.

Seo, Myeong-Gu, and W. E. Douglas Creed. 2002. "Institutional Contradictions, Praxis, and Institutional Change: A Dialectical Perspective." *Academy of Management Review* 27 (2): 222–247.

Sewell, Bradford H., and Robin M. Whyatt. 1989. *Intolerable Risk: Pesticides in Our Children's Food.* Washington, DC: Natural Resources Defense Council.

Sewell, William H., Jr. 1992. "A Theory of Structure: Duality, Agency, and Transformation." *American Journal of Sociology* 98 (1): 1–29.

Shapin, Steven. 2006. "Paradise Sold." *New Yorker*, May 15. http://www.newyorker.com/magazine/2006/05/15/paradise-sold.

Shapiro, Laura. 1989. "Suddenly, It's a Panic for Organic." *Newsweek*, March 27, 24.

Sikavica, Katarina, and Jo-Ellen Pozner. 2013. "Paradise Sold: Resource Partitioning and the Organic Movement in the US Farming Industry." *Organization Studies* 34 (5/6): 623–651.

Sinclair, Upton. (1906) 2004. *The Jungle.* New York: Simon and Schuster.

Singerman, Jesse. 2004. "Blooming Prairie: The Most Important Strategies Are Those That Strengthen Our Retail Members." *Cooperative Grocer*, September–October.

Sirota, Hy. 1970. "The Chain Store That Dared." *Organic Gardening and Farming*, August, 66–67.

Slater, Don. 1997. *Consumer Culture and Modernity.* Cambridge: Polity Press.

Sligh, Michael, and Carolyn Christman. 2003. *Who Owns Organic? The Global Status, Prospects, and Challenges of a Changing Organic Market.* Pittsboro, NC: Rural Advancement Foundation International—USA.

Smith-Spangler, Crystal, Margaret L. Brandeau, Grace E. Hunter, J. Clay Bavinger, Maren Pearson, Paul J. Eschbach, Vandana Sundaram, Hau Liu, Patricia Schirmer, Christopher Stave, Ingram Olkin, and Dena M. Bravata. 2012. "Are Organic Foods Safer or Healthier Than Conventional Alternatives? A Systematic Review." *Annals of Internal Medicine* 157 (5): 348–366.

Snow, David A. 2003. "Social Movements." In *Handbook of Symbolic Interactionism*, edited by Larry T. Reynolds and Nancy J. Herman-Kinney, 811–834. Blue Ridge Summit, PA: AltaMira Press.

Snow, David A., and Robert D. Benford. 1988. "Ideology, Frame Resonance, and Participant Mobilization." *International Social Movement Research* 1: 197–217.

Snow, David A., E. Burke Rochford, Jr., Steven K. Worden, and Robert D. Benford. 1986. "Frame Alignment Processes, Micromobilization, and Movement Participation." *American Sociological Review* 51 (4): 464–481.

Spillman, Lyn. 1999. "Enriching Exchange: Cultural Dimensions of Markets." *American Journal of Economics and Sociology* 58 (4): 1047–1071.

Stehr, Nico. 2008. *Moral Markets: How Knowledge and Affluence Change Consumers and Products.* Boulder, CO: Paradigm.

Stinchcombe, Arthur L. 1965. "Social Structure and Organizations." In *Handbook of Organizations,* edited by James G. March, 142–193. Chicago: Rand McNally.

Stoll, Steven. 1998. *The Fruits of Natural Advantage: Making the Industrial Countryside in California.* Berkeley: University of California Press.

Stolle, Dietlind, and Michele Micheletti. 2013. *Political Consumerism: Global Responsibility in Action.* Cambridge: Cambridge University Press.

Strauss, Anselm L. 1978. *Negotiations: Varieties, Processes, Context, and Social Order.* San Francisco: Jossey-Bass.

Strauss, Anselm L., Leonard Schatzman, Rue Bucher, Danuta Erhrlich, and Melvin Sabshin. 1963. "The Hospital and Its Negotiated Order." In *The Hospital in Modern Society,* edited by Elliot Friedson, 147–169. New York: Free Press.

Swaminathan, Anand. 1995. "The Proliferation of Specialist Organizations in the American Wine Industry, 1941–1990." *Administrative Science Quarterly* 40 (4): 653–680.

Swidler, Ann. 1979. *Organization without Authority: Dilemmas of Social Control in Free Schools.* Cambridge, MA: Harvard University Press.

———. 1986. "Culture in Action: Symbols and Strategies." *American Sociological Review* 51 (2): 273–286.

———. 2001. *Talk of Love: How Culture Matters.* Chicago: University of Chicago Press.

Szasz, Andrew. 2007. *Shopping Our Way to Safety: How We Changed from Protecting the Environment to Protecting Ourselves.* Minneapolis: University of Minnesota Press.

Thornton, Patricia H. 2004. *Markets from Culture: Institutional Logics and Organizational Decisions in Higher Education Publishing.* Stanford, CA: Stanford Business Books.

Thornton, Patricia H., and William Ocasio. 2008. "Institutional Logics." In *The Sage Handbook of Organizational Instutitionalism,* edited by Royston Greenwood, Christine Oliver, Kerstin Sahlin, and Roy Suddaby, 99–129. Thousand Oaks, CA: Sage.

Thornton, Patricia H., William Ocasio, and Michael Lounsbury. 2012. *The Institutional Logics Perspective.* New York: Oxford University Press.

Time. 1971. "The Profitable Earth." *Time* Magazine, April 12, 96.

Townley, Barbara. 2002. "The Role of Competing Rationalities in Institutional Change." *Academy of Management Journal* 45 (1): 163–179.

Turner, James S., and Ralph Nader. 1970. *The Chemical Feast.* New York: Penguin.

Utting, Peter. 2005. "Corporate Responsibility and the Movement of Business." *Development in Practice* 15 (3/4): 375–388.

Vos, Timothy. 2000. "Visions of the Middle Landscape: Organic Farming and the Politics of Nature." *Agriculture and Human Values* 17 (3): 245–256.

Weber, Klaus, Kathryn L. Heinze, and Michaela DeSoucey. 2008. "Forage for Thought: Mobilizing Codes in the Movement for Grass-Fed Meat and Dairy Products." *Administrative Science Quarterly* 53 (3): 529–567.

Weber, Klaus, and Brayden G. King. 2014. "Social Movement Theory and Organization Studies." In *The Oxford Handbook of Sociology, Social Theory, and Organization Studies: Contemporary Currents*, edited by Paul S. Adler, Paul du Gay, Glenn Morgan, and Mike Reed, 487–509. New York: Oxford University Press.

Weber, Max. 1949. "'Objectivity' in Social Science and Social Policy." In *The Methodology of the Social Sciences*, edited by Edward A. Shils and Henry A. Finch, 49–112. New York: Free Press.

———. 1978. *Economy and Society*. Vol. 1. Berkeley: University of California Press.

Weick, Karl E. 1993. "The Collapse of Sensemaking in Organizations: The Mann Gulch Disaster." *Administrative Science Quarterly* 38 (4): 628–652.

———. 1995. *Sensemaking in Organizations*. Thousand Oaks, CA: Sage.

Weick, Karl E., Kathleen M. Sutcliffe, and David Obstfeld. 2005. "Organizing and the Process of Sensemaking." *Organization Science* 16 (4): 409–421.

Whoriskey, Peter. 2014. "Think Your Milk and Eggs Are Organic? These Aerial Photos Will Make You Think Again." *Washington Post Wonkblog*, December 11. http://www.washingtonpost.com/blogs/wonkblog/wp/2014/12/11/think-your-milk-and-chicken-are-organic-these-aerial-farm-photos-will-make-you-think-again/.

Williamson, Oliver E. 1981. "The Economics of Organization: The Transactions Cost Approach." *American Journal of Sociology* 87 (3): 548–577.

Winne, Mark. 2010. *Food Rebels, Guerrilla Gardeners, and Smart-Cookin' Mamas: Fighting Back in an Age of Industrial Agriculture*. Boston: Beacon Press.

Wohl, Jessica. 2014. "Wal-Mart Aims to Push Organic Foods into the Mainstream." *Chicago Tribune*, April 10. http://articles.chicagotribune.com/2014–04–10/business/ct-walmart-organic-wildoats-0410–biz-20140410_1_wild-oats-organic-groceries-plum-organics.

Wyndham, Robert J. 1969. "Your Oranges Don't Shine." *Organic Gardening and Farming*, September, 66–67.

Youngberg, Garth, Neill Schaller, and Kathleen Merrigan. 1993. "The Sustainable Agriculture Policy Agenda in the United States: Politics and Prospects." In *Food for the Future: Conditions and Contradictions of Sustainability*, edited by Patricia Allen, 295–318. New York: John Wiley and Sons.

Zald, Mayer, Calvin Morrill, and Hayagreeva Rao. 2005. "The Impact of Social Movements on Organizations: Environment and Responses." In *Social Movements and Organization Theory*, edited by Gerald F. Davis, Douglas McAdam, W. Richard Scott, and Mayer Zald, 253–279. Cambridge: Cambridge University Press.

Zavetoski, Stephen, Stuart W. Shulman, and David Schlosberg. 2006. "Democracy and the Environment on the Internet: Electronic Citizen Participation in Regulatory Rulemaking." *Science, Technology, and Human Values* 31 (4): 383–408.

Zelizer, Viviana A. 1978. "Human Values and the Market: The Case of Life Insurance and Death in 19th-Century America." *American Journal of Sociology* 84 (3): 591–610.

Zerubavel, Eviatar. 1991. *The Fine Line: Making Distinctions in Everyday Life*. Chicago: University of Chicago Press.

Zilber, Tammar B. 2002. "Institutionalization as the Interplay between Actions, Meanings, and Actors: The Case of a Rape Crisis Center in Israel." *Academy of Management Journal* 45 (1): 234–254.

Zuckerman, Ezra W., Tai-Young Kim, Kalinda Ukanwa, and James Von Ritterman. 2003. "Robust Identities or Nonidentities? Typecasting in the Feature-Film Labor Market." *American Journal of Sociology* 108 (5): 1018–1073.

Zwerdling, Daniel. 1979. "The Uncertain Revival of Food Cooperatives." In *Co-ops, Communes, and Collectives: Experiments in Social Change in the 1960s and 1970s*, edited by John Case and Rosemary C. R. Taylor, 89–111. New York: Pantheon Books.

Index